Blood 'n' Thunder's
CLIFFHANGER CLASSICS

Ed Hulse
Editor

MURANIA PRESS   MORRIS PLAINS, NJ

First edition, July 2012

The essays herein were originally published in *Blood 'n' Thunder* magazine and are copyright © their respective years of publication (2002–2012) by Murania Press. Introduction copyright © 2012 by Ed Hulse.

All stills, posters and lobby cards reprinted herein are either in the public domain or believed to be covered for publication by the "fair use" provision of copyright law.

Except for brief passages for reviews and critical articles, no part of this book may be reproduced, stored in or introduced into a retrieval system, or transmitted in any form or by any means (electronic, mechanical, photocopying, or otherwise) with the prior written permission of Murania Press editor/publisher Ed Hulse, holder of copyright to this book and the essays contained herein.

Book Design: Chris Kalb

Special Thanks to Rex W. Layton, Daniel J. Neyer and Brian Taves for their contributions to this book.

ISBN13 978-1478189213
ISBN10 1478189215

CONTENTS

- 7 **Introduction**
  by Ed Hulse

- 13 **The Movie Serial: A Collector's Primer**
  by Ed Hulse

- 32 **The Iron Claw (1916 Pathé)**
  by Ed Hulse

- 42 **The Mysteries of Myra (1916 Pathé)**
  by Ed Hulse

- 52 **Patria (1917 Pathé)**
  by Ed Hulse

- 67 **The Jungle Goddess (1922 Export & Import Co.)**
  by Ed Hulse

- 79 **The Green Archer (1925 Pathé)**
  by Ed Hulse

- 95 **Gallery**

- 113 **The House Without a Key (1926 Pathé)**
  by Ed Hulse

- 128 **Tarzan the Mighty (1928 Universal)**
  by Ed Hulse

- 144 **The Last of the Silent Serial Teams**
  by Ed Hulse

- 153 **Jungle Mystery (1932 Universal)**
  by Brian Taves

166 **The Red Rider (1934 Universal)**
by Daniel J. Neyer

172 **New Adventures of Tarzan (1935 Burroughs-Tarzan)**
by Ed Hulse

185 **Tim Tyler's Luck (1937 Universal)**
by Daniel J. Neyer

193 **Gallery**

213 **The Lone Ranger (1938 Republic)**
by Ed Hulse

232 **The Secret of Treasure Island (1938 Columbia)**
by Rex W. Layton

244 **The Shadow (1940 Columbia)**
by Ed Hulse

256 **Drums of Fu Manchu (1940 Republic)**
by Daniel J. Neyer

264 **Daredevils of the West (1943 Republic)**
by Ed Hulse

276 **Adventures of Smilin' Jack (1943 Universal)**
by Ed Hulse

285 **Dissed and Dismissed: Ten Underrated Serials**
by Daniel J. Neyer

300 **Appendix: My Dinner with Nita**
by Ed Hulse

Introduction

I love serials. Always have, always will.

As a middle-aged man who remains enthusiastic about a cinematic form that generally targeted juvenile audiences, I've often found it difficult to explain my fondness for the chapter play and, frankly, have given up trying. The old maxim comes to mind: "For those who understand, no explanation is necessary. For those who *don't* understand, no explanation is possible."

My love affair with movie serials began in 1962, when I was nine years old. Growing up in northern New Jersey, I watched television stations that broadcasted from New York City. One of them, WPIX, ran an afternoon kiddie show hosted by a local celebrity who dressed like a cop and called himself Officer Joe Bolton. His daily program, which aired in the late afternoon just as kids were arriving home from school, offered cartoons, Three Stooges comedies, and serial chapters.

One day, having visited a friend's house to consummate a comic-book trade, I stayed long enough to see Officer Joe's "Funhouse" for the first time. The genial host's avuncular patter didn't particularly impress me, but the serial chapter—from Republic's 1952 epic, *Zombies of the Stratosphere*—gripped me from beginning to end. The hero, a guy named Larry Martin (played by Judd Holdren, as I later learned), was prosecuting a war against alien invaders using little more than his "rocket suit" and a ray-gun or two. Of course, the bullet-shaped helmet and leather-jacket rocket pack had been developed several years earlier for *King of the Rocket Men*, but I had no way of knowing that at the time. Nor did I have any idea that the episode's cliffhanging ending, in which an unconscious Martin lay slumped in the front seat of his speedboat while it sailed over the crest of a waterfall to plunge into the churning rapids below, was stock footage from *G-Men vs. the Black Dragon* (1943).

No, what really grabbed me was the mingling of frustration and anticipation I felt when the final shot cut to black and Officer Joe's beaming countenance once again filled the small screen. To found out what happened to Larry Martin, he explained, we'd have to tune in tomorrow at the same time. In those days, to avoid confusing young viewers, WPIX cut away after the cliffhanger ending, just before the end-title card that said "At This Theater Next Week." Instead, Officer Joe spelled out the next chapter title in a simple alphabetical code. That was the tease; once you'd decoded something along the lines of "Death Rides the Rails" or "Plunge to Oblivion," there was no way you were going to miss the following episode.

After seeing a few more chapters of *Zombies*, I was hooked. It was followed by *Radar Men from the Moon*, which brought back the rocket suit, now owned by a bland-looking fellow who called himself Commando Cody. At the time I didn't know that *Radar Men* had preceded *Zombies*, but it didn't matter. I was enthralled just the same.

Officer Joe's "Funhouse" ran Republic serials from the Fifties, and over the next year I saw them all. Other WPIX programs presented older serials, especially the Flash Gordons, which were on the air almost continuously, in one time slot or another, for the entire decade. During one glorious summer—it was either 1965 or '66—the station ran classic chapter plays every weekday morning: *The Phantom Empire* on Mondays, *Tim Tyler's Luck* on Tuesdays, *The Masked Marvel* on Wednesdays, and so on. They all delighted me, to varying degrees.

The fall of 1966 saw a competing station, WOR, launch a Saturday-afternoon program titled "Action Theater" or something along those lines. In two-hour time slots it ran the 100-minute feature versions of 26 Republic serials, hastily

INTRODUCTION

prepared by National Telefilm Associates (owners of the Republic film library) to capitalize on the success of the *Batman* TV show and the recent theatrical release of the 1943 *Batman* serial produced by Columbia. WOR's director of film programming, Chris Steinbrunner, was a serial fan from way back, but he didn't have to sell station management on the wisdom of leasing the NTA package. They offered no resistance. In those days the hip pop-culture trend was "high camp," and what could possibly be more campy than those old "cliffhangers," right? Meanwhile, I looked down my 13-year-old nose at the erstwhile hipsters who sneered and chuckled at serials. What did *they* know? For Chrissakes, they preferred Roy Lichtenstein's outsized paintings of comic-book panels to the real thing.

By this time I had practically memorized every word in every issue of *Screen Thrills Illustrated*, a short-lived companion magazine to Forrest J. Ackerman's *Famous Monsters of Filmland*. Publisher Jim Warren saw *Screen Thrills* as another catalog for the motley assortment of mail-order products he sold as "Captain Company." But editors Sam Sherman and Bob Price were determined to make the new zine a haven for serial lovers like me. They reprinted rare photos, wrote perfunctory articles on chapter plays, and occasionally interviewed old serial stars; every one of *Screen Thrills*' ten issues offered something new to me.

Around this time I also discovered Alan G. Barbour, a Queens, New York native who self-published his own magazines, targeted even more narrowly to hard-core film buffs. His chapbook-sized *The Serials of Republic* was indispensable to me because it listed casts and credits. By comparing character names to performer names while watching chapter plays, I was soon able to identify all of my favorite serial players and stuntmen.

What I didn't know back then was that all these people—Alan Barbour, Chris Steinbrunner, Sam Sherman, Bob Price—were friends and film collectors who assembled at various places (most often Alan's Queens apartment) to watch old

16mm prints of the classic cliffhangers. In fact, there existed in New York City an entire underground network of movie buffs, many of whom congregated at a tenement-basement "clubhouse" every weekend to screen old serials, Westerns, and "B" mysteries.

I met Chris Steinbrunner at the 1972 New York Comic Con, where he handled the film programming; at that holiday-weekend convention I saw *Adventures of Captain Marvel* for the first time. Chris invited me to join the club, rather pretentiously called the Cooperative Film Society, and for the next ten years or so I could be found there more weekends than not. Joining this group of aficionados also persuaded me that I just *had* to start collecting 16mm—a decision that kept me broke but happy for a good many years. Prints were hideously expensive, especially compared to the later videotapes, videodiscs, and DVDs. Complete serials in 16mm cost hundreds of dollars.

Back in the early Seventies I resolved to see every extant sound serial—which is all but a handful of the 231 produced. It was an undertaking I finally completed in 2009, after viewing the recently unearthed *Daredevils of the West* at the Lone Pine Film Festival. I still hold out hope that the few remaining "lost" serials, including *Tarzan the Fearless* and *Clancy of the Mounted*, will be found during my lifetime.

I began writing about episodic epics in 1966 with a series of articles published in *Photon*, a mimeographed fanzine devoted primarily to horror and science-fiction movies. The editor, Mark Frank, was not keen on covering serials, but I persuaded him to let me do so provided I draw some connection to fright-film icons. Hence my articles on *Shadow of Chinatown* (Bela Lugosi) and *Captain America* (Lionel Atwill), among others.

The Seventies found me attending various nostalgia-themed film festivals where I met—and in some cases developed long-lasting friendships with—actors, stuntmen, writers, and directors who toiled on some of my favorite chapter plays. During this period I was intensively researching serials, and interviewing the people involved in their making filled many gaps in my knowledge.

INTRODUCTION

When I started writing professionally in 1980, my knowledge of movies in general helped me secure a berth at the late, lamented *Video Review* magazine, which every month published hundreds of capsule reviews for the benefit of home tapers. At that time the major studios were just beginning to dip their toes into the video waters, and most of the titles they released on tape were relatively recent films. *Video Review* covered their product while also providing a valuable service to curious cinephiles who kept stocked up on blank tape. My first major article covering serials appeared in a 1981 issue.

Being involved in the planning of such film festivals as Cinecon, an annual event celebrating silent and early-talkie movies, enabled me to meet even more "picture people." In 1991, *Captain Marvel*'s Frank Coghlan Jr. helped me arrange a 50th-anniversary reunion of that classic serial's surviving participants, including director William Witney and cast members Louise Currie and Billy Benedict. The following year, at my behest, *Hop Harrigan* star William Bakewell persuaded his old friend Sally Blane to appear at Cinecon.

Most of the essays in this book, which originally saw print in the pages of my journal *Blood 'n' Thunder* (check it out at muraniapress.com) include first-hand information gleaned during those many encounters with survivors of Hollywood's Golden Age. I've never been interested in writing gushy, fact-free, sentimental articles on these films. I've always believed serials worthy of study and documentation, no matter how unimportant they have seemed not only to film historians but also to the people who made them. Chances are, many of you reading this book are familiar with the chapter plays covered herein. But I'm willing to bet that you'll learn a great deal about them you never knew or even suspected. If you love serials as much as I do, you'll enjoy the 20 essays that follow. And if you don't . . . well, this book might just be the beginning of a beautiful friendship, at the very least.

Ed Hulse
July 2012

The Movie Serial: A Collector's Primer

by Ed Hulse

Thousands of people have gathered for the opening of the Channel Tunnel, an underground roadway stretching from the Southern California mainland to beautiful Santa Alicia Island, a few miles off the coast. The malevolent 39-0-13, a master criminal who prefers to be known only by his prison number, has vowed to destroy the tunnel as part of his campaign to ruin its developer, prominent industrialist Horace Granville, whose testimony 15 years before put 39-0-13 behind bars.

In direct defiance of the archfiend's threats the Governor, accompanied by Granville's granddaughter Blanche, is taking the first car through the tunnel. What they don't know is that 39-0-13 has commandeered an offshore drilling rig and has for the last several days been boring through the rock strata just above the tube, painstakingly timing its rupture to occur during the Governor's opening-day ride.

Gene Townley, one of three circus acrobats who have sworn to apprehend 39-0-13, discovers the monstrous plot while struggling with the villain's henchmen on Santa Alicia Island. Realizing he has only minutes to warn the Governor, Gene steals a motorcycle and races through the tunnel toward the mainland in hopes of heading off the car. Before he reaches the halfway point, however, the weakened roof cracks and tons of ocean water pour through. With the cycle's throttle wide open, Gene speeds ahead with a gigantic wave of foaming sea water cascading behind him, rushing closer . . . closer . . . closer . . . .

"Don't Miss Chapter Two, At This Theater Next Week!"

That's what 1939 moviegoers saw on their local theater screens just before the end credits to "The Monstrous Plot," Chapter One of *Daredevils of the Red Circle*, a Republic serial in 12 pulse-pounding episodes. In those halcyon days of the motion-picture industry, the serial (or chapter play, as it was also known) was a staple of Saturday-afternoon matinees, where hordes of screaming children—and, in some cases, undiscriminating adults—could be found rooting for an endless procession of intrepid heroes struggling to foil an equally endless procession of diabolical villains bent on acquiring large fortunes, revenging themselves against society, or conquering the world.

The motion-picture serial existed to provide one commodity: thrills. For over 40 years, in more than 500 chapter plays, serial directors used every trick in the book to keep audiences on the edges of their seats. It was this ceaseless pursuit of nail-biting suspense that led filmmakers to devise the "cliffhanger" ending, building each 20-minute episode to a thundering crescendo climaxed by the spectacle of heroes and/or heroines facing imminent death.

But they always escaped.

Whatever fate befell the protagonist at chapter's end, he or she always got out of danger in the opening of the next week's episode, only to race through 19 more minutes of hair-raising exploits before being trapped once again in a deadly situation From Which There Could Be No Possible Escape.

Although no movie serials have been made in America since 1956, they are still very much with us thanks to DVD, videotape, and surviving 16mm prints. It's isn't the same as it used to be, of course. Watching those celluloid heroes of yesteryear battle with master villains is still fun, but not as much fun as seeing them from the balcony of the local Rialto. There are other differences as well. Home-video formats allow a viewer the luxury of running all 12 or 15 stanzas of a serial in a single sitting, if he's of such a mind, although there's a great deal to be said for taking one chapter at a time, the way those episodic epics were originally meant to be seen.

While some serials—particularly those of the early silent era—were produced on a fairly lavish scale, most chapter plays were made on minuscule budgets and shooting schedules charitably described as breakneck. To put this in perspective, consider the following comparison: *The Roaring Twenties,* a 1939 James Cagney film with a running time of 104 minutes, cost a modest $450,000 to produce, and was shot over a 12-week period. The aforementioned *Daredevils of the Red Circle,* with a total running time of approximately four hours, was shot in five weeks on a budget of about $175,000.

Serial makers were less interested in artistic achievement than mass production. The reasons for this were strictly financial. Chapter plays were rented to theaters for five to ten dollars per installment. They were come-ons, virtually given away by studios as an inducement to theater owners to book large blocks of more expensive feature-length films. Serial profits, then, were relatively small, and the studios were understandably reluctant to invest much time or money in them.

Moreover, sound-era serials were largely aimed at Saturday-matinee audiences, which consisted primarily of eight-to-15-year-old boys—not the type of crowd one could depend upon to sit through the latest Greta Garbo picture. Kids wanted action and melodrama, commodities the serial delivered in ample quantities. The suave villainy of a Basil Rathbone might be okay for a big-budget grownup feature, but it paled next to the depredations of hooded madmen who menaced the world weekly in most chapter plays.

The first movie serial was produced in 1912 by the Thomas A. Edison Company, at that time making films in the wilds of New Jersey. *What Happened to Mary* starred stage actress Mary Fuller and consisted of ten episodes, each complete in itself. It wasn't until the following year that Colonel William N. Selig, producer of *The Adventures of Kathlyn,* hit upon the strategy of ending episodes with suspenseful scenes calculated to compel curious moviegoers to return the following week to see how the perilous situation would be resolved. This dramatic device was instantly successful, but other serial makers adopted it only intermittently until around 1920, when the cliffhanger ending was incorporated into chapter-play structure on a full-time basis.

The serial most fondly recalled by most pre-World War I moviegoers is *The Perils of Pauline,* a 1914 opus starring Pearl White, a honey-blonde actress who became the first Queen of the Chapter Play. Surviving chapters, however, reveal *Perils* as appallingly crude—even for the period—and for the most part badly acted. Although there was a master villain of sorts, Pearl in her first episodic effort was menaced by a motley assortment of Indians, gypsies, wharf rats, and cheap hoodlums—none of whom would have lasted a round with 39-0-13.

In retrospect, it was Pearl herself who made a success of *Perils,* and she went on to star in eight subsequent chapter plays—nearly all of which have been lost to the ravages of nitrate decomposition, the eventual fate of all films made before 1949 and not preserved on stable acetate film stock. For this reason, it's difficult to evaluate most of the nearly 300 silent serials. Only a couple dozen survive in complete form, with an additional 20 or so represented by scattered episodes saved by archives like the American Film Institute and commercial film companies like Blackhawk Films, which for many years sold 8mm and 16mm dupe prints of odd chapters to private collectors.

In an attempt to emulate the success of Pearl White's serials, other producers came up with their own serial queens, the best of which were Ruth Roland and Helen Holmes. These intrepid ladies should be remembered today as the original liberated women, since their exacting and often dangerous exploits provided entertaining screen fare in the days before women smoked in public or voted in public elections.

By 1920, most film production had moved west and serials were made on sound stages, with exteriors lensed in what would become familiar Southern California locations. In addition, the serial makers set a large number of their cliffhangers in the past, with Western chapter plays—being cheap to make—accounting for a high percentage.

The apogee of the silent serial was reached with *The Green Archer* (1925), considered by many to be the finest of all chapter plays. Adapting a classic mystery novel by Edgar Wallace, Frank Leon Smith's screenplay concentrated on plot and atmosphere rather than action—a potentially risky approach for a serial writer to take during the thrill-hungry Roaring Twenties. The ten-chapter thriller was directed by Spencer Gordon Bennet, whose commitment to serial production spanned 40 years: Beginning his movie career as a stuntman on Pearl White chapter plays, he became a director in 1924 and single-handedly accounted for 20 percent of all cliffhangers made until 1956, when he wielded the megaphone for *Blazing the Overland Trail,* the last theatrical serial made in this country.

Bennet's specialty was fast action, but he extracted considerable suspense from *The Green Archer,* which focused on villainous Abel Bellamy (played by Burr McIntosh), an eccentric millionaire who imported a medieval British castle, brick by brick, to America. Unfortunately for Abel, the castle's ghost—a caped and masked archer clad in forest-green raiment—made the trip to these shores as well. His persecution of Bellamy for unknown reasons supplied the yarn's mystery element. Allene Ray and Walter Miller, a popular screen team at this time, took the leading roles in this third of their ten episodic epics, all but the first helmed by Spencer Bennet.

Serials featuring masked and costumed characters, whether heroes or villains, were extremely popular with audiences. One of Pearl White's earliest chapter plays, *The Iron Claw* (1916), teased its audience by daring patrons to guess the identity of The Laughing Mask, a mysterious helper who appeared regularly to rescue Pearl from the titular terror played by Sheldon Lewis. Each episode, in fact, ended with a shot of the mystery man, smiling into the camera as he began to lift the face-concealing cloth, followed by a screen-filling question mark and a title card asking, "Who Is The Laughing Mask?"

The mystery-man motif also dominated Universal's *The Riddle Rider* (1924), another silent-era classic, starring William Desmond as the editor of a frontier newspaper who became a riding terror to thwart the evil designs of ruthless schemers in Wyoming. Western serials as a rule tended to be rather prosaic, but Desmond's flamboyant heroics lifted *The Riddle Rider* above the norm. He reenacted the role in a 1927 sequel, *Return of the Riddle Rider,* and portrayed similar characters in 1928's *The Mystery Rider* and *The Vanishing Rider.*

The coming of sound meant little to serial production. For a very short time, the cumbersome recording equipment used by sound technicians inhibited the staging of action scenes, but once chapter-play producers realized that dialogue and sound effects could be dubbed in after filming, they continued in much the same way as before, with the usual reliance on master villains, secret panels, hidden treasures, and the other standard elements of serial storytelling.

Nevertheless, most of the silent era's serial-producing companies went belly-up. By 1930, when *The Indians Are Coming*—the first all-talkie chapter play—was released, most of the early production companies were already defunct: Vitagraph, Arrow, Rayart, others. Pathé ceased serial production and merged with Radio Pictures, the forerunner of RKO, leaving only Universal and Mascot to struggle for serial supremacy.

Mascot Pictures, founded in 1927 by former garment worker Nat Levine, had already made a name for itself by the time talkies arrived. Levine, always among the most pecunious of serial producers, peopled his chapter plays with two types of actors: those on the way up and those on the way down. He never utilized major stars because their salaries would consume too much of his shoestring budgets.

Casting his episodic epics in this way, Levine was able to secure the services of Walter Miller for two of Mascot's first three sound serials. A fan favorite during his Pathé years,

Miller was already sliding toward a long stretch of playing heavies when Levine tapped him for *The Lone Defender* (1930) and *King of the Wild* (1931). Earlier, the erstwhile Pathé leading man had starred in a part-talkie Mascot serial, *King of the Kongo* (1929), whose heavy was played by Boris Karloff, at that time still two years away from winning major stardom as the Monster in *Frankenstein*.

In 1932, Levine signed a three-picture deal with a young actor who had starred in a big-budget Fox feature, only to find himself scrambling for work when it died at the box-office. The film was *The Big Trail* (1930), and the actor was John Wayne. Levine saw in Wayne the type of handsome, athletic young lead that young serial fans worshipped and starred him first in *The Shadow of the Eagle* (1932), a circus-set melodrama with aviation thrills mixed in. Duke, as he was already called, had not yet developed his familiar persona, and his overdone histrionics in this serial make *Shadow* occasionally difficult to take.

Levine and Wayne had better luck with *The Hurricane Express* (1932), a mile-a-minute thriller that pitted daring Duke against The Wrecker, a mysterious villain who had sworn to ruin railroad tycoon Tully Marshall. Filled with the typical Mascot blend of fast action, improbable situations, and unbelievably corny dialogue, *Hurricane Express* is nonetheless the best of Wayne's three Mascot cliffhangers. It's also the most familiar to video fans, being available from several public-domain DVD and VHS companies, both in its original 12-episode format and as a feature-length version sloppily edited to 90 minutes.

Wayne's final chapter play, *The Three Musketeers* (1933), is also available on tape and disc. It's got the best premise of the triad, featuring Wayne as a modern-day D'Artagnan to three Foreign Legionnaires (played by Jack Mulhall, Raymond Hatton and Francis X. Bushman Jr.) charged with subduing a desert uprising led by masked native chieftain El Shaitan, or The Devil.

Another Levine discovery went from $75-a-week Mascot contract player to major Western hero, eventually starring in more than a hundred full-length movies and an eponymous TV series. Gene Autry was just another cowboy crooner until he came to Hollywood, where Levine saw in him a glimmer of personality that might register on screen. After casting Autry in a bit role in *Mystery Mountain,* a 1934 Western serial, Levine decided to take a chance on the earnest Oklahoma native by giving him the lead in one of Mascot's most outrageous episodic efforts.

The Phantom Empire (1934) was a curious hybrid of conventional Western and science-fiction fabulism. The rather preposterous plot (reportedly dreamed up by scripter Wallace MacDonald while under ether at his dentist's office) had Autry playing himself as a Western radio vocalist who discovers beneath his ranch the lost city of Murania, an advanced civilization located some 25,000 feet below the earth's surface.

In 1935, Levine sold Mascot to Herbert W. Yates, whose Consolidated Film Laboratories did most of the film processing for Hollywood's small independent production companies. Yates, having long cherished the hope of getting into production himself, merged several of these indie studios into the Republic Pictures Corporation, using as its base the San Fernando Valley plant Levine had recently leased from silent-comedy producer Mack Sennett.

Republic serials utilized most of the form's standard devices but refined their presentation. Directors Mack Wright, Ray Taylor, William Witney, John English, and Spencer Bennet kept things moving at top speed, carefully staging action sequences with top stuntmen like Yakima Canutt, David Sharpe, Tom Steele and others. These men, largely forgotten today, created most of the procedures and safety devices used by Hollywood stuntmen up to the present day.

Elaborate fight sequences—upon which, unfortunately, later Republic serials became far too dependent for thrills—were choreographed like dance routines and crisply photographed by such ace lens men as William Nobles, Jack Marta and Bud Thackery. Special effects in Republic serials were second to none in Hollywood, thanks to the innovative work of brothers Howard and Theodore Lydecker, who operated autonomously and specialized in the building and shooting of intricately detailed miniatures.

Additionally, Republic hired composers Alberto Columbo, William Lava, Paul Sawtell, Cy Feuer, and Mort Glickman to write original scores for its chapter plays. Prior to 1935, sound serials had little or no background music; the inclusion of music tracks added more money to budgets than most serial producers were willing to spend. Music libraries such as those operated by Abe Meyer and Lee Zahler rented "cues" to all takers for $50 each, but their stock melodies became familiar through overuse. At Republic, a good musical score was considered an invaluable asset, and budgets were stretched to allow for the writing of original compositions.

The end results of these collective efforts constitute the greatest body of serials produced during the form's four-decade history. Competing studios Universal and Columbia grudgingly supplied chapter plays to exhibitors as inducements to buy feature films, but Republic took pride in its serials and sold them as standalone products with all the enthusiasm most studios reserved for big-budget spectaculars.

Zorro Rides Again was the first joint directorial effort of William Witney and John English, the team responsible for most of the best Republic serials. Under their direction, actors were encouraged to play their roles without the condescension and hokum that occasionally crept into other chapter-play performances. Moreover, the two men complemented each other perfectly: Witney preferred shooting outdoor and action scenes while English opted to handle indoor and dialogue scenes, but both were equally capable in either capacity. Together they eventually perfected a homogeneous directorial style, turning out 17 top-notch serials between 1937 and 1941.

One of the team's best chapter plays was *The Lone Ranger* (1938). Already a nationwide favorite to millions of radio listeners, the Masked Rider of the Plains successfully made the transition from ether waves to silver screen along with his faithful Indian companion Tonto and his great horse Silver. The characters alone might have carried the serial through 15 episodes, but producer Robert Beche was mandated to come up with something special; Republic had spent a young fortune obtaining screen rights to the character, and Yates wanted a box-office blockbuster to justify the expense. Head writer Barry Shipman, working from a treatment penned by Oliver Drake, devised a subplot that actually commanded more attention than the Ranger's crusade against a Texas dictator with his own private army. The first chapter established our hero as the lone survivor of an ambush of Texas Rangers, and presented viewers with five nearly identical "suspects," any one of who could conceivably be the Lone Ranger.

No red-blooded serial fan could fail to be sucked into Republic's carefully devised guessing game. Shipman and company killed off three of the suspects, one by one, every few episodes, so that by the last chapter, only Allan King (played by Lee Powell) and Bert Rogers (Herman Brix) were left. To further obscure the character's "true" identity, the Lone Ranger's on-screen voice was dubbed by a different actor altogether, chosen for his vocal resemblance to radio's Ranger, Earle Graser.

The Lone Ranger was a huge success, attracting attention to Republic from exhibitors who had never before booked the studio's product. It eventually grossed over a million dollars, almost three times the amount normally expected from chapter plays.

The financial successes of *Zorro Rides Again* and *The Lone Ranger* encouraged Yates to purchase screen rights to numerous heroes from other media—especially the comic pages. Witney and English inherited several of these characters and brought them to life with unerring skill and panache.

In many cases, however, the screen versions of these four-color favorites differed substantially from their printed-page counterparts. Two-fisted crime buster Dick Tracy, for example, appeared in a quartet of Republic serials—*Dick Tracy* (1937), *Dick Tracy Returns* (1938), *Dick Tracy's G-Men* (1939), and *Dick Tracy vs. Crime Inc.* (1941)—but bore little resemblance to the character created by cartoonist Chester Gould. The comic strip's fanciful exploits and bizarre villains were ignored by Republic's screenwriters, who came up with their own colorful heavies. Tracy himself was identified as an FBI agent instead of a plainclothes police detective. But youthful audiences overlooked these deviations from Gould's comic strip. Action was almost non-stop and location shooting plentiful, indicating somewhat more generous budgets and shooting schedules. Ralph Byrd starred as Tracy in all four chapter plays, beginning an association with the character that continued in two 1947 feature films and a short-lived 1951 TV series.

Another outstanding comic-strip adaptation, *Adventures of Red Ryder* (1940), made a star of leading man Donald Barry, subsequently saddled with the nickname "Red," who went on to star in over 40 feature films for Republic during the World War II years. *Red Ryder* showed the Western serial at its best, with a virtually nonstop parade of chases, shootouts, and fistfights. The plot, a familiar but serviceable trifle about the efforts of an unscrupulous banker to run ranchers off their land in order to sell it to a railroad, was just sound enough to provide a strong framework for the excitingly staged and expertly photographed action sequences.

Republic's two finest comic-strip adaptations featured characters that originally appeared in Fawcett Publications' *Whiz Comics*. Both *Adventures of Captain Marvel* (1941) and *Spy Smasher (1942)* represent the chapter play at its very best, graced as they are with credible scripting, good performances, terrific action sequences, impeccable special effects, and atmospheric musical scores.

Adventures of Captain Marvel is held in particular esteem by serial collectors. Once again, the character as adapted for film bore little resemblance to his four-colored incarnation. Captain Marvel, for those of you who don't remember his comic-book exploits, was actually the alter ego of Billy Batson, boy radio announcer, who could transform himself into the costumed crusader by uttering the magic word "Shazam!" Former cowboy star Tom Tyler played the super-powered hero as a grim avenging angel, suspiciously fond of tossing evildoers off cliffs and skyscrapers.

According to Republic, Billy's power was the gift of an aged wizard who had for centuries guarded an ancient tomb in "a remote section of Siam near the Burmese border." In this crypt could also be found the Golden Scorpion, a device capable of turning any base metal into gold. A young and superstitious radio operator accompanying a scientific expedition in search of the tomb, Billy refused to desecrate the sacred ground, thereby convincing the wizard that he was worthy of being entrusted with Captain Marvel's powers to protect the newly unearthed Golden Scorpion from misuse.

The five scientists, having realized this ancient artifact would make them the richest and most powerful group of men in the world, wisely chose to divide amongst themselves five golden lenses needed to power the Scorpion. One of the men, however, decided he should have the device all to himself and embarked on a campaign to obtain the other lenses.

Special-effects wizard Howard Lydecker devised a life-sized papier-mâché dummy with arms and legs extended to match the comic-book pictures of Captain Marvel in the air. For a test on Republic's back lot, he affixed tiny casters to the dummy's wrists and ankles, then stretched lengths of piano wire from one point to another, a hundred yards or more distant, and strung at a slight downward angle. The papier-mâché Captain was placed on the wires and propelled forward, the casters rolling along the taut cords and the figure's weight giving it added momentum as it glided along. Lydecker's camera was tilted to the same angle as the wire to make it appear that the dummy moved parallel to the ground.

Witney and English augmented shots of the dummy with impressive takeoffs and landings performed by Tyler's stunt double, Dave Sharpe. In the average flying sequence, Tyler would take a few steps in close-up. The editors would cut to Sharpe, bounding into the air from concealed trampolines. Then they would cut to shots of the dummy in flight, intercutting close-up shots of Tyler suspended before a rear-projection screen that showed clouds flitting past. In this way, the illusion of flight was successfully created.

Captain Marvel was a smash hit, and the only thing that prevented Republic from using the character in a sequel was a lawsuit slapped on Fawcett Publications in 1941 by DC Comics, publishers of *Superman,* who claimed that the Captain's very existence infringed upon the Man of Steel's copyrighted status as the premier comic-book superhero. The suit dragged on for years, and Fawcett ultimately lost.

Spy Smasher, directed by Witney solo, starred Kane Richmond as erstwhile foreign correspondent Alan Armstrong, who adopted a secret identity to combat Nazi spies and saboteurs in the days just prior to America's entry into World War II. In a puckish twist to the comic-book series, Republic's screenwriters gave Alan an identical twin brother named Jack, who just happened to work for Admiral Corby, the U. S. Intelligence chief charged with running to earth a spy ring headed by "The Mask," a German former diplomat conspiring with American-born criminals. *Spy Smasher* was the *ne plus ultra* in Republic serials, a flawlessly executed fast-action chapter play with exhilarating fight choreography, daredevil stunt work, and explosive cliffhanger endings. Upon its completion in late 1941 Republic's executives deemed *Spy Smasher* the studio's best serial to date. None of the chapter plays that followed was able to better it.

Republic wasn't the only serial-producing studio that had good luck with characters drawn from the funny pages. Back in 1936, Universal had scored big with a serial that, arguably, remains the most fondly remembered of them all: *Flash Gordon.*

Alex Raymond's comic strip of the same name was a nationwide sensation when Universal licensed the screen rights in mid-1935, and the studio realized it would have to come up with something special to properly exploit the property. Obviously, the strip's basically juvenile audience militated against production of an extravagant feature-length film. On the other hand, the expense of creating elaborate special effects for rocket ships and mythical cities in space was judged by the studio to be more than a serial's budget could stand.

Eventually, Universal relented and allotted *Flash Gordon* more money than was expended on the typical chapter play. But producer Henry MacRae was still forced to cut corners. The special effects, actually very primitive for the time and not comparable to those achieved by the Lydecker brothers at Republic, cost less and looked it. Miniature rocket ships suspended on piano wire jerkily glided over unconvincing tabletop representations of extraterrestrial terrain. Numerous exotic costumes were made from scratch in order to duplicate those pictured in the comic strip, wreaking havoc with the wardrobe department's balance sheet. But MacRae saved money elsewhere by pulling relics from the studio prop department and redressing sets left over from earlier, more lavish Universal pictures, including *The Bride of Frankenstein.* Rather than commission original music for the serial, he had film editors recycle stock music recorded for such earlier features as *The Black Cat, Bombay Mail, The Invisible Man,* and *Werewolf of London.*

MacRae's economies extended to the cast. Olympic swimming champ Larry "Buster" Crabbe closely resembled the pen-and-ink Flash Gordon, so the Universal producer borrowed him from Paramount, where Crabbe had toiled as a lowly contract player for three years. For his role in a serial that spawned two sequels and grossed millions of dollars for Universal, Buster received his regular Paramount salary of $75 per week.

In what proved to be inspired casting, Universal contractee Jean Rogers, not yet 21, was assigned to play Flash's sweetheart Dale Arden. Irish character actor Frank Shannon was hired to play eccentric scientist Dr. Hans Zarkov and veteran screen heavy Charles Middleton won the role of Ming the Merciless, ruthless emperor of the planet Mongo and would-be dictator of the universe.

Universal's screenwriters drew extensively from the comic-strip continuity in fashioning 13 episodes of intergalactic adventures for Flash, Dale and Zarkov, who flew in the latter's homemade rocket ship to the planet Mongo, which seemed to be on a collision course with Earth as the serial began. Landing safely on the strange planet, the earthlings found it inhabited by bizarre alien races—Lion Men, Hawk Men and Shark Men, to name a few. All of Mongo's inhabitants feared Ming, who plotted to destroy Earth as the first step in his plan to conquer the universe. Flash eventually befriended many of the planet's oppressed minorities and led a revolt against the Emperor's forces, defeating Ming and saving Earth from destruction in the bargain.

Seen today *Flash Gordon* appears crude and campy, yet it was enormously successful, easily outgrossing both *Show Boat* and *Sutter's Gold,* Universal's prestigious big-budget features for the year. In almost constant theatrical reissue, sold early to TV, and available in several home-video formats, this serial was arguably the most profitable ever made, producing millions of dollars in profit. Crabbe, Rogers, Shannon and Middleton reprised their roles in a 1938 sequel, *Flash Gordon's Trip to Mars,* which was nearly as popular although not as imaginative as the first Flash opus. Jean Rogers was replaced by Carol Hughes for *Flash Gordon Conquers the Universe (1940),* third and last of this great trilogy.

Universal leaned heavily on comic-strip adaptations for its post-1934 serials, which on the whole were inferior to competing chapter plays from Republic. The Universal product was often padded with ancient stock footage—some of it dating back to the silent era—shoehorned into convoluted plots to save the expense of shooting spectacular sequences. Fights and chases were often completely unmotivated, with supporting characters often popping on screen like rabbits drawn from a magician's hat, their presence unexplained and often unacknowledged.

In *Red Barry* (1938), for example, second-billed Edna Sedgwick played a deposed Russian noblewoman trying to regain two million dollars in bonds stolen from her family. She appeared only fleetingly in the first stanza, when observing a murder, but was neither referred to by other characters nor given any dialogue to introduce herself. Yet in Chapter Two, introductory titles explaining the previous episode's events indicated that she had instigated much of the preceding week's action!

Other comic strips adapted to the serial screen by Universal included *Ace Drummond* (1936), *Radio Patrol* (1937), *Tim Tyler's Luck* (1937), *Buck Rogers (1939)* and *Adventures of Smilin' Jack* (1943), all of which can be numbered among the studio's better efforts.

After releasing three independently made chapter plays through its distribution channels, Columbia initiated in-house serial production in 1938 with a character lifted from the garish pulp magazines of the era. The title character of *The Spider's Web* (1938) didn't bother to engage thugs in fistfights: he just shot them down with his twin Colt .45 automatics. As ace criminologist Richard Wentworth (played by Warren Hull) often explained during *Web*'s 15 episodes, the police were too hindered by legal red tape to be helpful in combating super-criminals like the Octopus, whose evil tentacles reached out to seize control of the country by taking over its utilities and transportation system.

Aided by their "three faithful musketeers," Jackson (Richard Fiske), Jenkins (Don Douglas), and Ram Singh (Kenneth Duncan), Wentworth and his fiancée Nita Van Sloan (played by the breathtakingly beautiful Iris Meredith) dispatched no less than three dozen Octopus henchmen in what was arguably the shooting-est serial ever.

The Spider killed 12 heavies in the first two chapters alone. After submitting these installments for the Production Code seal of approval, Columbia was chastised by the Hays Office, which claimed the serial was far too bloodthirsty for kiddie consumption. With most of the film already shot, the editors were forced to make changes in completed episodes. Therefore, later chapters typically found the Spider, blazing gun in each hand, wading into rooms holding a half-dozen or more heavies. A close-up would show him firing numerous rounds toward the off-screen villains, and the subsequent cut pictured him striding across the room, now littered with barely visible corpses who had not been shown being struck by the Spider's bullets. Only by such editorial obfuscation was Columbia able to satisfy the Production Code's stricture forbidding excessive killing in kiddie-oriented movies.

The Spider's Web was hugely successful and got Columbia's in-house serial unit off to a good start, but the studio lost interest in the production of quality serials very soon thereafter, and its chapter plays were entrusted to shoestring producers whose primary interest was chiseling extra money for themselves out of already minuscule budgets. Large chunks of funds earmarked for Columbia's episodic thrillers went toward the purchase of screen rights to highly marketable characters from other media. Comic-book great Batman was featured in two serials, *Batman* (1943) and *Batman and Robin* (1949), but in both cases the results were dismal. In the persons of Lewis Wilson (1943) and Robert Lowery (1949), the Caped Crusader came off as rather less effective than the average Republic heavy. It didn't help that, in both cases, the character's most important accoutrements—his distinctive costume, his Bat Cave, his Batmobile—appeared to have been cheaply and hastily thrown together.

Columbia snagged the Man of Steel himself for a 1948 chapter play which, befitting his stature in the superhero pantheon, rated somewhat higher than most of the studio's episodic efforts. *Superman* starred Kirk Alyn in the title role and featured Noel Neill as reporter Lois Lane, a role she would reprise in a 1950 sequel—*Atom Man vs. Superman*—and later in the TV show starring George Reeves. Former *Our Gang* tough guy Tommy "Butch" Bond was cast as Jimmy Olsen, and sultry Carol Forman provided formidable villainy as the Spider Lady.

Unfortunately, producer Sam Katzman badly muffed the all-important flying scenes in his desire to do them as inexpensively as possible: Whenever the script called for Superman to take to the air, actor Kirk Alyn would stretch his arms skyward and turn into a poorly animated cartoon figure. A far cry from the elaborate effects used in Republic's *Captain Marvel,* the airborne shots in *Superman* failed to convince even the youngest viewers and provided a resoundingly sour note in an otherwise enjoyable serial.

In Katzman's defense, it should be stated that by 1950, when *Atom Man vs. Superman* was produced, the serial was already an endangered species. Television had just reared its ugly head, and the half-hour adventure series being made for the video screen bore more than passing resemblance to serial episodes—and were free to watch, besides. The handwriting was certainly on the wall by 1951, when Columbia bought screen rights to Captain Video, a hero who had originated on TV.

Moreover, production costs had risen alarmingly since the end of World War II, concurrent with the growing strength of Hollywood's labor unions. With serials losing ground at the box office, budgets were trimmed judiciously, resulting in an increasing reliance on stock footage. Republic, in fact, built entire chapter plays around spectacular footage shot for earlier serials, and went so far as to garb its actors in out-of-date hats, suits, and gowns to match scenes filmed a dozen or more years earlier.

To its credit, Republic *did* create at least one memorable serial hero for the post-atomic era. *King of the Rocket Men* (1949) starred Tris Coffin as scientist Jeff King, who flew across the California countryside in an atomic-powered rocket suit complete with bullet-shaped helmet. The Rocket Man character was revamped as Commando Cody, Sky Marshal of the Universe, in *Radar Men from the Moon* (1952), which added interplanetary travel to Republic's serial-situation repertoire. As imaginative as the character was, however, Republic's dependence on stock shots and stereotyped situations weakened the impact of *Radar Men*. While in the air he was great, but on the ground Cody and his adversaries ran around in the same pinstriped suits, snap-brimmed fedoras, and 1945 Nash roadsters used by several of their serial predecessors.

Republic and Columbia limped along until 1956, when both studios almost simultaneously threw in the towel on serial production. By that time, Republic had already sold much of its product to television, so the company's earlier (and better) cliffhangers were being seen by a new generation of serial enthusiasts. Universal and Columbia eventually did the same thing, and for many years the old serials were staples of TV syndication. The Flash Gordon epics have always been particularly popular, and when he died in 1983 Buster Crabbe was still getting fan mail for chapter plays he had made almost a half century earlier.

The old serials, seen today by sophisticated viewers without nostalgic attachments to the form or the characters, come across as pitifully threadbare in most respects. They're also seen as overly juvenile and campy—in other words, unacceptable viewing for adults. And yet, for those film buffs who still remember when they believed in the magic word "Shazam!" . . . who remember Flash Gordon's interplanetary jaunts with fondness . . . who lived a thousand battles and shared a thousand perils with those flying and fighting heroes . . . for all of these, the movie serial lives. For them, the larger-than-life adventures of the Serial Kings and Queens are still "To Be Continued."

The Iron Claw
(1916, Pathé Exchanges, Inc.)
by Ed Hulse

The surprise success of *The Perils of Pauline*, a 1914 chapter play distributed by the American branch of the French motion-picture company Pathé Freres (later Pathé Exchanges, Inc.), put to-be-continued thrillers on the pop-culture map. The serial melodrama, a cinematic storytelling format never really given its due by film historians, made moviegoing a weekly pastime for millions of Americans. And those Americans loved Pearl White, the athletic, light-hearted girl whose daring exploits had made *Perils of Pauline* a sensation.

Perils was followed by *The Exploits of Elaine* (1915), an Arthur B. Reeve crime story that introduced chapter-play fans to scientific detective Craig Kennedy and his arch-nemesis, The Clutching Hand. This 14-chapter serial, a considerable improvement on *Pauline*, smashed box-office records and spawned two sequels released back to back. Pearl's name on a theater marquee now guaranteed huge profits for Pathé. Before the year was out, production had begun on a new Pearl White chapter play, one unrelated to the *Elaine* cycle.

At that time, serials were commonly based on original stories by well-known authors whose popularity lent credibility to any motion-picture enterprise. Generally, the author penned a novelization that could be serialized in newspapers concurrent with the release of filmed episodes. *The Iron Claw* was credited to Arthur Stringer, a prolific writer who sold to both pulp-paper and slick-paper magazines. George B. Seitz, who had guided the *Elaine* serials to successful completion, translated Stringer's original story to scenario format. Direction was entrusted to actor Edward Jose (with Seitz pitching in as needed), and production began in the late autumn of 1915. The *Iron Claw* company shot on locations in New York City and across the river in New Jersey, where Pathé maintained a studio. Episodes were completed at the rate of approximately one per week, and principal photography was less than half finished when the serial went into theatrical release on February 27, 1916.

Unfortunately, *The Iron Claw* is a "lost" serial; only one complete chapter—the seventh—is known to survive. (It was released to the home-movie market many years ago by Blackhawk Films of Davenport, Iowa.) However, Stringer's novelization still exists in the form of tattered pages saved by a reader of the *Atlanta Constitution*, one of several hundred newspapers that ran *The Iron Claw* in their Sunday magazine sections. A comparison of the filmed Chapter Seven to its printed-page counterpart indicates that Stringer's prose version can be relied upon as a fair representation of what appeared on movie screens in 1916.

The Iron Claw, in which Pearl played heiress Margery Golden, was planned as a 15-episode serial. Each chapter told a complete story and ended with that week's dilemma having been resolved. "Cliffhanger" endings, with which movie serials became synonymous, had been employed as early as 1913, but they weren't widely used until after the First World War. There was no shortage of perilous situations and daring rescues, but every episode ended with Pearl and her allies safe for the time being.

The Iron Claw's most important contribution to the serial's development was its use of a masked mystery man to counter the villain's schemes and rescue Pearl whenever necessary. No such character had ever appeared in a chapter play, and his presence made *Iron Claw* irresistible to thrill-hungry moviegoers.

As written by Stringer, Chapter One opens with a lengthy prologue set on Windward Island, a sandy patch of land off the South Carolina shore. For nine years, Enoch Golden (played in the film version by John E. Dunn) has lived there, mining nitrate and slowly amassing a fortune. He has protected his plantation by erecting seawalls to keep the Atlantic from encroaching on the sand-covered fields during high tide. Isolation has taken its toll on his wife (Carey Lee), who eventually yields to temptation by romancing Ludwig Palidori (Sheldon Lewis), a visiting physician more interested in Golden's family jewels than his woman.

Interrupting one of his wife's midnight assignations, Golden immediately banishes the mother of his child from Windward Island; later, he has her "defiler" tortured. Palidori's left hand is crushed in a vise by Golden's loyal servants, who also sear his face with a branding iron. Thus disfigured, he is released by the embittered husband and given an hour to leave the island. But the miscreant, who has sworn revenge, hides himself until the arrival of high tide, at which time he destroys the seawalls, thereby flooding the island. As Golden and his servants prepare to quit Windward, the pain-maddened medico seizes the miner's young daughter, Margery, and spirits her away in a small boat. Golden spots Palidori and a confederate rowing toward the South Carolina shore with the girl between them. "She will live," Palidori yells back across the swirling water, "but she will live in a way that will leave you praying she had died!"

This is juicy, red-blooded stuff, written by Stringer in the most florid prose imaginable. Of course, subtlety was not highly valued by serial audiences, and in the years before censorship reared its ugly head, an ostensibly sympathetic character could be forgiven the crippling and disfiguring of his adversary—especially in the interest of getting a chapter play off to a rousing start.

Some 12 years pass before we get another glimpse of Palidori, now known as Jules Legar and nicknamed "the Iron Claw" for the pincer-like appendage affixed to the stump of his left forearm. He maintains headquarters in an underworld hideout known as the Owl's Nest, which Stringer describes as "an unsavory cellar room in one of the most unsavory sections of [Manhattan's] lower East Side." The Claw has just received the latest in a series of cryptic warnings: "Remember the Hammer of God, which smites, and crushes whom it smites." But there's no time to dawdle over foolish messages: Legar is about to deliver the captive Margery Golden—who, according to Stringer, is "a girl still in her teens, a girl with a look of inalienable innocence still in her mournful eyes"—to one of his henchmen, a coke-snuffing dandy named Casavanti. (In 1915, when *The Iron Claw* was written, serial scribes weren't particularly concerned with maintaining ethnic neutrality where villains were concerned. Legar and most of his followers are clearly supposed to be Italians; they deliver "spotted warnings" in the accepted Black Hand manner and, for the most part, prefer the stiletto to the pistol.) The Iron Claw has previously called Margery "a flower that is ripe for the picking," and Casavanti eagerly awaits her arrival. At the appointed hour, however, his designs are thwarted by the intervention of a masked, bewhiskered stranger (future director Harry Fraser, impersonating another cast member) who subdues the drug fiend and whisks away the surprised girl. Once they are safe, Margery asks, "Who are you?" Her savior replies, "I'm only a hammer . . . the Hammer of God."

This is the last line of Stringer's first chapter and, presumably, Seitz's first chapter as well. But the newspaper serialization omits the coda that appeared on each filmed episode: a medium-close shot of the mystery-man hero, over whose chuckling countenance is superimposed the words: "Who Is The Laughing Mask?" He lifts his hands as if to remove the mask, but the camera irises to black before he can do so.

The Iron Claw's opening installment impressed trade-journal reviewers, supposedly impartial critics who, in those years, invariably favored Pathé's chapter plays to those of other studios. "The author, Arthur Stringer, is blessed with an astonishingly fertile imagination," wrote Lynde Denig in the

March 4, 1916 issue of *Moving Picture World*. "For many years he has been contributing weird stories to American magazines, and he may be counted upon for just the quality of ingenuity required in a photoplay of this character." Denig concluded that *The Iron Claw* "bids fair to become the most popular serial made by Pathé." Harvey S. Thew, the *Motion Picture News* critic who would later become a screenwriter, agreed: "The serial should have a drawing power as great if not greater than any the Pathé people have yet issued." Subsequent episodes proved this to be the case.

Chapter Two opens at the mansion of Enoch Golden, now a millionaire industrialist whose personal tragedies have hardened his heart. He is, among other things, a slumlord—the first and last father of a serial heroine to hold that dubious distinction. We are introduced to his secretary, David Manley (Creighton Hale), whom Stringer calls "incorrigibly youthful and engagingly irresponsible," with a demeanor characterized as "more that of a schoolboy than a confidential secretary."

Later, after Davy leaves on an errand and the millionaire retires to his study, the erstwhile "Hammer of God" makes the first of what will be many surreptitious visits to the Golden home. At this point Stringer gives us a more complete word-picture of the item that gives our hero his unusual name: "Over the face of this intruder . . . was an odd-looking band of yellow cloth, cut in the form of a mask. The center of this, drooping apron-like almost to his upper lip, was marked by an inverted crescent, which at first glance lent to the partly covered face the faint suggestion of an ironically laughing mouth."

The Laughing Mask, as he's now known (the "Hammer of God" sobriquet will neither be used nor referred to again), has Margery in tow and presents the girl to her startled father. At first skeptical, Golden identifies his long-lost daughter by the scar of a sand-shark bite she sustained as a child on Windward Island.

Shortly thereafter, Legar uses a fiery ray to destroy several buildings owned by the millionaire. (*The Iron Claw*, influential as it was, can't lay claim to the first deployment of such an infernal machine; that honor belongs to *The Exploits of Elaine*.) Before the chapter ends, Manley discovers the ray's whereabouts and puts it out of commission, showing himself to be a man of action.

Two episodes into the story, a pattern was already becoming apparent. Male characters dominated the narrative. Pearl White—more than willing to perform daredevil stunts, and presumably this serial's drawing card—was clearly overshadowed, not only by the mystery-man hero but also by Creighton Hale, despite the fact that his character was meant to be played at least partially for laughs. Pearl had figured prominently in the 20 episodes of *Pauline*, along with *Elaine* and its two sequels, but *The Iron Claw* found her playing second-fiddle to the men, rather than vice-versa. If Stringer's newspaper serialization is to be believed, several chapters unfolded with glimpses of the high-paid star restricted to bland, obligatory "dialogue" scenes set in the Golden house.

Initially, Pearl drew moviegoers to theaters playing *The Iron Claw*, but it was the Laughing Mask who brought them back week after week. Pathé's filmmakers already knew that audiences determined to solve a mystery-man riddle would catch every episode lest they miss clues that might point to the character's true identity. What they learned from *The Iron Claw* was that the guessing game was eminently more enjoyable when the mystery man was a heroic character with whom viewers identified, and for whom they could cheer.

Chapter Three reunites Margery with her errant mother, who has spent years in exile, distraught over her child's fate but unable to get succor from her stone-hearted husband. The climax of that episode famously featured a car chase which ended with one auto jumping an open drawbridge—a rousing stunt that reportedly elicited cheers from 1916 audiences seeing it for the first time. In the next installment, Legar enters the Golden home through "a neglected coal chute" and forges a note framing the Laughing Mask for the robbery of $50,000 in gold from a Golden-influenced bank. The Mask reclaims the stolen gold and eventually returns it, but he is blamed for the crime anyway. This is another innovation: The masked hero, already deemed a suspicious character by well-meaning but dull-witted detectives, is forced to carry out his plans while dodging the police.

Chapter Four also introduces the first of several male characters who might be the Laughing Mask: Golden's attorney, John Sibley, by all accounts a clever and resourceful fellow. As he recedes into the story's background, Stringer presents a more likely suspect: Count Luigi Da Espares, an impoverished young nobleman in America to raise money by selling family heirlooms and art treasures coveted by Golden. The gallant Count seems particularly solicitous where Margery is concerned. Could he be the Laughing Mask? Well, no. The end of Chapter Eight finds him crushed beneath Golden's shattered vault, dislodged from its second-floor resting place in a massive explosion set off by the Claw.

As the serial moves along, Margery Golden takes a more active role in the crusade against Legar and his minions, but the bulk of the fighting still falls to the Laughing Mask, who invariably appears whenever he's needed most. The action is swift and varied, with Chapter Ten's memorable, climactic struggle taking place in a setting that would become a popular serial battleground: a working foundry, in which Claw and Mask have an extended chase and fight along girders crisscrossed above huge cauldrons of molten steel. Stringer, presumably at the behest of Jose and Seitz, came up with a slew of varied, picturesque sites at which key action sequences could be staged. The use of real locations would come to typify serial production on the East Coast, and Pathé writers eventually plotted entire chapter plays around specific areas with visual appeal. (The 1922 *Go Get 'Em Hutch*, for example, took place almost entirely in and around New York Harbor.)

In April of 1916, with only eight episodes of *The Iron Claw* in general release, Pathé vice-president and general manager Jacques A. Berst announced that the serial—at that time still in production—would be extended to 20 chapters in response to enthusiastic letters and telegrams from exhibitors. An anonymous *Motion Picture World* correspondent, reporting on Berst's decision, said that theater owners had been excited about *Claw* from the beginning. "When the first two episodes were screened [for members of the trade], it was seen at once that the serial possessed all the elements that make such a picture great. . . . The mystery and suspense have been well sustained and it is a fact that the more recent episodes have been even stronger than at first."

Jose and company plowed forward, with Stringer engaged to write an additional five installments. He continued to introduce situations that became serial staples. In Chapter Thirteen, for example, he had the Laughing Mask imprisoned in a locked room. With no phone, and no other way of contacting friends on the outside, the masked man strips the insulation from two electrical wires and rubs the exposed edges together. This short-circuit causes the hotel lights to flash, enabling our hero to send a message of dots and dashes; this is finally recognized as Morse code by a hotel detective who frees the prisoner.

In the next episode, the Laughing Mask commandeers a trolley car to escape Legar's henchmen. Chapter Fifteen finds him chasing the Claw first by motorboat, and then by rail. Over the course of the next several weeks, he is hurled over a cliff, trapped in a quarry, and plunged into icy waters. And then, at the end of Chapter Nineteen, he does something quite unexpected. At Margery's insistence, with his back to the camera, the mystery man removes his mask. "Transfixed with wonder," begins the terse last paragraph of Stringer's newspaper installment, "Margery stood gazing upon the face of her companion. A little cry broke from her lips—a cry that might have signified either joy or sorrow."

How 1916 readers and audiences must have wondered whose face Margery saw! And how long the intervening week must have seemed to those who could barely wait to learn if they had correctly guessed the Laughing Mask's true identity, his face hidden beneath that crescent-shaped cloth and phony mustache-and-whiskers makeup.

In Chapter Twenty, the Iron Claw makes one last, desperate attempt to revenge himself on Golden and family. He plans to infect them with virulent bacteria, chemically enhanced for extra potency, that causes death in mere minutes by accelerating and toxifying the aging process. The Laughing Mask and Margery track the madman to his laboratory and confront him one last time. In this final hand-to-claw struggle, Legar cuts himself, and some of the virus from a broken test tube gets into his bloodstream. Transfixed with horror, Margery and the Mask watch their adversary turn into a shriveled, attenuated, white-haired corpse before their eyes. A return to the Golden mansion, where police are awaiting an explanation, is all that's needed to clear everything up.

The subsequent revelation that David Manley was the Laughing Mask probably surprised thousands of moviegoers. Earlier in the serial, Davy and the mystery man had been seen within seconds of each other, and the masked avenger had bobbed up in places the secretary could not possibly have reached. In explaining himself, Davy reveals that several of his friends periodically doubled for the Mask—not a difficult deception to carry out, given the nature of the disguise. The false whiskers, slouch hat, and long overcoat effectively concealed their identities.

Even in Stringer's dialogue-heavy denouement, several key questions remained unanswered. Why did Davy feel it necessary to become the Laughing Mask at all? How did he come to have so much knowledge about the inside workings of Legar's gang? And why didn't he do more to secure the Golden mansion, which was subject to so many home invasions that he and the Claw's henchmen should have been punching a time clock on their way in and out?

Logic never was a serious requirement for writers of movie serials. They were charged with creating memorable characters and devising fantastic plots. In many cases, they succeeded admirably. *The Iron Claw* was enormously popular, and not just because it was a Pearl White vehicle. Harry Fraser found that out while making a public appearance in character at a New York theater. Pearl and Sheldon Lewis were, of course, surrounded by admirers, but it was Fraser to whom most of the customers flocked, every one of them trying to raise his mask and get a peek at the face beneath.

The Mysteries of Myra
(1916, Pathé Exchanges, Inc.)
by Ed Hulse

The *Exploits of Elaine* cycle, running to 36 episodes in total, was produced by brothers Theodore and Leopold Wharton, show-business veterans who quickly saw the potential in motion pictures. Prior to making the Pearl White chapter plays, the Ithaca-based sibling had produced films starring the popular team of Francis X. Bushman and Beverly Bayne. Although the first of the *Elaine* trilogy had been shot largely in New Jersey, *The New Exploits of Elaine* and *The Romance of Elaine* were mostly filmed in the brothers' new plant in Ithaca's Renwick Park, on the southern tip of Cayuga Lake, on the site of an old amusement park.

In an innovation that actors welcomed, the state-of-the-art Wharton studio eschewed wholesale deployment of Klieg lights, those intense carbon-arc lamps that in constant and close-up use frequently produced scorched retinas in actors, who were often sidelined for days after coming down with bad cases of "Klieg eye." Instead, the Whartons outfitted their stage with light banks that took 1000-watt Mazda bulbs. An *Ithaca Journal* story about the plant reported that the filmmakers "have the dimming process figured out to a nicety—a feature that is sadly neglected by many of our largest film manufacturers."

The Whartons in those days enjoyed extensive cooperation from the locals, who not only allowed the filmmakers to shoot outside their homes when necessary but also loaned their furnishings when the dressing of sets required items not stored at the studio.

Specialists in every aspect of production were employed on a full-time basis. Cameramen included Ray June (who would become one of Hollywood's most respected cinematographers), Harry Smith, Joseph Dubray, Levi Bacon, William Pyles, and John K. Holbrook. Leroy Baker assisted them with special lighting effects and optical work. Production designers Archibald D. Chadwick and E. Douglas Bingham supervised construction of sets, and prop man Howard Cody built whatever he couldn't otherwise procure.

The New Adventures of J. Rufus Wallingford (1915), a series of loosely connected two-reelers based on the humorous yarns by George Randolph Chester, was produced entirely in Ithaca, proving to Pathé's satisfaction that the Whartons' production facility matched in technical quality of output any studio currently operating on the East Coast. The firm commissioned another serial from the brothers.

At this time William Randolph Hearst's influence on Pathé serials was still being felt. Hearst wanted product to release through his International Film Service, which operated in conjunction with Pathé, and he helped finance the Whartons in exchange for a financial interest in their next chapter play. The brothers resolved to produce something different: an episodic epic that would offer audiences the ultimate in thrills and chills . . . a serial built entirely around the supernatural. Its villains would employ every trick known to practitioners of the black arts.

To devise a storyline that would convincingly incorporate elements of occultism the Whartons engaged Hearst columnist and astrologer Hereward Carrington (1880-1958), described in one press release as "the greatest exponent of psychic phenomena, authority on spiritualism, and author of *The Problems of Psychical Research*." In his youth a great skeptic, Carrington through his extensive investigations and experiments had come to believe in the paranormal. He made its study his life's work and became known as the field's preeminent scholar.

Available evidence indicates Carrington devised his story late in 1915. The Whartons turned it over to Goddard, who in January of 1916 began writing his scenarios for what was then titled *The Mysteries of Mona*.

The story opened with a secret order of devil worshippers—operating from a hidden headquarters known as "the Black Lodge"—that employed occult powers in an attempt to control 19-year-old Mona Mason, whose sensitive nature and latent psychic ability made her particularly susceptible to such influences. Mona's late father had been a long-time member of the Black Order, whose Grand Master had already caused the deaths of her two sisters, who killed themselves on their 20th birthdays while under his control. According to John Mason's will, should all three daughters die before attaining their majorities, the family fortune would go to the Black Order. (An odd codicil, that. Even if Mason's executors didn't suspect the Order of foul play, the bequest would leave Mrs. Mason—still alive and living with Mona—out in the cold.)

Dr. Payson Alden, a scientist and psychic researcher with encyclopedic knowledge of the black arts, took upon himself the responsibility of championing Mona. Together they battled the Black Order and its Grand Master to a standstill, despite continual interference from Arthur Bayliel, ostensibly Mona's friend but secretly a member of the Order. Over the course of 15 episodes, Mona and Alden employed everything from simple hypnosis to astral projection and thought transference to fend off the devil worshippers.

For reasons not known, Goddard eventually changed Mona Mason to Myra Maynard and Arthur Bayliel to Arthur Varney. Myra's age at story's beginning was lowered from 19 to 17; her sisters were said to have committed suicide on their 18th birthdays, not their 20ths. Although the serial itself is lost except for several intriguing fragments, the scenarios have survived. They reveal that Goddard worked closely with Carrington; the scenarist's descriptions of sets, props, costumes, symbols, and rituals were taken from books, drawings, and photographs supplied him by the psychic researcher. Even a cursory reading of the scenarios makes evident the Whartons' desire that their scenarist render faithfully such fantastic details as had been uncovered by students of the occult.

As Goddard kept writing, the Wharton publicity machine began churning out news articles for movie-industry trade journals and local media outlets. *Myra*'s story was hailed as "a new theme in moving pictures." To further distinguish this latest production, the articles and advance ads for *Myra* routinely labeled it "a feature series" rather than a serial.

Leo Wharton, speaking to the *Ithaca Journal*, maintained the serial would offer reasonably convincing simulacrums of psychic phenomena reportedly witnessed by reputable scientific agencies and dedicated researchers. "The average layman," he averred, "and even the most rabid movie fan, does not seem to realize that every episode of the *Myra* series is authentic.

"For instance, we have it on very good authority that the Black Lodge, so vividly portrayed in *The Mysteries*, really exists. Also we have the word of dozens of good men and true that they have seen astral bodies enter and leave living bodies. Neither the Black Lodge nor the astral body is a figment of anyone's imagination, and all along, both authors and producers have striven not only for realism but for authenticity."

In casting the title role it was necessary to find a girl whose ethereal beauty, obvious sensitivity, and pantomimic skill could "sell" Myra's unique qualities and endear her to audiences. The part ultimately went to Jean Sothern, then just 21 years old but already a veteran performer. A child actress with considerable experience in vaudeville and on the legitimate stage, she made three feature films in 1915 for William Fox. The best of these, *The Two Orphans*, was based on the same Adolphe-Philippe D'Ennery—Eugene Cormon play later filmed by D. W. Griffith as *Orphans of the Storm*. Jean played the blind sister Louise, the part handled so beautifully by Lillian Gish in the Griffith version.

The Whartons scored a major coup in hiring Howard Estabrook to play the serial's hero, Dr. Payson Alden. Detroit-born Estabrook, who broke into show business locally after a stint as cashier in the county treasurer's office, became the toast of Broadway as a result of his first major role, the lead in *Brown of Harvard*. No stranger to moving pictures, he won acclaim for his starring performances in *Officer 666* (1914) and *The Four Feathers* (1915). Later he turned to writing and snagged an Oscar for his script to *Cimarron* (1931).

Cornell-educated actor Allan Murnane was hired to portray Arthur Varney. M. W. "Mike" Rale was cast as the Grand Master. Both were members of the Wharton stock company and had appeared in the *Elaine* cycle. Leo's wife Bessie, a perfect dowager type, took the role of Myra's gray-haired mother. Other parts went to Ithaca residents who had appeared in earlier Wharton productions.

With the first scenarios in hand, the cameramen spent two solid weeks experimenting with lighting effects and double exposures prior to the commencement of principal photography. *The Mysteries of Myra* would rely heavily on photographic trickery to persuade audiences that they were witnessing supernatural phenomena. Eerie atmospherics were further enhanced by extensive tinting of release prints. For example, Chapter Seven's scenario called for the Grand Master to direct his spirit to enter the Maynard home and materialize under a red light. (Red light, according to occult lore, being conducive to materialization and violet light being "antagonistic.") At that point he was to enter Myra's room and turn on the gas in an attempt to asphyxiate her. Anticipating the attack, Alden had outfitted the room in a way that flooded it with violet light when the Master threw the gas switch, causing the villain to dematerialize "in great agony." The red-light effect was achieved with tinting. The violet light effect, which called for a higher level of brilliance, was produced by strategically placed Cooper-Hewitt lights, resulting in a brightly exposed image tinted in lavender on release prints.

Myra's unusually complicated special effects necessitated far more time and effort than the Whartons had expended on previous serials. In one trade-paper story, Leo claimed that "nearly every piece of film used in this picture has to be run through the camera twice—this on account of the double-exposure work necessary. It's almost like producing two pictures at once, only it's a lot more trouble." (Although most sources list both brothers as *Myra*'s directors, Goddard's scenarios are sprinkled with frequent asides to "Mr. Leo," indicating that the older Wharton sibling did the lion's share of the megging.)

Some of the most intricate effects were accomplished by mechanical rather than photographic means. A levitation scene, which required the use of a derrick for lifting, taxed the patience of cast and crew. Positioning the derrick, blocking the scene so as to conceal its presence, lighting the set, rehearsing the actors, and getting a usable take consumed an entire day. For one shot.

Occasionally, unanticipated events caused a stir during shooting, providing the press agent with fodder for news items needed to fan the flames of anticipation. One minor mishap got considerable play in both the trade papers and the *Ithaca Journal*. In filming a scene for Chapter Three that called for Myra to be hypnotized by Alden, Sothern engaged in a little method acting—quite unintentionally. The Whartons had built a hypnosis machine that, reportedly, was an exact duplicate of one frequently used in experiments by Cornell professors and psychology students. A large revolving wheel fitted with mirrors designed to catch and refract light into a patient's face, it proved surprisingly effective. According to the press account of the scene's shooting:

"The lights were dimmed in the laboratory, the switch was turned, and to the soothing purr of an electric motor the huge wheel with its myriad mirrors glancing, refracting and blending the lights, began to revolve at high speed. . . . After a proper length of time, Dr. Alden (Howard Estabrook) was directed to bring Myra (Jean Sothern) back to earth again. To the great amazement of all, Miss Sothern failed to carry out her part. . . . She had actually been hypnotized." Estabrook, the account maintained, "shook her violently" to rouse her from her stupor.

Meanwhile, Hearst lost no time promoting the International's involvement in production and distribution. One trade-paper ad quoted him as saying: "The knowledge we have gained of public taste, of popular requirements in the publishing business, we will apply to the motion picture business."

The association of Hearst's International with the Whartons, Inc. was announced at a special Ithaca Rotary Club luncheon held some weeks after production commenced. Other issues were addressed there as well. Responding to early criticism of *Myra*'s theme and some of its heroine's predicaments, guest speaker Howard Estabrook reassured the locals that the finished film would not prove objectionable. "The Whartons," he said, "have never produced a scene that you couldn't take your children to see . . . and the Wharton studio is, always has been, and will always be a place where any man's daughter or wife or mother would be as much at home as in her own home."

On the night of April 19 the Whartons, with the assistance of Hearst's right-hand man Arthur Brisbane, arranged a preview of the first two chapters in New York City. The event drew some 1,487 attendees: exhibitors, distributors, representatives of the trade papers, and local media people. By all accounts the screening was a huge success. Afterward Wid Gunning, editor of *Wid's Daily*, polled the most prominent audience members and sent the Whartons a telegram: "*Myra* tremendous hit. All exhibitors and reviewers emphatically enthusiastic. Congratulations." Based on that enthusiasm, International immediately secured 703 bookings in the greater New York territory alone. A subsequent screening at Chicago's Princess Theatre drew some 900 people and elicited a similar response.

The trade-paper reviewers offered fulsome praise. *The Moving Picture World*'s Lynde Denig reported of the Wharton brothers' New York exhibition: "They scored so obviously, so decisively that to speak of their success is not expressing an opinion, but reporting a fact." Denig went on to say: "*The Mysteries of Myra* dispels the fear that the possibilities of the motion picture serial have been attained. Here is a story, unusual and interesting, possessing a pseudo-intellectual twist that raises it above melodrama; but not too far above—trust William Randolph Hearst for that."

Writing for *Motion Picture News*, Oscar Cooper opined that "[The Whartons] have supplied some of the most novel camera work so far seen on the screen. Splendid effects are gained by clever use of dissolves, double exposures, and fades; and these are reinforced by two-color treatment in many of the scenes. The atmosphere of mystery is created well and a high order of technical achievement is presented in the first two episodes."

Moviegoers flocked to theaters to see the latest Pathé-released serial, which went into general release on April 24, 1916, and if they expected the hairs on the backs of their necks to stand up, they weren't disappointed. Here was a veritable cornucopia of spine-tingling, blood-curdling thrills, generated by depictions of occult phenomena most viewers never heard of, much less witnessed.

Chapter One finds Myra under the Grand Master's telepathic influence, saved by Payson Alden at the last possible second from committing suicide with a ceremonial dagger found in a secret room built by her father under the Maynard mansion. Chapter Two has her imperiled by one of Varney's gifts, an exotic flower that blooms only at night and releases a poisonous white vapor.

The third chapter introduces viewers to the Auroscope, first in a series of pseudo-scientific devices employed by Alden in the detection of occult phenomena. An assortment of glass lenses filled with a chemical called Dicyanin, the Auroscope filters out ordinary light and allows its user to see the "aura" of a person standing before it. Myra, it turns out, has a well-developed aura—a discovery that reinforces Alden's earlier appraisal of her psychic predisposition.

In several chapters, Myra and the Grand Master temporarily switch bodies by virtue of putting themselves in trances that release their "astral forms." This enables the Master to make repeated attempts on Alden's life while inhabiting the girl's corporeal form.

The Black Order's murder methods were seemingly limitless. In Chapter Nine, Varney develops the skill of slowing Myra's heartbeat by a form of telekinesis. She is half dead before Alden figures out what is happening.

One of the most interesting episodes is Chapter Twelve, "The Elixir of Youth." It opens with the Grand Master temporarily transforming two superannuated subjects into attractive young people with a few drops of his niftiest elixir. They are charged with eliminating Myra; failing to do so will cause them to revert to old age. The newly rejuvenated woman loses her youth when she stands over a "sacred pentagram" Alden has hidden under a rug. Her husband, meanwhile, has lured the sleepwalking Myra to a nearby lake. His occult powers enables both of them to walk on water along a reflected beam of moonlight. When she refuses to yield to his advances, he vanishes into thin air and she plunges into the lake's icy waters. Alden, having learned of the plot from the old woman, races to the lake, commandeers a motorboat, and rescues the floundering girl just in time.

Apparently, *The Mysteries of Myra* was originally intended to comprise more than 15 episodes. The surviving scenario for Chapter 15—as scripted, a tepid installment—ends with the Grand Master and Varney still at large. The final scripted subtitle reads: "Next Week—The 16th episode of *The Mysteries of Myra*." But the fifteenth chapter that went into national release on July 31 was completely different, according to a synopsis printed in the August 19 issue of *Moving Picture World*.

Titled "The Thought Monster," *Myra*'s final installment deals with the Black Order's fiendish creation, a huge and powerful creature described as "a sort of Psychic Frankenstein." Sent to kill Myra and Alden in the latter's laboratory, the Monster comes very close to doing so in a slam-bang sequence that must have horrified 1916 audiences. As the girl cowers, Payson shoots the rampaging thing at point-blank range to little effect. Luring the beast away from Myra, he barricades himself behind a door and hastily swings his hypnosis machine into position. When the creature smashes through, his gaze is held by the whirling wheels and Alden gets him under control.

By this time Payson has abandoned any thought of bringing the Black Order to justice. So he commands the Thought Monster to return to the Black Lodge and destroy his vile creators. Suspecting as much, the Grand Master and Varney take protective measures. Armed with peculiarly shaped flashlights—which, the synopsis says, emit death rays—they await the thing's homecoming. In the ensuing battle, the Monster all but destroys the Order's Council Chamber, hurls Varney across the room to his death, snatches up his trick flashlight, and engages the Grand Master in a death-ray duel that ends with both combatants simultaneously vaporizing each other. Safe at last, Myra and Alden live happily ever after. That is, we have to *assume* they do, because there was no sequel to *The Mysteries of Myra*. We can find no evidence suggesting it did poorly; indeed, some trade ads published well into the initial playoff period featured raves from exhibitors who had booked the serial early on. But there were also reports that *Myra*'s devil-worshipping theme and occult trappings incensed small-town exhibitors in socially and culturally conservative areas, where local religious institutions wielded more influence than big-city journalists. It's probably reasonable to assume the Whartons' first production for Hearst was both popular and profitable—just not as much so as the Pearl White serials.

Patria
(1917, Pathé Exchanges, Inc.)
by Ed Hulse

Early in the summer of 1916, William Randolph Hearst—having played major albeit behind-the-scenes roles in the preparation of numerous films over the last few years—decided to jump into production with both feet. The already-legendary newspaper magnate could afford to bankroll motion pictures reflecting his own ideas and was determined to see them made. To this end he contracted the Whartons in 1916 to produce a "preparedness" serial—but unlike most such films, including Pathé's *Pearl of the Army*, his would avoid demonization of the Central Powers and target other nations he perceived as potential enemies. Hearst's German friends had convinced him that the United States need not fear the Kaiser; Uncle Sam's enemies were much closer. Let Europe fight its own battles, Hearst reasoned. His opposition to U. S. participation in the First World War was fierce and President Woodrow Wilson, who considered America's entry in the conflict inevitable, was a frequent target of vitriolic editorials written either by Hearst or his editors.

One of the wilder conspiracy theories of the day held that Japan, interested in bringing America to heel so as to further its domination of the Pacific, was secretly working with revolution-plagued Mexico to invade the United States from the south. Hearst's ranch in the Chihuahua province had already been seized and looted by Pancho Villa's raiders, and what was left of the Mexican government seemed indifferent to the wealthy American's outrage. So Hearst didn't need much convincing that here lay a greater threat.

"The Chief," as his closest employees referred to him, envisioned a scenario in which a fashionable New York debutante, the last of a patriotic family with roots dating back to the American Revolution, willingly abandoned society life to pit herself against Japanese and Mexican conspirators bent on waging war against the United States. He already had someone in mind to play the lead. . . .

One night in early 1913 Hearst and his wife Millicent invited famous ballroom dancers Vernon and Irene Castle to join them for dinner at their lavish apartment in New York's Clarendon building. The Castles had recently invented dance steps that were the rage of Manhattan's café society, and the Hearsts were eager to learn them. In her chatty 1958 autobiography, *Castles in the Air*, Irene wrote that after dinner had been finished the Hearst butler wasted little time rolling back the drawing-room carpet and turning on the gramophone. "Vernon danced with Millicent Hearst," she recalled, "while I danced with W. R. He had a very keen mind and if I showed him a step *once*, he remembered it. He also had that spring in his knees that is vital to a good dancer, and we thoroughly enjoyed the evenings we spent at his house."

Hearst and Irene Castle also shared a love of dogs, so she remained friendly with "W. R." after British-born Vernon returned to his homeland when World War I began and became a pilot in the Royal Flying Corps. Irene had already appeared in motion pictures, both alone and with her husband, and Hearst thought her ideally suited to play the heroine of his proposed serial. She took the role, committing to 20 weeks work at a salary of $1500 per week. Before the chapter play was done she would earn every penny.

To flesh out the story he had conceived, Hearst turned to popular fictioneer Louis Joseph Vance, whose literary creations included the Lone Wolf. Vance later recalled being contacted by an International Film Service employee who relayed the proposition rather off-handedly: "Mr. Hearst wants to star

Mrs. Vernon Castle in a serial having for its main theme the need of national preparedness for war. We're not in any hurry, but we'd like to have the first six or seven episodes in detailed continuity by tomorrow morning at the latest."

Vance put meat on Hearst's skeleton of a plot, adding enough characters to fill out 15 chapters. His novel-length thriller, titled *Patria—The Last of the Fighting Channings*, would be serialized in the Hearst newspapers. He forwarded episode synopses to Charles W. Goddard and John B. Clymer, who turned them into scenarios. The Wharton brothers, Theodore and Leopold, agreed to produce the chapter play for Hearst and accepted the princely sum of $500 per week—which they split—for their efforts.

Patria begins in the resort town of Newport, where recently orphaned Patria Channing, heiress to both an immense fortune and the largest munitions plant in America, is about to celebrate her coming of age. She has been considering an offer of marriage from Rodney Wrenn, the son of her friend and chaperone. But things change when she meets Captain Donald Parr, late of the United States Army and now doing secret service work for the government.

The Captain's attraction to Patria is genuine, but it also happens to bear on his mission. Parr has been keeping his eyes on Baron Huroki, chief of Japan's intelligence, and Senor Juan de Lima, a Mexican gentleman of mysterious means. Working together on a scheme to invade the United States from its southern border, the plotters have attempted to purchase an immense supply of munitions to be shipped secretly to Mexico—but the only firm capable of filling their order, the Channing concern, adheres strictly to a policy of selling its goods only to the American government and nations friendly to it.

Hoping that intimidation will succeed where his straightforward business proposition has failed, Huroki has his aide Kato send a threatening letter to Peter Ripley, the principal trustee of the Channing estate, who resides in the old family mansion in New York City. On the eve of Patria's birthday,

Ripley writes a letter informing the girl of the sacred trust that now devolves to her. Beneath the Channing house is a vault containing one hundred million dollars in gold—a fortune placed there by one of Patria's ancestors, to be used only in defense of America. Its disposition now falls to her. Shortly after completing the missive, he discovers one of Huroki's men skulking around the house. In the brief confrontation that follows he shoots the spy but is mortally wounded. With his life ebbing away, the elderly trustee phones Patria in Newport and summons her to the old family homestead.

At the birthday party being thrown for her by Mrs. Wrenn, the frightened girl confides in Don Parr, who volunteers to get her to the train station in time to catch the midnight express to New York City. Senor de Lima, hoping to gain control of the Channing fortune and munitions works by forcing Patria to marry him, attempts to kidnap the girl but is held at bay until Parr comes to the rescue. Huroki and Kato then attempt to wreck the Manhattan-bound train, but the heiress and her new beau escape unharmed.

Chapter Two opens with Patria and Don reaching the Channing mansion too late: Ripley is dead. Finding the letter the faithful trustee wrote her before being attacked, Patria reads about the hidden defense fund and willingly shoulders the responsibility of administering it. The remainder of this episode, and the next, details the efforts of Patria and Don Parr to protect the gold, the existence of which Huroki and de Lima are aware.

Chapter Four introduces a popular nightclub dancer named Elaine, a dead ringer for Patria who is hired by Huroki to impersonate the young heiress to his benefit. That subplot, wrapped up in the sixth episode, is followed by another involving Patria's jealous suitor, Rodney Wrenn. Huroki apparently stumbles on a successful means of undermining the girl when he sends underlings to infiltrate the munitions-plant workforce and persuade the men to strike. Eventually, Patria exposes the spies and appeals to the patriotism of her employees, who agree to undergo military training under Parr's command. The former Captain vigorously drills the Channing workers, turning them into a highly disciplined paramilitary force that easily repulses a surprise attack leveled against the plant by Huroki and soldiers he and de Lima have smuggled into the country, disguised as menial workers.

Following the abortive insurrection, which takes place in Chapter Ten, *Patria* shifts its focus to the Channing-owned ranch on the Rio Grande. Baron Huroki, exposed as an enemy agent, now resides in Mexico and devotes the rest of the serial to mobilizing his allies below the border and, finally, launching the long-planned invasion, which is beaten back during a pitched battle of startling ferocity.

Production commenced in the summer of 1916. Irene Castle arrived in Ithaca on July 11 and immediately rented a well-appointed house in Cayuga Heights, not far from the Cornell University campus. The other principals soon joined her. Captain Parr was played by Milton Sills, a 34-year-old actor with numerous Broadway shows but only a handful of film appearances to his credit. The scion of an affluent family, Sills attended the University of Chicago on a scholarship and, following post-graduate work, returned there as professor of philosophy and psychology. He spoke four languages and had already written a book on philosophy when the acting bug bit him. Probably the most intellectually gifted leading man in the silent-film era, he had no affinity whatsoever for chapter-play melodrama and soon came to regard his serial work as an onerous chore. "For my many sins," he later wrote, "I did penance for nine months of my life in *Patria*." The stolid Sills was, however, an effective leading man and with very few exceptions did his own stunts, fully earning the $400 per week paid him by the Whartons.

Swedish actor Warner Oland, who had previously worked for the brothers in Pearl White's *The Romance of Elaine* (1915) and the *Beatrice Fairfax* series (1916), was cast as villainous Baron Huroki. Another Broadway veteran, he did not share Sills's aversion to blood-and-thunder melodrama and continued to play Oriental characters (including Dr. Fu Manchu and

Charlie Chan) for the remainder of his quarter-century film career.

George Majeroni took the role of Juan de Lima, and Wharton regulars Allan Murnane and M. W. "Mike" Rale were cast as jealous suitor Rodney Wrenn and Huroki's trusted aide Kato respectively.

Patria's first ten episodes were shot largely in Ithaca, with brief side trips to Buffalo, Fort Lee, and New York City. A nightclub sequence in Chapter Four was staged in Times Square's popular Montmartre Club, but the cinematographers failed to get sufficient light in the large ballroom, and the resulting poor exposures forced the Whartons to retake these scenes in the New Amsterdam Theater's famous rooftop nitery. (This footage happens to survive, by the way, and Rudolph Valentino is clearly visible as a dress extra in several shots.)

Although delicate by nature and slight of frame—almost birdlike, in fact—Castle quickly got into the spirit of the piece and insisted on doing most of her own stunts. Chapter after chapter called for her to be manhandled and perform strenuous physical feats, and as a result, according to Louis Joseph Vance, "She grew deeply versed in the lore of liniments and bandages and surgeons' plaster. But never once did she complain or shirk any of the hazardous risks which the scenario called upon her to chance."

After reading about Irene's feats in her correspondence, Vernon Castle implored her to ask for doubles in potentially dangerous scenes, including airplane flights, chases on horseback, and assorted leaps and fights. But the plucky actress soldiered on. In mid-August the Whartons rented the *Sandoval*, a naval-militia gunboat, for a one-day shoot on Lake Ontario. Irene joined Milton Sills in diving from the deck into the water. Doing a similar stunt not long afterward, she plunged into Cayuga Lake and blacked out after hitting the unexpectedly cold water. Crew members immediately dove into the lake to fish her out, and she spent two days recovering from the ordeal.

Although Castle was determined to prove herself equal to the challenges associated with starring in a rough-and-tumble serial, the physical demands of her role proved increasingly unnerving and eventually wore her down. Filming was briefly postponed several times, giving Castle time to recover her strength and soothe her frayed nerves. She later wrote: "I was not called on for any acting except to look terrified occasionally, and on those occasions I didn't need to act [because] I was."

Through his minions, Hearst kept close tabs on the production and periodically ordered last-minute script changes related to sudden brainstorms. In one instance, recognizing the publicity value of keeping noted clotheshorse Castle in the rotogravure pages of his papers' Sunday sections while the serial was being produced, Hearst decided he needed shots of the actress garbed in the latest fashions. Goddard bristled at a memo from "the Chief" insisting he immediately concoct a scene in which Patria briefly disengages herself from the story's action to try on some clothes. "There is no excitement in this incident," he fired back. "It is merely a reason for showing [Castle] dolled up and giving a little relief from the swift and thrilling stuff that goes before and after. I have been unable to devise anything exciting where Patria can be dolled up which will not involve retaking of scenes on Ithaca sets or gumming up the plot."

The Whartons were generally well liked in Ithaca, whose residents often appeared as extras in crowd scenes and even rented furniture and props to the filmmakers. But as *Patria* dragged on, their patience surely *must* have been tried. In late September the brothers purchased a mansion at the corner of Meadow and State Streets and burned it to the ground for a thrilling sequence. Dozens of townspeople and several companies from the Ithaca fire department stood by while cameras rolled and actors darted in and out of the flaming building. Some weeks later, in mid October, the Whartons bought and blew up a railroad boxcar on a siding just outside town. Shortly after that, some 250 locals were hired to play rampaging strikers that ransacked and razed the Channing munitions plant.

As filming progressed, tensions escalated between Hearst and the Whartons. A rift eventually developed, although to this day the cause remains a mystery. Likely the break was a result of cumulative irritants. In any event, a report in the November 25, 1916 issue of *Moving Picture World* stated that Castle, Sills, and Oland were on their way to Los Angeles to film the remaining five episodes of *Patria*. "[B]ecause of the varied scenery in and around Los Angeles, some of which is typical of Mexican border scenes, the International Film Service decided to transport the *Patria* company to this region," wrote columnists G. P. Von Harleman and Clarke Irvine. "Most of the scenes taken here will be exteriors, which will include a number of battle scenes to be taken in and around San Gabriel Canyon. The company also will be taken to the desert for some 'locations.'" The item went on to say that Louis Joseph Vance himself would be overseeing production, which was expected to continue until "nearly Christmas."

Patria's plot called for a climactic border confrontation between the heroine's private army and the allied Mexican-Japanese forces, so moving the company to Southern California was certainly justified in the interest of verisimilitude, but Hearst's naming of Vance as unit manager could only have been seen as a slap in the face to the Whartons.

Vance engaged Jacques Jaccard to direct the final five chapters. Having just finished *Liberty, a Daughter of the U. S. A.* for Universal, Jaccard brought some of that serial's principal players along when he assumed helming responsibilities on the Hearst chapter play. *Liberty* leading lady Marie Walcamp, his protégé, was hastily written into the story. Her character, Bess Morgan, was a rancher who joined Patria and Donald Parr in battling the conspirators and mounting armed resistance to the planned invasion.

Filming proceeded slowly, pushing *Patria* ever further behind schedule. Castle, whose contract with Hearst expired shortly before Christmas, had commitments to fulfill back east, so additional sequences featuring Walcamp were devised to keep things moving. In a nod to current conditions on the border, Vance even brought Pancho Villa into the plot. The real-life bandit and revolutionary was played by 31-year-old

Wallace Beery, at that time transitioning into dramatic roles after working in comedy shorts for the past several years. (He would reprise the role to great acclaim 18 years later in M-G-M's feature film, *Viva Villa!*)

Castle biographer Eve Golden claims *Patria*'s star disliked Jaccard because he lavished too much attention on and allotted too much screen time to Walcamp. That might have been dictated by Castle's limited availability during December and January. She demanded extra compensation from Hearst when production extended into the early months of 1917.

Patria's final scenes weren't lensed until early April, many weeks after the serial went into release. Jaccard had saved for last the staging of a massive battle sequence that began in Chapter 14 and stretched into the 15th and final episode. For this lavishly mounted confrontation he hired hundreds of extras and rented actual military weaponry kept in an armory specially built for that purpose. Modern warfare was accurately depicted down to the last particular, with tanks, dirigibles, and airplanes being deployed to sensational effect. Jaccard had several miles of trenches dug and protected by barbed wire, in accordance with plans drawn up by U. S. military men hired as consultants. Several buildings were blown to bits and a plane deliberately crashed to add thrills to the siege. The director also shot night-for-night scenes lit only by explosions and flares. A *Moving Picture World* news story on the filming of this sequence called it "wonderfully spectacular" and "almost unbelievably realistic."

Having already invested $90,000 in *Patria* and eager to secure bookings for the as-yet-still-uncompleted chapter play, Hearst in late November ordered prints of the first three installments struck for exhibition in key venues. Some 900 people—including the Chief himself and Irene Castle, along with many of New York's most prominent citizens—attended a widely publicized screening in the grand ballroom of the lavish Ritz-Carleton hotel on November 20, just days before the star left for California. A full symphony orchestra was hired to accompany the opening chapters, and the audience of media, society, and financial heavyweights burst into sincere and generous applause when Castle made her first appearance on screen. After the third-chapter fadeout, when the ballroom lights came up, *New York Evening Journal* editor Arthur Brisbane—Hearst's right-hand man—introduced La Castle to the crowd, which gave her a standing ovation lasting several minutes. The following night, a trade screening at the Strand Theater attracted more than a thousand exhibitors from as far away as Philadelphia, Boston, and Washington, D. C. Their reaction was equally enthusiastic. Previews in other big cities—such as those at the Hotel Alexandria in Los Angeles and the Davenport Hotel in Spokane—generated similarly positive response.

Not surprisingly, reviews in the Hearst papers were hyperbolic raves. The *Los Angeles Examiner*'s critic, for example, called the serial "a super motion picture of unrivaled artistic beauty and epoch-making magnificence." But others *not* beholden to Hearst were complimentary as well. *Variety*'s "Jolo" labeled *Patria* "a certain hit" and characterized it as "probably the best feature of its kind ever produced. . . . The suspensive interest is always interestingly depicted, in modern fashion." *Moving Picture World*'s Ben H. Grimm was slightly more reserved: "*Patria* gives, through a view of its first three episodes, indications that it will be well received by audiences who have an appetite for melodrama. This appetite will be satisfied if the audiences are willing to forego the seasoning of logicality in their melodramatic food." It is worth noting that the few brickbats were tossed by reviewers from newspapers hostile to the Chief. The *New York Telegraph*'s critic, for example, panned *Patria* outright. It was "frankly anti-Mexican and anti-Japanese in line with William Randolph Hearst's policies," he sniffed.

Business was brisk from the start. Pathé's sales department worked feverishly to write business and scored a major coup when the serial was booked into the big-time Keith and Orpheum vaudeville houses, which catered to audiences more upscale than those that typically followed chapter plays. First-run exhibitors reported increasing attendance with each succeeding episode. In a news story appearing in the February 10, 1917 issue of *Moving Picture World*, Pathé attributed this to its "unprecedented advance advertising campaign," "the drawing power of Mrs. Castle's name," and "the compelling power of Louis Joseph Vance's story." Press releases reprinted telegrams sent to Pathé by such prominent exhibitors as Walter H. Seely, whose 2600-seat Piccadilly Theatre was the toast of Rochester, New York. "We find it necessary to cancel *Patria* or enlarge our house," wired Seely facetiously. "Playing to more than capacity. What do you advise?"

Buoyed by favorable reaction to the serial—especially from exhibitors—Hearst and the International announced it would conduct "the most stupendous advertising and publicity campaign ever launched in connection with a motion-picture serial." In addition to the prose serialization, which was booked into 25 leading newspapers, the Hearst Sunday sections devoted three full pages to *Patria* immediately preceding the chapter play's national release. Ad cuts in multiple configurations, ranging from tabloid quarter-page all the way up to broadsheet full-page, were made available to papers with the biggest circulations in the nation's 30 largest cities. Other ads and announcements appeared in Hearst's widely circulated "slick" magazines, *Cosmopolitan, Harper's Bazaar, Good Housekeeping*, and *Hearst's Magazine* among them. The campaign was expected to reach tens of millions of Americans before it ended, and the International's 15 domestic exchanges, working in concert with Pathé, wrote up thousands of bookings.

Patria went into general release on January 14, 1917. Around that time, British Naval Intelligence intercepted and decoded a top-secret dispatch from Berlin to the Mexican government. This document, known as the Zimmermann Telegram, urged Mexico to join the war as Germany's ally against the United States, which would America to defend her southern border rather than deploy troops to Europe. President Woodrow Wilson, who favored intervention despite his public pose of neutrality, released the Zimmermann communiqué to the press and used it to generate support for the country's immediate entrance into the conflict. Congress declared war on April 6, 1917.

Japan's recently cemented alliance with the United States was dealt a blow when Ambassador Hanrihara complained bitterly about *Patria*, which had been given a publicity boost by current events and reportedly was playing to packed houses. Pressure from those in diplomatic circles slowly intensified as nervous bureaucrats demanded Pathé withdraw the serial from circulation.

On the first of June, Secretary of Commerce William Redfield suggested the President himself intervene. Wilson sampled the chapter play before writing Pathé's Jacques Berst on June 4. He claimed he had just "seen portions of the film entitled *Patria* in Keith's Washington, D. C., vaudeville palace and was disturbed by the character of the story. It is extremely unfair to the Japanese and I fear that it is calculated to stir up a great deal of hostility which will be far from beneficial to the country, indeed will, particularly in the present circumstances, be extremely hurtful. I take the liberty, therefore, of asking whether the Pathé Company would not be willing to withdraw it if it is still being exhibited."

Berst was in a spot. *Patria* had been financed with Hearst money and Pathé's distribution deal with the International gave the tycoon total autonomy with regard to content. He wrote Wilson on June 8, informing the President that Hearst's International had already invested "a great deal of money . . . in the making, advertising, and marketing of this picture." Hearst biographer David Nasaw, writing in *The Chief: The Life of William Randolph Hearst* (New York: Houghton Mifflin Company, 2000), infers that Wilson next consulted the State Department counsel, who after investigating the matter concluded that the American government had no legal right either to censor the serial or insist upon its withdrawal from the marketplace. Yet the President pressed his case, importuning Berst again in August and this time appealing directly to the

Pathé executive's patriotism. He wanted *Patria* pulled from the nation's theaters but, as a fall-back position, suggested the chapter play could be altered to mollify critics and defuse the situation: "It would seem desirable to omit all those scenes in which anything Japanese appears, particularly those showing the Japanese and Mexican armies invading the United States, pillaging homes, kidnapping women and committing all sorts of other offenses. I trust this will be found possible, and if not, I again venture to ask whether you are not prepared to withdraw the film entirely from circulation."

Apparently Berst repeated that no alterations to prints of *Patria* could be made without Hearst's approval, because Wilson next wrote to the Chief's attorney and chief legal adviser, Grenville MacFarland. Hearst's relations with the administration were frosty at best, and presumably the powerful publisher saw no upside in further antagonizing Wilson. On August 23, MacFarland assured the President that the requested changes would be made, "though with great difficulty."

Intent on avoiding costly retakes, Hearst opted to make cosmetic changes instead, ordering selected trims and commissioning the remaking of text titles that had identified various heavies as Japanese. The new title cards gave Mexican names to *all* of the serial's malefactors, regardless of their apparent ethnicity. This strategy had risible if not downright ludicrous results. Baron Huroki became Senor Manuel Morales and Kato was renamed Pedro—despite the fact that both were repeatedly shown wearing kimonos, drinking tea, and living in apartments furnished with such plainly Japanese items as tatami, fusuma, and shoji. It is inconceivable that these substitutions fooled a single viewer—yet Pathé allowed prints thus doctored to go back into circulation.

In October the revised chapter play was screened for State Department officials and members of the Japanese Embassy, who found *Patria* much improved but still objectionable. Another round of correspondence—this one less insistent—produced no further concessions from International and the matter was dropped. By that time the serial was out of the nation's first-run theaters and making the rounds of small-town houses. Hearst's already rocky relations with the Wilson administration took a serious downturn as a result of *Patria*, the last serial in which he would have any hand. Fortunately, the controversy had no lasting effect on Pathé's fortunes.

In the end, it was the Whartons who took the biggest beating on *Patria*. Primarily to keep Hearst from interfering with production and making capricious changes to approved scripts, they had insisted from the start that he pay for any and all retakes resulting from his meddling. The Chief, however, saw things differently and refused to reimburse the brothers, who were ultimately forced to sue him for $39,000 in costs incurred during reshoots. And in addition to losing their connection to the International Film Service, the Whartons somehow alienated Pathé, with which they had enjoyed a profitable relationship. Theodore and Leopold decided to distribute subsequent Wharton productions themselves, an ill-advised gambit that backfired and severely diminished their standing in the industry.

In 1942 Hearst's organization officially dissolved the International Film Service. A handful of *Patria* chapters, all that survived after a quarter century of careless storage and the resulting deterioration, were donated to New York's Museum of Modern Art, which eventually preserved them—but only after additional decomposition had taken place. Not a single episode is complete from main title to end title, but most of Chapters Two, Three, Four, and Ten was saved. Today, a screening of this footage—about an hour's worth—validates those 1917 critics who praised *Patria*. It really is an outstanding chapter play. The production values are well above average, while the direction, photography, and editing is of a high order.

Castle makes an extremely appealing heroine, and while she lacks the natural ebullience and athleticism associated with such popular serial queens as Pearl White, Ruth Roland, and Helen Holmes, she does not seem particularly ill at ease in her role. The famous dancer is well represented in the surviving footage, most notably in a suspenseful sequence from Chapter Three:

Having discovered the loss of her gold, removed by Huroki men who bored through the wall of an adjoining house to penetrate the secret chamber of the Channing home, Patria confronts a Japanese henchman left behind to cover the villains' tracks. He overpowers the girl and ties her to a chair, then lights the fuse to a bundle of dynamite. The resulting blast is supposed to damage both buildings severely and thus remove any trace of the robbery. After the heavy leaves, Patria squirms in her chair and eventually loosens one arm enough to slip a dainty hand into a pocket. Withdrawing a pistol and literally shooting from the hip, she manages to sever the burning fuse just before the dynamite explodes. This melodramatic gimmick has been used countless times since, but apparently it was sufficiently novel at the time of *Patria*'s making to be cited by several critics as an example of this serial's thrills.

The Jungle Goddess
(1922, Export & Import Film Co.)
by Ed Hulse

The motion picture serial, which had been instrumental in making moviegoing a weekly habit for millions of Americans, had also become a lightning rod for criticism by the beginning of the Roaring Twenties. Moralists and educators decried the chapter play for its seeming glorification of crime and violence, and took umbrage at what they saw as incessant depictions of torture, murder, drug use, and assorted depravities. By 1921 these complaints achieved critical mass, forcing serial producers to tone down their products or risk losing the all-important youth trade. Since most gripes were leveled at urban-based crime thrillers, producers began turning out chapter plays with exotic settings and perils deriving from natural menaces—fires, floods, landslides, wild animals, and so on.

One outgrowth of this self-censorial product modification was a cycle of jungle-based serials. It began with the February 1920 release of *The Lost City*, a 15-episode adventure produced by Colonel William N. Selig and distributed on a territorial basis by sibling entrepreneurs who called their eponymous concern Warner Brothers. Selig, a Chicago-based filmmaker who moved to Hollywood with the bulk of the burgeoning industry, had pioneered the jungle serial with 1913's *The Adventures of Kathlyn*, the first chapter play to employ "cliffhanger" endings. He was known throughout the industry as the owner of an extensive collection of animals, rented for use by nearly every studio at one time or another. The Colonel signed Juanita Hansen, late of Universal, as his leading lady and put his extensive zoo to good use.

An unqualified success later released in feature-length form as *The Jungle Princess*, *The Lost City* was followed in theaters by *The Son of Tarzan* (also 1920), the first episodic drama adapted from the works of Edgar Rice Burroughs, who took a back seat to nobody where jungle-based action was concerned. The National Film Corporation release was generally faithful to ERB's novel; it has survived and merits closer scrutiny. For now, suffice to say that *Son of Tarzan*'s success helped perpetuate the cycle.

The brothers Warner subsequently released *Miracles of the Jungle* (1921) and *A Dangerous Adventure* (1922), which performed admirably at the nation's box offices but cost more than *The Lost City* to produce. The latter was the last serial handled by the Warners, who began concentrating on feature-film production and built their small company into a major studio. Between these two chapter plays, the Weiss brothers' Numa Pictures Corporation made and distributed *The Adventures of Tarzan*, a loose adaptation of Burroughs' second Ape Man novel, *The Return of Tarzan*. Although this serial also was popular, some exhibitors said it relied too much on the charismatic leading character—played by Elmo Lincoln, who originated the role in a 1918 feature—and didn't have as many animal thrills as earlier entries in the cycle.

For reasons lost to history, Colonel Selig became disenchanted with the Warner brothers after completing *Miracles of the Jungle* for them. (Most likely he was unhappy with the share of film rentals they paid him.) Knowing they planned to make a follow-up with or without his help, he decided to top them by producing what he grandiosely claimed would be the jungle serial to end all jungle serials. He commissioned the writing of an original screen story that, among other things, would employ modern-day contrivances in primitive jungle settings. Then, early in the fall of 1921, he started planting stories about this new opus in the trade papers.

"The script for *The Jungle Goddess*," said Selig in one of

these articles, "calls for action, plenty of action, taking our leading characters in a swirl of complications across three continents. The speeding train, the submarine, the airplane, and the radio are all called upon to play their parts in furnishing thrills for this chapter-photoplay.

"But I am going further than anyone has ever gone before to make a real animal-jungle masterpiece serial. I am putting wild animals into scenes hitherto thought impossible. I am coupling the terrors of the jungle with the actualities of modern life."

We'll never know whether it was Selig or his scenarists, Agnes Johnston and Frank Dazey, who came up with the storytelling innovation that distinguished *Jungle Goddess* from its contemporaries. At that time serials generally had one villain, who surrounded himself with as many henchmen as were necessary to implement his diabolical schemes. Occasionally additional collaborators were brought into the fold, and sometimes the villain had a female partner, but in general there was a single miscreant behind whichever depredations animated the plot. *The Jungle Goddess* opened by identifying one villain, who disappeared from view before the first reel had ended and was not seen again until the last chapter. A succession of subsidiary villains presided over no less than four separate and distinct subplots; each was dispatched after committing his allotted outrages.

Selig, an old hand at the serial game, must have known that exhibitors were already complaining about insufficiently plotted chapter plays that bogged down in mid-stream and resorted to illogically protracted and repetitive situations to pad the requisite number of episodes. His new serial would avoid that trap by introducing new characters and changing locales every few installments while adhering to the basic theme established in the first chapter. The story began in darkest Africa, moved to the open seas for two episodes, and then shifted to India and other Far Eastern locales before returning to Africa.

Production got underway early in September 1921 following the two-month construction of a huge jungle fortress set dominated by a massive stone idol (nearly three stories high) resembling a god seated on his throne. The idol's hollow base was big enough to house 20 lions, which would be deployed effectively in the opening episode. Selig hired James Conway to direct; having helmed *Miracles of the Jungle* with E. A. Martin, Conway knew his way around animals and was capable of staging the thrilling scenes in which they would be involved. Gabe Pollack was signed as Technical Director; presumably he worked with cameramen Harry Neumann and Eddie Beasley on the framing and lighting of scenes.

By this time Selig's zoo included some 470 animals—lions, tigers, leopards, chimpanzees, crocodiles, giraffes, exotic birds, and small monkeys, among others. Representatives of every species on hand would be seen in the new production, and Conway was issued a mandate to use them in stunts previously unattempted by filmmakers.

Heading the large cast were Elinor Field and Truman Van Dyke, attractive and personable performers who had worked in movies for several years without achieving real stardom. After essaying minor ingénue roles in a string of undistinguished program pictures, Field had played a few leads for the new Metro company before being hired by Selig. Van Dyke portrayed juveniles in several features prior to landing the second male lead in *The Red Glove*, a 1919 Universal serial starring Marie Walcamp. Supporting roles were taken Olin Francis, Lafe McKee, George Reed, William Phelps, Marie Pavis, and H. G. Wells. (No, not *that* H. G. Wells.)

Principal photography on the 15-episode serial took about four months, yielding roughly one complete chapter each week, as was then the industry standard. Although we don't know for certain how much was spent on *Jungle Goddess*, it's safe to say that Selig didn't pinch pennies. The frequent changes of locale necessitated the building of many substantial sets—temples, palaces, caves, and so forth—and the action set pieces were costly and time-consuming to stage.

Selig didn't offer his lavish new production to the major

serial distributors. He elected to place it with the New York-based Export & Import Film Company, an independent outfit that distributed motion pictures via the territorial, or "state rights," method. Very enthusiastic about the serial's quality, Export & Import president Ben Blumenthal contracted to release any other films Selig might produce over the next three years. Then he undertook the task of selling *Jungle Goddess* to the various sub-distributors that comprised the state-rights marketplace.

"In placing *The Jungle Goddess* on the Independent market," stated an E&I official to *Exhibitors Trade Review*, "we believe we are offering the greatest wild-animal jungle serial ever made. Every exhibitor knows Colonel Selig. Every exhibitor has faith in him and regards him as the peer of wild-animal serial makers. They know him from past successes and will book this serial on his name alone. Colonel Selig has promised that *The Jungle Goddess* will be his chapter-picture masterpiece."

Ordinarily it would be easy to dismiss Selig's promise and the E&I's statement as routine hyperbole of the kind employed in the promotion of every serial. Apparently, however, it was the truth. In early February, Selig delivered the final episode to the New York organization and Export & Import began offering it for sale to the various territories. Within a few short weeks, trade papers were flooded with news items reporting this or that sub-distributor had acquired *Jungle Goddess* for his territory. The subs arranged special screenings of the first three chapters for exhibitors they serviced, and the theater men were bowled over by what they saw. Selig had made good his boast: The new serial featured animal stunts that had never been seen before, and the visually stunning early episodes bespoke a heretofore-unseen lavishness of production for this type of chapter play.

The Jungle Goddess wasn't entirely immune to complaints about content, inasmuch as the title character became a lust object for several of the minor villains, but by and large the serial was "clean," relying on daredevil stunts (both with and without animals) for its thrills.

The Export & Import Film Company spent plenty to advertise the serial in the leading movie-industry trade journals, which responded with uniformly enthusiastic (and, one suspects, altogether heartfelt) reviews. Raved *Motion Picture News*: "*Jungle Goddess* quite surpasses them all when it comes to measuring out thrills by releasing a bunch of wild-animal stunts.... The atmosphere is well suggested. It is a fascinating jungle picture and exhibitors in the states-rights field are certain to lug their money bags to the bank after playing it." The *Exhibitors Herald* reviewer gushed, "Probably few of even the wildest flights of fancy by writers of thrillers ever conceived as many intricate near-death situations as did Agnes Johnston and Frank Dazey . . . [The serial] should prove a lucrative booking attraction."

Moving Picture World called *Jungle Goddess* "one of those episode productions that has a logical plot, plenty of human interest, and is literally choked with hair-raising, recklessly sensational stunts in which wild beasts play a most prominent role. *The Jungle Goddess* establishes a high mark in serials."

Exhibitors and moviegoers felt the same way, making *Jungle Goddess* the most profitable independent serial of the 1920s. Its initial theatrical playoff extended well into 1924; favorable word-of-mouth and glowing reports from theater owners persuaded exhibitors who hadn't booked it originally to hop on the bandwagon. Some sub-distributors, having purchased territorial rights in perpetuity, made spot bookings throughout the decade, and the serial was re-released in 1928 to capitalize on the revival of the jungle cycle sparked by the previous year's *King of the Jungle* (starring former Tarzan Elmo Lincoln) and *Perils of the Jungle* (starring future Tarzan Frank Merrill).

Slightly more than half of a deteriorating 35mm nitrate print of *Jungle Goddess* reposes in the UCLA Film & Television Archive, patiently awaiting preservation. A screening of this footage reveals that the raves were justified; even by today's standards some of the serial's action scenes are eye-poppers, and its production values are plainly superior to those of other surviving chapter plays of the period.

The Jungle Goddess begins with a glimpse of four-year-old Betty Castleton (played as a child by Vonda Phelps), identified as the daughter of an English nobleman and the richest heiress in South Africa. She's celebrating the fourth of July with a young male companion. Her unscrupulous, scientist James Scranton (H. G. Wells), hopes to gain control of her fortune and to this end has hired several ruffians to spirit the girl away. They interrupt Betty's play and whisk her to a hot-air balloon. The girl is deposited safely in the basket, which is loosened from its moorings. Before the henchmen can finish climbing aboard, they are attacked by a lion while they dangle from the mooring ropes. Lion and men struggle as the balloon slowly rises, but all three eventually plunge to earth. (Nearly every critic who reviewed the serial mentioned this shocking scene.)

The balloon drifts for more than a day before floating over a village inhabited by a cult of lion worshippers. High priest Beta Oom (George Reed) is about to make a human sacrifice to the lions when another native spots the balloon and brings it down with a flaming arrow. Miraculously, Betty escapes unharmed and thus is believed to be the white goddess whose arrival was predicted long ago. To test the girl's "divinity," Beta Oom has her placed in the sacrificial arena with a huge stone idol known as "the God of Fire" for the blazing beams that issue from its eyes. As the lions warily approach this strange-looking little creature, Betty pulls a bunch of firecrackers from her pocket and ignites them in an incense burner. She tosses them at the snarling beasts, which scatter when the firecrackers explode.

The amazed savages accept Betty as their goddess and raise her among themselves. Fifteen years later, we see her (now played by Elinor Field) clad in animal skins, ruling the tribe with kindness rather than fear—much to Beta Oom's chagrin. Her closest friends, whom she has nicknamed, are the giant chieftain "Thunderman" (Olin Francis) and the diminutive trickster "Tom-Tom."

Unbeknownst to Betty, who has all but forgotten her origins, her childhood friend Ralph Dean (Truman Van Dyke) has grown to manhood and embarked on a quest for his little playmate. He searches for months, inspired by the legend of a white girl ruling savage lion worshippers deep in the jungle. Ralph finally finds the village, only to be attacked by lions subsequently repelled by Betty's elephant friend Wapu.

Overjoyed to find the girl safe, Ralph persuades her to leave the jungle and return with him to civilization. An eavesdropping Beta Oom uses this information to inflame the tribe, and in short order Ralph is restrained while Betty is carried into the arena and placed in the lap of the stone idol. As Ralph stares in amazement, the idol's eyes blaze, and lions released from its hollow base try to climb into its lap, where Betty huddles in terror. As the chapter draws to a close, one of the idol's massive arms moves and opens a stone hand to seize the frightened girl.

Chapter Two begins with the thrilling rescue of Betty by Wapu, who stomps the nearest lion to death and scatters the others while Thunderman and Tom-Tom pry Betty from the idol's fingers. Ralph is released and the chief denounces Beta Oom, who is driven into exile.

Most serials would have squeezed five or six chapters, at least, out of the conflict between Beta Oom and the white people. But *The Jungle Goddess* breaks with tradition by immediately killing off several prominent supporting characters introduced in Chapter One. On her way back to civilization with Ralph, Betty is menaced again by the high priest, who has trained one of two particularly intelligent chimpanzees to wield a knife. Tom-Tom rescues his beloved goddess but loses his life to the enraged Beta Oom. Later in the chapter Thunderman falls to his death, leaving Ralph at the mercy of lions while the temporarily blinded Betty drifts down river in a canoe heading toward a waterfall.

In Chapter Three the two chimps trained by Beta Oom rescue Betty by hanging from a tree limb and plucking her from the canoe as it floats by. Ralph evades the lions and fights the maddened high priest, who himself falls victim to the snarling beasts. Betty and Ralph befriend the chimps and resume their journey.

Chapter Four introduces a new subplot and a new villain. Captain Nordhoff, skipper of the cargo ship *Katrinka*, comes ashore when his vessel is becalmed off the African coast not far from Ralph and Betty. His crew captures a slew of animals—including Betty's pet elephant Wapu—and stows them aboard with the intent of selling them in Singapore. Coming across the erstwhile goddess and her rescuer, Nordhoff offers them passage to the nearest port. Once aboard the *Katrinka*, however, the brutish captain shows his true stripes: Ralph is put in chains and Betty repeatedly forced to fend off her captor's lecherous advances. This, apparently, goes on for some time, as the voyage is represented to be a lengthy one. The episode climaxes with Ralph, freed to stand watch on deck while the crew rests below, being stalked by a Bengal tiger released from his cage by the scheming Nordhoff.

The fifth chapter opens with one of the chimps filching a gun from a drunken sailor and bringing it to Betty, who shoots the tiger just in time. She and Ralph manage to barricade themselves in a cabin while the chimp frees all the animals. The seamen are either killed by the animals or forced to jump overboard. Captain Nordhoff is seen being brutally mauled by a tiger. The blood-crazed beasts then try to force their way into the cabin where Ralph and Betty are hiding.

The next episode sees yet another shift in gears. With nobody at the wheel, the *Katrinka* runs aground on a reef. The frightened animals leap over the side and clamber ashore (even Wapu the elephant, whose departure from the ship couldn't have been easy). Once they are certain the animals have all quit the vessel, Ralph and Betty make their own way to shore. Before long they come across a Hindu, evidently of high caste. Somehow the *Katrinka* has made its way to India!

The serial's next major villain, Rajah Obar Sen (Lafe McKee), spends several chapters trying to persuade Betty to marry him. When she refuses, he puts her under a spell by means of a magic crystal. Unable to break the spell, Ralph enlists the aid of Archie Vale, a member of the India Aero Patrol, in an attempt to secure medical help for the girl.

Subsequently Vale falls victim to one of the Rajah's assassins and Ralph is menaced by hungry tigers while trying to climb the side of a building by rope. Betty is eventually restored to her senses, although shortly thereafter a leopard imperils her as Ralph, tied to a tree, awaits death at the jaws of a crocodile.

Chapter Nine, in which Ralph kills the Rajah by hurling him from a high balcony, ends on a very unusual note. Instead of the human protagonists it's the female chimp that is threatened in the cliffhanger ending. Cornered by tigers, she is rescued at the beginning of Chapter Ten by Wapu, who uproots a tree with his trunk and hurls it at the cats.

Ralph and Betty fall under attack by Thugs but are rescued by a "leopard woman," who turns out to be the long-lost daughter of missionaries. Another villainous high priest, Ram Wang, is introduced in Chapter Eleven. He's dispatched fairly quickly, though, and the young lovers finally make their way through the wilderness to a seaport town. Upon wiring Betty's relatives that he has found her, Ralph learns that the scheming Scranton (remember him?) has substituted another girl for the real Betty Castlemon; in this way he has maintained control of her fortune.

Betty realizes there's only one way to prove her identity beyond a reasonable doubt: by recovering her old clothes and personal belongings from the village of the lion worshippers. She tells Ralph that Thunderman enshrined these items. And so they're off to Africa!

Back in the jungle, their trail is dogged by a man on horseback identified in an intertitle as "a Masked Rider." (And you thought masked riders only turned up in Westerns!) The race for Betty's belongings consumes the next two chapters, with the Masked Rider getting them just before natives still loyal to the girl seize him. Sentenced to death, he begs her to intercede on his behalf in return for his assistance in helping her prove that she's the real Betty Castlemon. Unmasked, he proves to be one of the ruffians hired by Scranton in Chapter One to kidnap the four-year-old heiress. He has remained in the service of the unscrupulous uncle all these years, but now he is prepared to help the girl.

In a dramatic but non-lethal confrontation, Scranton's perfidy is exposed and he surrenders meekly. Ralph and Betty settle down to a life of luxury, ending one of the Twenties' most remarkable serials.

Surviving episodes of *The Jungle Goddess* are extremely impressive, combining above-average production values with clever staging of animal-action scenes that can still elicit gasps. The acting leaves something to be desired, but nobody can say that the serial didn't deliver what it promised. Curiously, for a serial made after the cries for censorship had been raised, it's pretty lethal: Barely a chapter goes by without a fatality, and some of the human-animal tussles are quite graphic.

The Jungle Goddess, as mentioned previously, remained in release far longer than its contemporaries and was extraordinarily profitable. In fact, it continued making money into the sound era. In 1935 an enterprising independent producer hired a Hollywood crew to shoot a 12-chapter serial built entirely around extensive stock footage from *The Jungle Goddess*. This new chapter play, titled *Queen of the Jungle* and distributed by Screen Attractions Corporation, relied to an extraordinary extent on thrilling scenes from the earlier film. Leading lady Mary Kornman, who normally appeared on screen as a blonde, wore a black wig to make her resemble Elinor Field. Silent-movie stunt star Reed Howes, a former male model in Arrow collar ads, was a little stockier than Truman Van Dyke but bore a superficial resemblance to him. Lafe McKee, who played the lecherous Rajah in *Goddess*, was hired for the new production; curiously, though, no stock footage of him was lifted from the Selig serial.

The talkie segments of *Queen* were lensed on a tiny soundstage dotted with potted plants and very small trees. In scene after scene Howes, Kornman, and other cast members trudged back and forth across this makeshift set; never once did the later production go outdoors for shooting. But director Robert F. Hill—himself a veteran serial helmer with two Tarzan chapter plays to his credit—gamely matched newly shot material to lengthy clips from *Jungle Goddess*. He did a pretty good job on what had to have been a minuscule budget, but the end results fooled nobody. *Queen of the Jungle* limped into release, was quickly forgotten, and became relegated to non-theatrical screenings in 16mm prints.

The Green Archer
(1925, Pathé Exchanges, Inc.)
by Ed Hulse

Edgar Wallace, the prolific British author whose fiction-writing career got off to a sensational start with the 1905 publication of *The Four Just Men*, already had 34 novels and a dozen volumes of short stories to his credit when one of his very best mysteries, *The Green Archer*, was published in 1923.

Replete with melodramatic situations and suspenseful chapter endings, Wallace's spine-tingling tale first appeared as a serial in *The Detective Magazine*, a bi-weekly British pulp, between July 20, 1923 and January 18, 1924. At roughly 150,000 words—nearly three times as long as most of his later novels—*The Green Archer* required 14 installments. The magazine's readers received it enthusiastically. A 1924 hardcover edition was issued by the British publishing house of Hodder & Stoughton, which reprinted it 43 times over the next quarter-century.

Wallace's American publisher, Boston's Small, Maynard & Company, issued the popular story stateside early in 1924. While not quite as successful as its British counterpart, Small, Maynard's two-dollar edition went back to press twice before the New York-based A. L. Burt Company licensed the reprint rights and marketed an inexpensive (75 cents) version produced from the Boston publisher's plates. American readers were delighted with Wallace's latest page-turner, and *The Green Archer* remains a favorite of those who collect the works of this prolific author.

The story opens in London, where expatriate American newspaper reporter Spike Holland is assigned to interview one of his countrymen, an eccentric millionaire named Abel Bellamy. Having acquired his fortune by questionable means, Bellamy came to England many years before and purchased Garre Castle, a Berkshire landmark said to be haunted by the ghost of a medieval archer dressed in green—a 15th-century poacher caught and hanged by Garre's original owners.

A blustery brute with no friends, Bellamy reportedly spends every night in his castle, wandering the ancient halls and taking double-portion meals alone in his library, behind locked doors. An anonymous letter from one of the tycoon's servants to Holland's editor hints that the Green Archer is abroad once again, prowling the castle and grounds late at night.

With Bellamy expected at the Carlton Hotel for a meeting, Spike arranges a sit-down but first conducts a previously scheduled luncheon interview with another Carlton guest, philanthropist John Wood, who expresses curiosity about the people at a nearby table. The reporter identifies them as well-to-do Walter Howett, his daughter Valerie, and an amiable idler named James Featherstone. The Howetts reportedly plan to lease Lady's Manor, an old estate adjoining Garre Castle.

Later, as he approaches Bellamy's room, Spike witnesses the enraged millionaire's ejection of an obstreperous visitor. This man, a retired prison warder named Charles Creager, says he can give Spike a *real* story about Bellamy. Holland agrees to visit the disgruntled pensioner at his cottage that night.

Begrudgingly granting the interview, Bellamy dismisses the report of a recent Green Archer sighting in the castle. Spike suspects there's more to the affair at Garre, though, especially since the millionaire's secretary, Julius Savini, is a well-known swindler. He concludes that the situation bears investigating.

Later that day, the reporter visits Creager's home and finds the ex-warder dead—a long, green arrow buried deep in his chest. Does this mean the Green Archer really exists? And if so, why would he want to kill a retired prison guard?

Barely four short chapters into the story, Wallace has

already introduced the main characters, hinted at the existence of dark secrets, and given his readers a gruesome murder over which to puzzle.

We learn more about the characters as the story progresses. Valerie Howett seeks a missing woman named Elaine Held, about whom she believes Bellamy knows much. Savini, supposedly on the straight and narrow, is actually stealing money from his employer. Featherstone, the indolent playboy, exhibits an unusual interest in Garre Castle and its current occupants. Walter Howett, while constantly fretting that Valerie might run afoul of Bellamy, seems to be playing a dangerous game of his own. And John Wood, who has devoted his life to the welfare of children, secretly mourns the fate of one particular child affected long ago by Abel Bellamy's cruel machinations.

Hovering over these secretive people is the Green Archer, a spectral figure who appears providentially to rescue those menaced by Bellamy and his cronies. Wallace regularly drops clues to the identity of this avenging angel. For example: After shooting at and apparently wounding the Archer, Bellamy finds a bloodstained handkerchief bearing the initials "V. H." Later on, Walter Howett is shown to be proficient with bow and arrow. Then, while imprisoned by Coldharbor Smith, one of Bellamy's henchmen, Valerie is liberated by Savini—who appears mere moments after the abductor is slain with a green arrow.

Readers familiar with the author's general themes and storytelling techniques would not have much trouble guessing the Green Archer's identity. But as he so often does, Wallace withholds important information from his audience, thereby maintaining suspense straight through the final chapter, in which the last-minute disclosure of vital facts finally clarifies motivations and ties up loose ends.

Among those readers originally enthralled by *The Green Archer* in 1924 was Frank Leon Smith, a former newspaperman who had spent many years writing scenarios for motion-picture chapter plays released by Pathé Exchanges, Inc., the film distribution company known informally as "the House of Serials."

Smith, whose duties initially included copy-editing of intertitles and rewriting of others' scripts to get them approved by Pathé's Scenario Committee, aligned himself with veteran writer-director George B. Seitz in 1919. Seitz, whose involvement with Pathé serials dated back to 1914 and the legendary *Perils of Pauline*, headed his own New York-based production unit.

A writer himself, Seitz appreciated Smith's work and starred in as well as directed two chapter plays penned by the ex-newspaperman. *Bound and Gagged* (1919) and *Pirate Gold* (1920) were exceptionally well received by reviewers and audiences alike; the former was the only serial whose episodes were unanimously praised by Pathé's notoriously critical Film Committee.

In 1923, within a period of just a few months, Pathé lost its three top serial stars: Pearl White, Ruth Roland, and Charles Hutchison. White's departure saddened the many co-workers who liked her, but few tears were shed when Roland (whom Smith once called "an authentic bitch") and Hutchison said goodbye. Those two were missed only by members of the Sales Department, who'd had no trouble convincing exhibitors to run the enormously profitable Roland and Hutchison serials.

Without big names on which to piggyback routine plots and already-clichéd action set pieces, Pathé's serial producers instituted a policy of purchasing literary properties that could be adapted to episodic format. In fairly short order the company produced and released serials based on James Fenimore Cooper's "Leatherstocking" tales, Emerson Hough's *The Way of a Man*, Mary Hastings Bradley's *The Fortieth Door*, and Albert Payson Terhune's *Black Caesar's Clan*.

Smith, who thought *The Green Archer* "a grand yarn," urged Pathé to purchase screen rights from Wallace. (Years later he claimed the rights cost Pathé $1500, and while there's no evidence to support his contention, the figure seems reasonable.) The title's acquisition was announced in movie-industry trade journals and the chapter play scheduled for release during the 1925-26 season.

At that time the Seitz unit, unlike most producing films for Pathé distribution, operated autonomously with little or no interference from "the front office." The consistently high quality of his serials guaranteed Seitz and his co-workers immunity from meddlesome executives.

In addition to writing scenarios, Smith acted as production supervisor. He chose locations and helped cast the principal players. Occasionally he blocked out scenes on paper to make things easier for the director. In short, he assisted in every conceivable way. "I worked closely with my directors," Smith later recalled, "but also with set designers, prop men, and wardrobe men. I was a nut on detail. Prop men respected this, and made sure every knife, revolver, or other weapon—or any other prop, for that matter—was exactly what I wanted."

Although George Seitz loved making serials and had the instinctive feel for melodrama that made him good at it, he accepted an offer from Paramount to assume responsibility for the studio's Zane Grey Westerns. These big-budget "A" movies commanded more respect than the chapter plays, which increasingly were geared to younger and/or less sophisticated moviegoers. His last serial was *Sunken Silver* (1925), the adaptation of Terhune's novel about treasure hunters in Florida. Before leaving Pathé, however, Seitz helped Smith persuade the company brass to maintain the same "hands off" policy with his successor. The unit continued to function with Seitz's assistant, Spencer Bennet, as director.

Spencer Gordon Bennet had been an important member of the Seitz team for years. A handsome, athletic, fearless young man, he joined Pathé in 1914 as a stuntman. Seitz used him frequently, not only as stunt double but bit player as well. Bennet was a quick study and an attentive, enthusiastic worker, and by 1920 he had been promoted to Assistant Director. He continued to play supporting roles, though, and had been assigned a substantial part in *Sunken Silver*.

Bennet learned from Seitz the technique of visualizing fully edited sequences in his head and then filming only those shots needed to realize his vision. "Cutting in the camera," as he called it, was an invaluable skill for a serial director to develop: it saved time, money, and film stock.

In a 1968 letter to film historian Kenneth Scott, Smith called Bennet "an ideal partner for me." He went on to say: "We had many the session on policy. He agreed with me on the importance of plausibility, to the degree of instant believability. [Bennet said,] 'If we're convincing in the small details, the audience will be with and for us when we come up with something wild.'"

Some Pathé producers and supervisors were chiselers who deliberately cheapened their product so as to pocket as much extra money as they could squeeze from already-constricted budgets. Smith and Bennet, like Seitz before them, took pride in their work and stubbornly refused to cut corners. If the budget allowed expenditures of $10,000 per episode (as was generally the case during the mid Twenties), they would spend the entire $10,000 to get the best possible results.

The first Smith-Bennet collaboration, *Play Ball* (1925), reunited recently crowned serial queen Allene Ray (a Seitz discovery) with leading man Walter Miller, an experienced silent-film actor who had worked in early short subjects directed by D. W. Griffith. Smith's original screen story embroiled rookie baseball player Miller and millionaire's daughter Ray in a conspiracy with international implications.

T. C. Kennedy's review in *Motion Picture News*, one of the most prestigious trade journals, called the serial "Major League in performance as well as background . . . acting, settings, and photography are of real feature quality." Kennedy further wrote: "Spencer Bennet, who has had a sound training in serial making under George B. Seitz and others, wins his spurs as a top-notch director with this effort."

Released in the middle of baseball season, *Play Ball* was sufficiently well enough received to reassure Pathé executives that the Smith-Bennet unit could be counted upon. With *Wild West*, a C. W. Patton production directed by Robert F. Hill, slated to follow *Play Ball* on Pathé's release schedule, Smith and Bennet would have ample time to prepare and shoot *The Green Archer*.

Although Smith remained enthusiastic about Edgar Wallace's

story, writing the serial proved unexpectedly difficult. While on location in Florida for *Play Ball*, he was shocked by the sudden death of his 35-year-old wife. Devastated, Smith returned to New York to arrange the funeral. But with both his own and Bennet's futures on the line, he forced himself to complete desperately needed scene revisions, which were forwarded to the unit via telegram and Special Delivery mail.

Still heartbroken and (by his own later admission) drinking heavily, Smith forced himself to complete the scenarios for *The Green Archer*'s ten episodes. Ironically, they were among the very best he had ever written. He later attributed his inspired work to "Pathé's confidence in me and the harmony of my association with Spencer Bennet." Smith couldn't bring himself to disappoint his friends and co-workers, especially since Pathé had purchased screen rights to *The Green Archer* at his instigation.

Shooting a serial in England was, of course, out of the question, so in adapting Wallace's story Smith changed its location to New York's Hudson River Valley. According to his version, Bellamy had the old castle taken apart stone by stone, shipped to America, and reassembled in a rustic area overlooking the Hudson. (This wasn't as far-fetched as it might seem today. In fact, during the Gilded Age several millionaires erected castle-like domiciles in the area. Even today, one of them can be glimpsed from New York's Tappan Zee Bridge.)

Otherwise, Smith's scenario remained remarkably faithful to the novel, retaining all its major incidents and most of the minor ones while adding sequences designed to enhance the mystery and reduce the need for explanatory intertitles. In Chapter One, for example, Smith substituted a country club for London's Carlton Hotel; in this setting he could justify the inclusion of an archery match, which would demonstrate to the audience that many of the principal characters were proficient with bow and arrow.

According to episode synopses submitted contemporaneously to the Library of Congress for copyright purposes, the archery tournament is Smith's only significant addition to the events depicted in Wallace's first four chapters. As the serial's Chapter One draws to a close, Spike Holland is just about to get Creager's information when the Green Archer appears at a window and looses the fateful arrow. Initially stunned by the killing's boldness, Spike hesitates before dashing outside for another look at the Archer. When he does, he runs smack into a highly agitated Valerie Howett clutching a bow in her hand. She faints at his feet as the episode fades to black.

At the beginning of Chapter Two, Featherstone suddenly arrives and spirits Valerie away after imploring Holland to keep silent about her presence at the crime scene. Later, in another memorable incident taken from Wallace's story, Bellamy shoots at the Green Archer and subsequently finds a bloodstained handkerchief. Shortly thereafter, Featherstone turns up at Dodge House (the renamed Lady's Manor) with a minor bullet wound. The episode closes when Valerie, entering her kitchen, comes upon the Green Archer—who zings an arrow straight at her.

Smith marveled at Wallace's ability to shift suspicion from one character to another, and he included most of the British author's red herrings in his scenario. The end of the serial's first chapter, for example, hints that Valerie is the Archer, who wears a bizarre mask and long, flowing robe. Chapter Two's situations briefly intimate that Featherstone is the ghostly killer, but almost immediately thereafter he's revealed as an undercover operative for the New York State Police. Other episodes point fingers at Howett, Savini, Wood, and Lacy (another of Bellamy's henchmen, and a participant in the archery contest).

Chapter Three introduces Coldharbor Smith, a river-front café proprietor who does most of Bellamy's dirty work. He brings two vicious guard dogs to the castle, and by episode's end the trespassing Valerie is caught between the hounds and the Green Archer, who slays the dogs at the beginning of Chapter Four. Additionally, that installment explains why Bellamy always brings meals into his library: We see him raising a trap door and carrying food into the dungeon below.

Chapters Five and Six revolve around the kidnapping of

Valerie by Smith, ordered by Bellamy to put a stop to her meddling. At the end of the sixth episode, Featherstone locates and boards the schooner on which the girl has been held prisoner. He dashes into her cabin and finds Coldharbor Smith dead, a green arrow protruding from his breast.

Chapter Seven opens with Valerie's rescue by Savini, whose long-suffering wife is blackmailed by the enraged Bellamy into becoming his housekeeper. The millionaire learns that his secretary has been working both sides of the fence.

In Chapter Eight, Bellamy's prisoner is finally located and freed by the Green Archer, who secrets the former captive in an abandoned cottage nearby for safekeeping. Believing the Savinis responsible for his loss, Bellamy locks them in the dungeon cell. He then instructs Lacy to disguise himself as the Archer and lure Valerie to the castle. The ruse works, and by the end of Chapter Nine Featherstone has joined her and the Savinis. Exposed as a villain, and with nothing left to lose, Bellamy plans to dynamite the castle and kill the people who have brought his plans to ruin. Featherstone's failure to report to his superiors prompts a siege of the castle by a detachment of State Troopers.

The real Green Archer slips into the castle, confronts Bellamy, and kills him. The prisoners are freed, loved ones reunited, and the remaining questions answered. In the closing scene, Featherstone catches up to and accosts the Archer, who after all has killed several people. But the officer can't bring himself to arrest the man who has righted so many wrongs, and with Valerie at his side, he watches John Wood speed away in a motorboat and sink his mask and green robe—no longer needed—into the Hudson River.

Most movie serials of the silent era (and later) emphasized action: fights, chases, shootouts, daredevil stunts. Many chapter-play writers reserved their ingenuity for the devising of "cliffhanger" endings that imperiled heroes and/or heroines. In adapting *The Green Archer*, though, Smith refused to sacrifice plot development on the altar of elaborately contrived, illogical action sequences. His script was dramatically cohesive from first episode to last, and the characters were extricated from their end-of-chapter predicaments without resorting to the outrageous deceptions most serial writers employed. As dictated by company policy, the finished scripts were submitted to Pathé's Scenario Committee, whose imprimatur was needed before budgets could be finalized and principal photography scheduled.

Smith and Bennet cast Allene Ray and Walter Miller in the leads; box-office returns on *Sunken Silver* had demonstrated that fans liked them. *Play Ball*, then in release, was reaffirming their popularity. Burr McIntosh, the heartless heavy of D. W. Griffith's *Way Down East* (1920), was signed to play Abel Bellamy. Oily, sinister-looking Frank Lackteen, who had menaced Ray in *The Fortieth Door* (1924) and the aforementioned *Sunken Silver*, took the key role of Savini. Wally Oettel, another unit regular, drew the part of Spike Holland.

Interior sets, including Bellamy Castle's massive main hall (modeled after the one in Britain's famous Cromley Castle), were constructed at Pathé's Astoria, Long Island studio. Smith had written actual Hudson Valley locations into the script, and exterior scenes were shot on the Storm King Highway and the Bear Mountain Bridge—still familiar landmarks to residents of the Empire State. The Sound View Golf and Country Club in Great Neck, Long Island granted Bennet permission to shoot Chapter One's archery contest on its premises.

Bellamy Castle and Dodge House were represented in part by actual castles along the Hudson; the owners graciously allowed Pathé's unit to film on their estate grounds, a decision one of them later regretted when his beautifully maintained lawn was destroyed by State Troopers on horseback galloping across. Additionally, Bennet commissioned the construction of two large facades—a false castle front and a crenelated tower—on a bluff affording a picturesque view of the Hudson.

Principal photography commenced in August and proceeded without undue difficulty. Earl B. Powell, an expert archer who had coached Douglas Fairbanks during the production of *Robin Hood* (1922), instructed Bennet's actors in the use of bow and arrow, supervised the staging of the archery contest, and doubled for the Green Archer when exceptional marksmanship was required. (Powell, by the way, also served as resident archery advisor for the pulp magazine *Adventure*.)

Cinematographer Edward Snyder, a charter member of the Seitz unit, was assisted by two young men working on their first motion picture. The first assistant cameraman was Linwood Dunn, a talented and inventive young man related to Bennet by marriage, who stayed with the serial unit when it went to Hollywood and with *Queen of the Northwoods* (1929) graduated to Director of Photography. He later became RKO's optical-effects guru and worked on such classic movies as *King Kong*, *Gunga Din*, *Citizen Kane*, and *The Thing*.

Snyder's second assistant, whose older brother was an actor, used his sibling's adopted surname. As Stanley Cortez, he became a Director of Photography in 1936 and used his early stints on inexpensive "B" pictures (including *The Lady in the Morgue* and *Bombay Clipper*) to experiment with unusual lighting effects. Cortez became one of the industry's most respected cinematographers, with such influential films as *The Magnificent Ambersons*, *The Night of the Hunter*, and *The Naked Kiss* to his credit.

Snyder and his assistants enhanced the eeriness of numerous castle sets with spooky lighting. Scenes taking place at night inside Bellamy Castle were shot with a very simple, atmospheric effect: bright moonlight streaming through latticed windows to create cross-hatched shadows on the walls.

Some ingenuity was required to keep the Green Archer's identity a secret. In Chapter Nine of Wallace's book, Abel Bellamy briefly comes face to face with his nemesis, who is described as "[a] tall, thin, green figure, with a dead white face . . . green from head to toe, a vivid, startling skin-tight green that could not be mistaken. Green everywhere, save that white face that stared blankly."

Smith incorporated this encounter into his Chapter Two, but with eight more episodes to go, he realized it wouldn't do to show the Archer's true face. The mystery would be gone.

Wallace's phrase "dead white face" suggested an unnatural countenance, so Smith engaged Polish artist Wladyslaw Theodore Benda—whose papier-mâché masks had been prominently featured in Broadway plays and were popular accessories at masquerade balls—to create a phony face for the mystery man. For one hundred dollars Benda constructed with a suitably grotesque mask, which reportedly elicited gasps from startled moviegoers when the Archer first appeared on screen. That, and the flowing robe worn over his green tights, effectively obscured the character's identity.

Pathé's Publicity Department worked overtime to gin up interest in the chapter play. In October, with production still underway, Ray and Miller took time off to address New York radio listeners in a specially arranged broadcast from station WRNY. Later that month, Pathé threw a press party at the Long Island studio. The occasion: Ray's coronation as "Queen of Serials." Guests were driven in deluxe motor buses to the studio, where they listened to a Harlem jazz band, witnessed an exotic Oriental dance (performed by Walter Miller's wife), and participated in an archery contest. Burr McIntosh delivered a scripted speech, after which Bennet placed a prop crown on Ray's head as cameras flashed.

By this time the trade magazines were being flooded with ads for *The Green Archer*, and in these journals the Publicity Department placed news stories in which Pathé sales executives predicted great things for the latest Smith-Bennet serial.

Shooting wrapped in November. The last major sequence lensed was a lengthy car chase that at one point showed speeding drivers crossing the famous Bear Mountain Bridge.

With Chapter One's national release scheduled for December 6, editing was already underway. Bennet's "cutting in the camera" approach left the editorial department—also entrusted with rewriting intertitles to compensate for scene deletions and gaps in continuity—little to do but assemble the shots in their proper sequence.

As the finished episodes were screened for unit members and Pathé's Film Committee, Bennet and Smith realized they had a hit on their hands. So did everyone else. The firm's Publicity, Advertising, and Sales Departments got behind *The Green Archer* in a big way. "Absolutely strikes a new high note in serial production!" screamed one ad. "In sets, mounting, photography, and locations it's EQUAL TO THE FINEST FEATURES!" The hyperbole locomotive chugged ahead at full steam:

"Positively proclaiming the Dawn of a New Day in Serial Quality!"

"This oozes class like a Tiffany Store front!"

"As a feature it would be great. As a serial it is a sensational, surprising triumph!"

Amazingly, the reviewers all agreed. Opined Edward G. Johnson in *Motion Picture News*: "Mystery, romance, thrills, and suspense! They are all here—in fact there is everything that goes toward the making of a corking good serial in this latest one from Pathé." *Exhibitors Trade Review*'s Michael L. Simmons wrote: "Of essential importance in the success of a serial is its power to reach a climactic interest at the end of each episode, this stimulating the spectator's desire to see the succeeding number. This, *The Green Archer* does with intriguing regularity."

Booking requests flooded Pathé's exchanges. Public interest was stimulated by ads placed in such important, nationally circulated magazines as *The Saturday Evening Post*—magazines that didn't normally promote serials. In February 1926 Small, Maynard reprinted Wallace's novel and won more converts.

The first exhibitors who booked *The Green Archer* were wildly enthusiastic and encouraged their brothers to hop on the bandwagon. Trade-journal testimonials in sections like the *Exhibitors Herald*'s "What the Picture Did for Me" printed dozens of glowing recommendations from theater owners who reported attendance surges whenever *Green Archer* episodes ran.

Typical of such effusive praise was that rendered by Ben Morris, manager of the Olympic Theatre in Bellaire, Ohio. "For us," he wrote in the *Herald*, "[*The Green Archer*] is the best serial we have had in years, and we've run them all. Each chapter built up and the finish brought a record-breaking house for the season. The picture is consistent and the air of mystery well maintained throughout. If you run serials, get this one."

The Green Archer became the most profitable Pathé serial in years; not since the glory days of Pearl White and Ruth Roland had one of the company's chapter plays been so successful. For the remainder of the decade, Pathé would tout its serials, especially those directed by Bennet and starring Ray and Miller, as coming From the Company/Stars/Director Who Brought You *The Green Archer*!

Allene and Walter went on to star in seven more Pathé cliffhangers for Bennet. Their two 1926 vehicles, *Snowed In* and *The House Without a Key* (the latter based on Earl Derr Biggers' first Charlie Chan novel), were both scripted by Smith. Their 1928 version of Edgar Wallace's *The Terrible People* was an earnest but ineffectual attempt to make lightning strike twice in the same place.

Pathé's final chapter play was also the last to feature the team of Allene Ray and Walter Miller. *The Black Book* (1929), directed by Bennet, reunited the stars with their most frequent on-screen nemesis, Frank Lackteen, but aroused very little interest at the nation's box-offices. Talkies were in, silents were out, and Pathé was a shell of its former self, having been eviscerated the previous year by corporate raider Joseph P. Kennedy. (Yes, *that* Joe Kennedy.)

Pathé Exchanges, Inc. eventually ceased to be, although the company's fabled rooster trademark was seen on pictures released by RKO Radio Pictures as late as 1931. Allene Ray's oddly pitched voice and overwrought acting style doomed her career; she starred in a few Poverty Row talkies in the early Thirties and then disappeared. She died in 1961. Rumor had it she spent her last years working as a drugstore cashier.

Walter Miller, a talented actor with a fine voice, easily made the transition to sound, occasionally landing plum supporting roles in prestige pictures like *Street Scene* (1931). He worked most frequently in Westerns and serials, especially those produced by Henry MacRae at Universal during the early and mid Thirties. Miller died of a heart attack after doing a fight scene in a 1940 Gene Autry movie.

Spencer Bennet's economical shooting habits made him very much in demand among parsimonious producers. After leaving Pathé in 1929, he went on to direct some 50 feature films—all of them inexpensive "B" pictures—and 30 more serials, including the last one produced in Hollywood, *Blazing the Overland Trail* (1956).

(Unlike some directors of serials and "B" pictures, who in later years dismissed their work as uninspired drudgery, Bennet remained inordinately proud of *The Green Archer*. He was referring to it in a 1963 letter to film historian Alan G. Barbour when he said: "Of all the serials I have directed [which numbered 52 over a 30-year period], there is just one that stands out quite vividly." In the same letter he opined that release prints of *The Green Archer* should have been tinted in the Pathécolor process, which would have made the chapter play "perfect.")

In 1931 Columbia Pictures Corporation bought the Pathé library, including the 79 chapter plays released by the company from 1914 to 1929. *The Green Archer* was one of several that Columbia remade in the early Forties, but this version bore little resemblance to Wallace's novel. Director James W. Horne played it for laughs, cramming all 15 episodes with fistfights and car chases but instructing his actors to overplay even the minor scenes. The end result was nothing more than a burlesque of the best silent serials. Horne's approach didn't sit well with everybody: leading lady Iris Meredith, who played Valerie Howett, flatly refused to discuss the film when asked about it some 35 years later.

Germany's tremendous post-war resurgence of interest in Edgar Wallace produced a lengthy series of well-mounted, feature-length movie adaptations beginning in 1959. *Der Grune Bogenschutze* (*The Green Archer*), released in 1960, was among the very best of the lot. Beautiful Karin Dor made a fetching Valerie Howett, Klaus-Jurgen Wussow a stoic Jimmy Featherstone, and Eddi Arent an amusing Spike Holland. Best of all was Gert Frobe, whose portrayal of Abel Bellamy could have been a template for his turn as the titular terror of *Goldfinger* (1963). Despite some ill-advised attempts at comic relief—mostly furnished by Arent—the film maintained a spooky atmosphere and brought Wallace's story to life rather faithfully.

A succession of vault fires ultimately destroyed the Pathé negatives. As a result, the 1925 *Green Archer* is considered a lost film. A complete print was known to exist in France as recently as 1960, but even that appears to be gone now. All that remains of what might be the finest movie serial of the Twenties is a tantalizing fragment: the last three reels (approximately 33 minutes) of the "work print" to an unreleased five-reel feature version. Those reels, currently stored at UCLA's Film and Television Archive in Hollywood, condense material from the last three chapters. The Archer appears several times and, of course, his final showdown with Abel Bellamy is a joy to behold. The superior production value is plainly evident in this footage, which makes it even more frustrating that the entire serial is apparently lost to the ages.

Based on a comparison of the existing footage to episode synopses on file at the Library of Congress, it seems likely that the feature version's first two reels—inexplicably separated from those salvaged by UCLA's archivists, and presumably lost forever—condensed the expository material in Chapters One and Two. The lengthy subplot involving Bellamy's cohort, waterfront rat Coldharbor Smith, was undoubtedly jettisoned.

Edgar Wallace's novel was reprinted in hardcover by Norton in 1965. The new edition bore an introduction by well-respected book critic and mystery writer Vincent Starrett, whose Jimmie Lavender tales appeared in the Doubleday-owned pulp *Short Stories*. Unfortunately, the "revised" *Green Archer* was severely edited. The Small, Maynard and A. L. Burt editions ran to 383 pages, the Norton condensation only 191— a pruning of more than half the wordage. Rather an ignominious fate for one of Wallace's finest works. Even at that, his novel fared better than the Smith-Bennet serial.

Pearl White, first and most popular of the serial queens, in 1914.

Flash Gordon (1936) made Buster Crabbe the undisputed king of serials.

GALLERY

Hugh Sothern escapes Lee Powell and Herman Brix in *Fighting Devil Dogs* (1938).

The Spider's Web (1938): Iris Meredith surveys Warren Hull's handiwork in Columbia's best chapter play.

Villainous Sheldon Lewis brandishes his latest loot in *The Iron Claw* (1916).

The Mysteries of Myra (1916): Allan Murnane leads the devil worshippers.

GALLERY 101

Howard Estabrook comforts Jean Sothern in *Mysteries of Myra*.

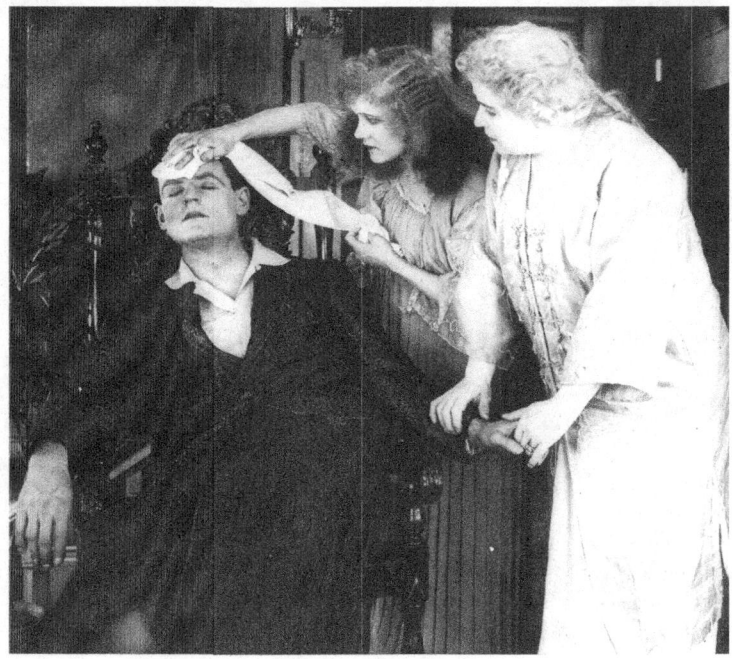
Sothern ministers to Estabrook after his struggle with occult forces.

Patria (1917): Celebrated dancer Irene Castle starred as a patriotic heiress.

GALLERY   103

Patria: Warner Oland's Baron Huroki (center) conspires with Mexican rebels.

Huroki and his henchman hatch a dastardly plot with Patria's double.

One of many elaborate advertisements placed in movie-industry trade papers.

The Jungle Goddess (1922): Elinor Fair and her protector, Truman Van Dyke.

Elinor Fair attacked by rampaging water buffalo while trying to ford a river.

Walter Miller and Allene Ray in their biggest hit, *The Green Archer* (1925).

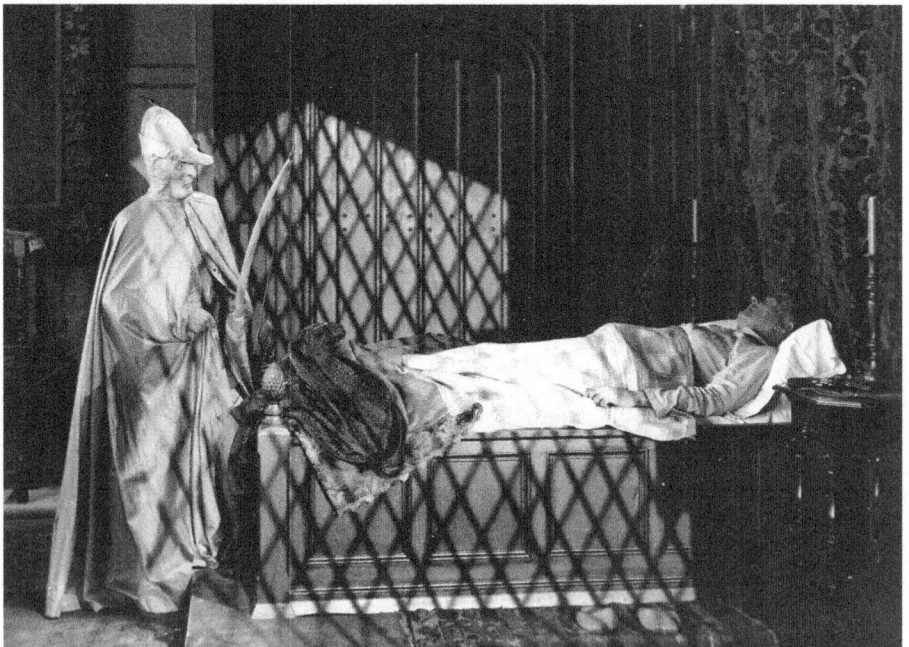

The Green Archer pays a midnight visit to Abel Bellamy (Burr McIntosh).

Director Spencer Bennet (left) in posed publicity shot with Ray and McIntosh.

The Green Archer: Walter rescues Allene again, this time with a trooper's aid.

Scene 38.

Dan's living room. Shaded light effect from windows. Make it interesting, shifty lighting, but enough to distinguish characters and action. Chan comes on swiftly, silently from side room which he has been investigating, looks off toward front door, then withdraws to side of room. A Jap house boy in white coat crosses to front door. Kam crosses to front door from direction of kitchen.

Scene 39.

Dan's living room. From another angle as seen from front door. The Winterslip party, Barbara, Minerva, John, Amos and Jennison come on. The Jap boy and Kam come on and are directed by Minerva to take care of the hand luggage. Barbara breaks down rather badly, and has to be attended by Minerva. John is very attentive, and to Jennison's disgust, manages to be Johnny on the spot. Attends Barbara.

Scene 40.

Dan's living room. Foreground Chan watching, quietly, sympathetically.

Scene 41.

Dan's living room. Minerva, Amos, John, Barbara and Jennison. Minerva is the boss. She says what is going to happen next. They must take Barbara to her room. Minerva and John support Barbara and cross to stairs and exit with her. Jennison hesitates. Wants to follow, but for the moment is uncertain. Turns to Amos. Amos begins pacing the floor nervously. Jennison hesitates and then exits to upstairs. The servants - Kam and the Jap, come on with baggage and go up stairs.

Scene 42.

Dan's living room. Chan watching quietly. Looks off at the retreating parties and then off at the pacing Amos.

Scene 43.

Dan's living room. Amos pacing the floor nervously. Suddenly looks off, discovering Chan. Stares off at him.

Scene 44.

Dan's living room. Foreground Chan. He smiles off at Amos and speaks:

516-Spoken title...
"Pardon me very much. I am Detective Sergeant Charles Chan. I make very quiet investigation in nice way."

Original *House Without a Key* script page introducing Charlie Chan.

GALLERY

House Without a Key: Miller and Ray apprehend henchman Frank Lackteen.

Walter and Allene seem apprehensive about George Kuwa (playing Charlie Chan).

Frank Merrill played the title role in *Tarzan the Mighty* (1928), a huge hit.

The Fire Detective (1929) starred Hugh Allan (hatless) and Gladys McConnell.

Edward Cecil (left) and Frank Lackteen trapped in *The Tiger's Shadow* (1928).

The House Without a Key
(1926, Pathé Exchange, Inc.)
by Ed Hulse

The *Green Archer*'s extraordinary success impacted its distributor, Pathé, in several ways. First, it restored luster to the company's slightly tarnished reputation as a supplier of top-quality movie serials. Second, it boosted the marquee value of stars Allene Ray and Walter Miller, whose fan base swelled considerably during *Archer*'s theatrical playoff. Third, it guaranteed the autonomy of the independent serial-production unit jointly headed by writer/supervisor Frank Leon Smith and director Spencer Bennet.

Pathé had increased its reliance on chapter plays adapted from popular novels, counting on well-known literary properties to generate audience interest following the departures of the company's top serial stars—Pearl White, Ruth Roland, and Charles Hutchison. It was Smith who had urged the company to purchase screen rights to *Archer* and Albert Payson Terhune's *Black Caesar's Clan*, which was the basis of the first Ray-Miller vehicle, *Sunken Silver* (also 1925). Early in 1926, Pathé's Serial Sales Manager, E. Oswald Brooks, encouraged the veteran scenario writer to recommend another mystery story, one the firm could produce as a Ray-Miller follow-up to *The Green Archer*.

As it happened, Smith already had his eye on a yarn that

had created a sensation when serialized in *The Saturday Evening Post* during January and February of 1925. *The House Without a Key*, a murder mystery set in Hawaii, delighted *Post* readers with its facile blending of romance, adventure, suspense, and humor. Written by former newspaperman Earl Derr Biggers, whose previous novels included *Seven Keys to Baldpate* (1913) and *The Agony Column* (1916), *House* concerned the murder of a wealthy islander whose larcenous past had finally caught up with him. Although Biggers built his yarn around the murdered man's nephew and the chief suspect's daughter, one of his secondary characters—a Chinese-Hawaiian police detective named Charlie Chan—all but overshadowed the young lovers. *Post* readers demanded more of Charlie, and Biggers was already working on a second Chan story when Pathé came calling.

(Earl Derr Biggers and Frank Leon Smith, as it turned out, were old acquaintances. Both worked on the *Boston Traveler* in the days before the First World War: Biggers as a humor columnist and the younger man as an editor of the comic pages. "He used to offer me a quarter to get off his desk and stop talking to him," Smith recalled years later.)

Pathé obtained screen rights to *House Without a Key* while Smith and Bennett were engaged on *Snowed In*, the Ray-Miller serial scheduled for summer release. Smith had written the original screen story, which revolved around a series of mail-plane robberies in the snow-covered Sierras. He once called it "a small, personal *tour de force*, as I wanted to see if I could build a serial like a stage play, with all entrances and exits carefully planned, and with dramatic unity."

When that serial wrapped, Smith turned his attention to the Biggers novel, breaking it down into the customary ten installments. He eliminated several minor characters, streamlined Biggers' plot, and injected physical action into what was, essentially, a very talky piece. His scenarios for the early episodes, particularly, followed the novel closely. Charlie Chan, who first appears approximately one quarter into the Biggers yarn, made his serial entrance in Smith's scenario for

Chapter Four. He was accorded roughly the same prominence in both versions of the story, although Smith downplayed the clever aphorisms that helped make the character so appealing in the prose version.

Work on *House* halted abruptly in April at the request of Pathé's Assistant General Manager John E. Storey, who had something else in mind for Smith and Bennet. After weeks of negotiation, he had finally secured the services of prizefighter Gene Tunney, a handsome ex-Leatherneck scheduled to challenge Jack Dempsey for the heavyweight championship. Tunney's manager, Billy Gibson, warned Storey that any motion picture starring the fighter would have to be completed well before summer's end: the bout with Dempsey was set for September 23rd, and Tunney would need time for intensive training.

Having gotten his job solely because he was a personal friend of Pathé Vice President Elmer Pearson, Storey did not enjoy the respect or confidence of many people at the company. He threw his weight around and insisted that unit producers find work for his movie-struck younger brother, Tom. Nonetheless, his landing of Gene Tunney was a public-relations coup promising myriad opportunities for exploitation. It was decided to star the fighter in a ten-episode serial, which could later be whittled down to feature length for exhibition in theaters that didn't book chapter plays. Storey hoped to rush the serial into production and begin distributing it before the fight, capitalizing on nationwide publicity surrounding the bout. Since Smith and Bennet were turning out Pathé's best serials, they were instructed to write, prepare, and shoot a Tunney vehicle on the quick. The fighter, already drawing a salary of $3000 per week, was due to arrive in Hollywood shortly, and there was no story.

Smith, who detested the Storey brothers, bitterly resented the high-handed manner in which he and Bennet were ordered to drop *House Without a Key* and do John Storey's bidding. The director, an easygoing extrovert who could adapt to anything, took the assignment in stride, but the fiercely independent

Smith chafed under this new responsibility. He quickly banged out a continuity that had little verve or originality and helped Bennet shoot the serial, titled *The Fighting Marine*, as expeditiously as possible. Tunney cooperated fully and enthusiastically, but as an actor he was hopeless.

The Fighting Marine was released nationally on September 12, less than two weeks before the Dempsey-Tunney fight. Pathé charged through the nose for it, and many exhibitors felt they were being taken advantage of. Fortunately, Tunney won the championship, and *The Fighting Marine* did enough business to justify the expenditures all around. A seven-reel feature version was released in October. By that time, Smith and Bennet were once again in the thick of *House Without a Key*.

As was his custom, Smith wrote the *House* scenario with certain actors in mind. Frank Lackteen and Harry Semels, old cronies of Smith and Bennet (as well as their Pathé mentor, George B. Seitz), were picture-perfect for the menacing characters they were hired to play. Natalie Warfield, who had added the comedic touch to *Snowed In*, was Smith's first choice for a spinster role. John Webb Dillon, another *Snowed In* supporting player, was considered ideal for one of the red-herring characters.

A newcomer to serials, Japanese-American actor George Kuwa, was cast as Chan. He wasn't right for Charlie at all, physically speaking. Biggers had described the detective thusly: "He was very fat indeed, yet he walked with the light dainty steps of a woman. His cheeks were as chubby as a baby's, his skin ivory tinted, his black hair close-cropped, his amber eyes slanting." Kuwa, by contrast, was slight of frame and narrow of face. The book's Charlie was habitually pleasant, but Kuwa (judging by stills from the serial) seemed rather dour.

Shooting in Hawaii was out of the question for a modestly budgeted serial, so Smith expended considerable time and effort to find locations that could pass for Waikiki. Some exteriors were shot on Santa Cruz Island off the California coast near Santa Barbara. To represent the novel's Reef and Palm Hotel, Smith chose a veteran's home in Sawtelle, between Hollywood and Santa Monica. The main barracks, ringed with palm trees and neatly trimmed lawns, certainly looked like a Hawaiian hostelry. A lavishly appointed home near Malibu stood in for the titular dwelling. (Interestingly, there's a real "House Without a Key" on Waikiki: It's a popular beachfront restaurant adjoining the Halekulani Hotel. Tourists congregate there for informal meals, cocktails, and entertainment. On most evenings hula dancers gyrate under a century-old Kiawe tree outside.)

With the scenario completed, the cast selected, and the locations chosen, Smith walked out on the independent production unit he and Bennet had nurtured. Afflicted with pleurisy, increasingly irritated with John Storey, and still mourning his dead wife, he had contemplated bolting upon completion of *The Fighting Marine*. Not wanting to leave his longtime friend and collaborator in the lurch, Smith waited until he had completed pre-production work on *House*. "I'd had my fill of movies," he said later. "I'd built up a good [financial] reserve and I wanted to get back to [writing] short stories. . . . The fun was gone and I was too damned independent to care for Hollywood and studio fears, compromises, and politics." In fact, he did not abandon Hollywood immediately; first he took a job as story editor for Paramount. Leaving Tinseltown, apparently, was not nearly as important to him as getting away from the Storey brothers.

Dismayed by Smith's defection but committed to doing the best possible job, Bennet hurled himself into the shooting of *House Without a Key*. Fortunately, the heavy lifting had already been done. The scenario was remarkably detailed; the cast included many former co-workers with whom Bennet had great rapport; and Smith had planned for practically every contingency before abandoning the project. It remained only for the director to shoot the scenes as written. Principal photography began in late summer and continued through autumn, with chief cinematographer Edward Snyder and first assistant Linwood Dunn—the future special-effects guru related to Bennet by marriage—manning the cameras.

Like the vast majority of Pathé's serials, *The House Without a Key* is a lost film. However, a copy of Smith's unusually well-crafted scenario survives and warrants synopsizing in some detail.

Chapter One opens as does Biggers' novel, with aristocratic Boston spinster Minerva Winterslip (played by Natalie Warfield) admiring the picturesque beach at Waikiki. She has come to Hawaii to visit her feuding brothers, who haven't spoken to each other in 20 years. Dan Winterslip (E. H. Calvert) has done well for himself, although he is the most feared and hated man in the islands. Wealthy and powerful, he lives in a palatial home known as "the house without a key." His brother Amos (John Webb Dillon), along with friend and partner James Egan (Jack Pratt), runs the Reef and Palm, a modest hotel for tourists. They are convinced Dan amassed his fortune illegally—and at their expense—although Amos refuses to tell Minerva exactly what crime his brother committed. The Winterslips own adjoining properties that Amos separates with a barbed-wire "spite fence," over which he has not stepped in two decades.

Having failed in her attempt to reconcile the brothers, Minerva contents herself with visiting each regularly during her stay. And there's another Winterslip on the way: John Quincy (Walter Miller), the son of another sister living in Boston and by all accounts a very proper young man. At Dan's behest, John Quincy has stopped in San Francisco to retrieve an old box of ohia wood from his wealthy uncle's home on the mainland. Sailing for Hawaii on the *S. S. Matsonia*, John is seen reviewing a letter sent to him by the islander. It ends ominously: "Take the box aboard ship, and when you are at sea, throw it overboard. My life and safety depend on you."

Also sailing on the *Matsonia* are Dan's daughter Barbara (Betty Caldwell) and his attorney, Harry Jennison (William Norton Bailey). The lawyer has proposed to Barbara but for some reason Dan has expressly forbidden their marriage. There is one other passenger on board with an interest in the Winterslip family: Carlotta "Cary" Egan (Allene Ray), the daughter of James, partner of Amos and co-owner of the Reef and Palm. She has just graduated from a California college and can't wait to be reunited with her father.

One of the stewards, a sinister character named Bowker (Charles H. West), befriends John Quincy after the ship gets underway. But he's clearly up to no good, and while rummaging through John's bags he finds both Dan's box and the letter. Although it's not disclosed in Chapter One, Bowker is in cahoots with Kaohla (Frank Lackteen), a former cabin boy on Dan's old ship, the *Maid of Shiloh*. Kaohla, who does odd jobs at the house without a key, thinks he knows what the box contains: proof that Dan Winterslip committed a serious crime some 20 years ago.

John Quincy is immediately attracted to Cary, but during their first conversation she rebuffs him. Later, she explains that since John's uncle Dan wronged her father terribly, she is naturally suspicious of anyone named Winterslip. Puzzled and hurt, John Quincy expresses his hope that they can be friends.

That night, with the *Matsonia* far out to sea, John prepares to heave the wooden box overboard as per Dan's instructions. Cary spots him from the deck and follows. Before John can complete his task, he is attacked by three men and pitched overboard. Chapter One ends with him struggling to stay afloat as the *Matsonia* recedes into the distance.

Chapter Two opens with Cary recovering the box and crying, "Man overboard!" The ensuing commotion frightens off John's attackers and he is pulled from the sea. With the box safe in her stateroom, Cary hopes she can persuade John to open it in her presence; she seems to know its contents have something to do with her father's grievance against Dan Winterslip. The delay incurred by John's rescue prevents the *Matsonia* from making port on time and it is forced to drop anchor in the Honolulu harbor. Bowker and his henchmen make another attempt to secure the box, whisking it from the girl's room just as Cary and John arrive. In the chase and fight that follows, our hero is almost killed by a heavy block-and-tackle and Bowker drops the box over the ship's side—into the arms of Kaohla, waiting in a canoe below.

The first two chapters also include brief sequences that show Dan Winterslip narrowly escaping death. He is nearly hit with a thrown knife and barely dodges a heavy hammer dropped from his roof. In Chapter Three his luck runs out. Shortly after Cary and John lose the box to Bowker's henchmen, Dan calls the Reef and Palm and insists James Egan come immediately to his home. Egan tells Amos Winterslip that Dan has called for a showdown, and voices his willingness to oblige.

A few minutes later, in Dan's upstairs guest room, Minerva is awakened by a commotion. Joined by one of the servants, she enters Dan's sleeping porch just as a figure is slipping over the porch rail. The only thing visible on the intruder is a wristwatch with a luminous dial, missing the numeral "3." Dan lays dead, sprawled across his bed. The servant notices a trail of water droplets leading to and from the railing. "Man had wet feet!" she concludes.

Smith's handling of the water clue is masterful, a model of silent-era storytelling in which necessary information is conveyed entirely in pantomime. Prior to Dan's death, just following the fateful phone call to Egan, a series of scenes indicates that one of four men could be the murderer. First, Egan is shown stepping into a deep puddle of water after crossing the spite fence. Then, Amos is shown getting doused when a hotel waiter drops a large pitcher of water at his feet. Kaohla, returning from his trip to the *Matsonia*, leaps into the surf to beach his canoe. And Saladine (Harry Semels), a mystery man who's been skulking around both Winterslip properties, gets drenched to the knees by a wave as he spies on Kaohla from behind a large rock on shore. Thus are the seeds of suspicion planted.

The third episode ends with the *Matsonia* docking the following morning. Barbara Winterslip breaks down after being informed that her father has been murdered, and Minerva takes charge of the girl. James Egan, arriving to greet Cary, is stopped by Police Captain Hallet (Scott Seaton) and arrested for the murder of Dan Winterslip.

Chapter Four opens with Cary proclaiming her father's innocence and John Quincy incurring Minerva's displeasure for taking the girl's side. It develops that Egan sent Cary a radiogram urging her to prevent John from disposing of the ohia box. The case against him is circumstantial but strong nonetheless: his bitter feud with Dan Winterslip was no secret, he was known to have made an appointment with Dan just minutes before the murder, and witnesses say his feet were still wet when he returned to the Reef and Palm.

Charlie Chan enters the serial in a scene that finds the Winterslips and Jennison attempting to console the heartbroken Barbara. He introduces himself by saying: "Pardon me very much. I am Detective Sergeant Charles Chan. I make very quiet investigation in nice way." Jennison doesn't think much of the new arrival, but Amos sets him straight: "Charlie Chan? He's supposed to be the shrewdest detective in the islands."

John Quincy doesn't know Egan but finds it difficult to believe that anyone related to Cary could have committed murder. This makes him a minority of one in the house without a key. Chan befriends the young Bostonian and tries to be supportive. "At present hour all are dark and mysterious," he says. "We must make bright shining light beam on guilty party."

As the story progresses it becomes apparent that Jennison, Kaohla, and the steward Bowker are partners in some criminal venture. Kaohla buries the ohia box on the headlands near the spite fence, safe from prying eyes but easily retrievable if and when desired. Amos Winterslip disappears; his absence arouses suspicion even though there's no direct evidence against him. Kennedy (Clifford Saum), one of the Matsonia crew members hired by Bowker to attack John Quincy, attempts to blackmail Jennison and is lured into a dynamite trap that kills him and very nearly takes the lives of John and Cary as well. Saladine, still staying at the Reef and Palm, falls under suspicion and fights John after the latter notices a white band on his tanned wrist—a telltale sign that he once wore a wristwatch.

In Chapter Eight, a group of kids playing "pirate" dig up the mystery box, which eventually comes into Chan's possession. He opens it in Dan's house while surrounded by Cary, John,

Minerva, Barbara, and Jennison. Inside is the 1906 log book for the *Maid of Shiloh*, Dan's old schooner. Cary asks Chan to read the handwritten entry for the fourth of December. It says: "At anchor, Pearl Harbor. This day, my brother Amos and his partner, James Egan, delivered to me an ohia wood box containing coins and jewelry amounting approximately to $100,000. I am to deposit this to their account in Sydney."

Remembering that Kaohla was Dan's cabin boy, Minerva summons him to testify. He nervously tells them that the Maid was scuttled off the coast of Australia before the box could be deposited in the bank at Sydney. Cary insists Dan stole the hundred thousand, as her father and Amos always believed, and used it as seed money to grow his own fortune. Hiding the log book was a necessity, because it proved Dan had accepted the shipment. But concealing it in the ohia box was foolish because possession of the box indicated Dan had gotten the money as well.

Barbara, having finally realized her father was no saint, swears to a grateful Cary that she will repay every penny owed to the Egans, with interest. This declaration annoys Jennison, who rather obstreperously reiterates his belief in Jim Egan's guilt. It has become obvious to John that the lawyer is primarily interested in Barbara for the fortune she will inherit, and he challenges Jennison on this point. In the lovers' quarrel that follows, Barbara breaks off her engagement, infuriating the attorney.

In Chapter Nine, Jennison decides to quit the islands and arranges to sell the illegal merchandise he's been peddling with the help of Kaohla, Bowker, and others. Jennison has been running drugs, and a fire sale is quickly arranged for cash customers. The crooked lawyer bundles his money and departs to a steamer bound for the mainland. John is lured to the distribution center and captured, but he has left a message for Cary to meet him there and she brings Chan and the police. In the ensuing melee Cary spots a well-tanned arm bearing the luminous wristwatch with the missing numeral. The chapter ends as she reaches for it, crying, "The watch! The watch!"

The final episode opens with the roundup of the drug ring, among whose members is a native wearing the watch. He claims to have fished the timepiece out of the harbor after seeing it thrown from the *Matsonia* the night Dan Winterslip was killed. Bowker, fingered as the man who tossed the watch overboard, claims it was given to him by Jennison.

John Quincy overtakes the steamer in a fast launch, climbs aboard, locates Jennison, and engages him in a knock-down, drag-out brawl. The lawyer, having gotten the better of John, is about to kill the younger man when Chan, thrusting a gun through the cabin porthole, apprehends him.

Back at police headquarters, District Attorney Greene (John Cossar) pieces the story together from the testimony of various witnesses. Dan Winterslip had learned Jennison and Kaohla were running drugs; that's why he opposed Barbara's engagement to the lawyer. Saladine is identified as a Federal narcotics agent who knew early on that Kaohla was involved and thought Dan might be, as well.

Jennison, who knew about the log book, schemed to get it so he could force Dan to consent to the marriage. Realizing this, Dan sent the wire asking John Quincy to get the box and throw it into the ocean. That would effectively checkmate Jennison. Moreover, Dan planned to change his will, disinheriting Barbara if she married the lawyer. Jennison learned about this while on the *Matsonia*.

While the steamer lay anchored outside the harbor, Jennison—who once won an award as the best swimmer in the islands—swam to shore, made his way to Dan's house, and killed him just before Egan arrived for his appointment. Then he swam back to the ship. Realizing that he could be identified by the luminous wristwatch, which Minerva and the servant had seen, he gave the timepiece to Bowker with instructions to throw it overboard.

Somehow Dan found out that Egan, having learned about John's mission, wired Cary to prevent the young man from deep-sixing the box. He called Egan and demanded a showdown, but the Reef and Palm's co-owner arrived at the house without a key just after the murder had been discovered. Thinking his partner Amos—who knew about the meeting—might have beat him to the house and killed Dan, Egan allowed himself to be falsely accused rather than risk incriminating his old friend.

Chan is delighted to have helped in clearing Egan and thus facilitating the romance of John and Cary, who are contemplating marriage as the serial ends.

Smith's scenario for *The House Without a Key* is generally faithful to Biggers' novel but differs in important ways. To begin with, Cary Egan does not sail to Hawaii with John Quincy, Barbara, and Jennison; she arrives on another steamer. The ohia box is stolen from John at Dan's old home in San Francisco, not aboard the *Matsonia*, and it turns out to have been the property of one Thomas Brade, a rather unsavory character who amassed great wealth and kept it in the wooden chest. Winterslip's fortune, in the Biggers story, includes the money stolen from Brade, who died mysteriously while on board the *Maid of Shiloh*. His son, who bears the same name, arrives in Honolulu just prior to Dan's murder and becomes one of the prime suspects.

Other fairly significant characters were excluded from Smith's adaptation. Dan's girlfriend, former actress Arlene Compton, has been widowed several times under mysterious circumstances. Her husbands, it seems, were all quite wealthy. She is identified as the recipient of a valuable brooch that was among Brade's jewels; it is the first piece of evidence connecting Dan Winterslip to the theft of the ohia box and its contents. Captain Arthur Temple Cope, an admirer of Minerva's who knew both Winterslip brothers and James Egan in the old days, prompts Egan to confess that he knew about Dan's thievery and threatened to expose him. During the showdown that preceded Winterslip's murder, the Reef and Palm owner had accepted a check for five thousand dollars in return for his silence—a check that, upon reflection, he decided he couldn't cash.

While Chan plays a slightly larger role in the novel, it's

interesting to note that in neither version does he question all the suspects or elicit the most damaging testimony. Captain Hallet handles the key interrogations, and the climactic revelations are made in response to questions posed by District Attorney Greene. Charlie works behind the scenes, as unobtrusively as possible. He does, however, force the killer to make an incriminating break: when Greene advises Jennison to confess and throw himself on the mercy of the court, the lawyer refuses. Charlie drops a pencil and bends over to pick it up. From his hip pocket protrudes the butt of a revolver. Jennison snatches the gun, puts it to his head, and pulls the trigger. But the hammer clicks harmlessly: Chan has removed the bullets. He deliberately dropped the pencil at just the right psychological moment, guessing the murderer would make a grab at it.

House Without a Key was released nationally on November 21, 1926. It was among the last Pathé serials to benefit from extensive advertising in the major trade journals. Double-page spreads and color inserts heralded the chapter play's coming with typical hyperbole: "Better than *The Green Archer!*" . . . "A mystery as deep as the ocean. You pick man after man as the murderer, only to admit that you are baffled!" . . . "Powerful drama with sensational climaxes, superbly produced." . . . "A cast equal to those in the finest features. In quality and entertainment a picture equal to any." . . . "Pathé is proud of this serial. Not only is it a great mystery story, but it's a production that sparkles with brilliancy."

The initial reviews, while not quite as enthusiastic as those garnered by *The Green Archer*, were certainly favorable. "Judging by the first installments," wrote Paul Thompson in *Motion Picture News*, "Pathé serial followers are in for as good a time as they had with *Snowed In*, *The Fighting Marine*, and others acted, directed and written by the same invincible cooperative organization assembled by Pathé." *Moving Picture World*'s C. S. Sewell opined, "Here is a serial that, judging from the exceptionally good opening chapters, looks like a corker that will immensely please the fans. . . . There is a continual succession of exciting action and thrills with the usual carried-over suspense. . . . Here is a serial that lends itself exceptionally well to exploitation."

Exhibitors who booked the serial were generally happy with it; some were considerably more than happy. "The best serial I have run," reported R. W. Hempstone, manager of the Waverly Theater in Poolesville, Maryland, to *Exhibitors Herald*. "Increased attendance about 15 percent and holding them." As a rule, though, theater owners rated *House* just below *Archer*.

Curiously, the Charlie Chan chapter play has acquired the reputation of having been a disappointment. Film buff Ed Connor, writing about Ray and Miller in a *Films in Review* article titled "The Serial Lovers," had this to say about *House*: "The serial was ambitiously cast and slickly done but the absence of a strong mystery character like the Archer, or [*Snowed In*'s] Redfield, was keenly felt, and *House Without a Key* was not so successful as the two preceding ones with Ray and Miller." Another buff, George Geltzer, echoed Connor in his *FiR* career study of Spencer Bennet, "40 Years of Cliffhanging," dismissing the Chan serial with one brief sentence: "Bennet, meanwhile, directed *The House Without a Key*, which, lacking a strong menace, did not turn out so well." Kalton C. Lahue, in his pioneering silent-serial history *Continued Next Week* (Norman, Oklahoma: University of Oklahoma Press, 1964), said of *House*: "It was another fine effort by the cast and Spencer Bennet, but the [ohia] chest did not take the place of a strong character of mystery in sustaining interest."

Frank Leon Smith himself, reflecting on *House Without a Key* in a 1958 letter to Connor, couldn't muster much enthusiasm for the film. "I have since felt," he wrote, "that I should have thrown out much of Biggers' stuff and reshaped the thing from the start. [The novel] was not one of Biggers' best, and it wasn't good serial stuff."

These are puzzling appraisals. Assuming that *House* hewed closely to Smith's scenario (and there's every reason to believe so), it was most likely an excellent serial. Smith's adaptation lacks the intricacy of Biggers' original but is far more complex than the average chapter play. The situations are not only well developed but plausible as well, and plausibility was a quality not generally found in serials. *House*'s action sequences are organic to the story and not dragged in by the heels simply to pep up an episode. The chapter endings are suspenseful and the "takeouts" don't resort to the blatant cheating so often seen in sound-era chapter plays. And the serial is blessedly free of so-called "comic relief."

Moreover, *The House Without a Key* sports a relatively mature and (dare we say?) sophisticated plot. There are no secret formulas, hidden passages, hooded villains, or super-scientific death-dealing devices. At all times the plot is motivated by one simple question: Who killed Dan Winterslip? Aside from the subplot about drug running—introduced late in the game—there's nothing to distract the audience from the story's central riddle. When the Biggers novel was remade in 1933 as *Charlie Chan's Greatest Case*, a talkie starring Warner Oland as the detective, scripters Lester Cole and Marion Orth included several characters Smith omitted from his version, but they were forced to telescope the narrative to hold the film's running time to 70 minutes. The serial's total running time would have been 200 to 220 minutes, providing Smith a lot more footage in which to advance the plot and point the finger of suspicion at various suspects.

With so *many* silent serials lost, it might be difficult at this late date to shed tears for *The House Without a Key*. But the evidence suggests that Smith, Bennet, and company created something special. Aside from its historical significance as the film that introduced Charlie Chan to movie audiences, *House* is noteworthy as a chapter play that attempted to transcend the market-driven, self-imposed limitations of the movie-serial format as it existed in 1926. For that reason alone, its loss is keenly felt.

Tarzan the Mighty
(1928, Universal Pictures)
by Ed Hulse

If Universal Pictures president Carl Laemmle had not been such an ardent practitioner of nepotism, his studio would never have produced the brace of Tarzan serials that enthralled moviegoers in the waning days of the silent-movie era and earned scads of money for Universal.

Laemmle's brothers-in-law, Julius and Abe Stern, followed the erstwhile clothing-store manager into the motion-picture business not long after he opened his first storefront theater in 1906. Reportedly, they were partners in Carl's Independent Moving Picture Company, which evolved into the Universal Film Manufacturing Company. Some accounts credit them with helping Laemmle finance the 1912 purchase of the large North Hollywood tract—actually an old chicken ranch—that became Universal City. The Sterns held various positions in the company during its formative years. In 1915, for example, Julius served as general manager of East Coast operations; at that time some Universal releases were still being shot in New York and New Jersey.

A year later, the brothers formed the Century Film Corporation, an independent production entity that supplied comedy short subjects for distribution by Universal. Then, in 1919, Julius and Abe partnered with Louis and Oscar Jacobs to create the Great Western Producing Company, which turned out several serials distributed by "Big U." These three chapter plays—*Elmo the Mighty* (1919), *Elmo the Fearless* and *The*

Flaming Disc (both 1920)—starred Elmo Lincoln, the screen's original Tarzan.

Enter Louis, Max, and Adolph Weiss. Having crashed the movie business in 1917 as New York-based exhibitors, they formed the Numa Pictures Corporation two years later for the sole purpose of producing Tarzan films. From the ape-man's creator, Edgar Rice Burroughs, they licensed motion-picture rights to *The Return of Tarzan*, second novel in the series. In an unusual deal, ERB gave Numa the option of making two films from the same book. The first—initially titled *The Return of Tarzan* but ultimately released as *The Revenge of Tarzan*—was distributed by the Goldwyn Distributing Corporation, which paid Numa an advance of $100,000 for the privilege. The Weiss brothers were to receive a percentage of the film's profits as well, but Goldwyn's accounting of the revenues left something to be desired and the siblings vowed to self-distribute their next Tarzan film.

Believing they could achieve better box-office results by returning Elmo Lincoln to the role that made him a star, the Weiss brothers engaged the Great Western Producing Company—which still had Lincoln under contract—to make their second *Return of Tarzan* adaptation. This time around they elected to produce a serial, which was titled *The Adventures of Tarzan*. They formed the New York-based Adventures of Tarzan Serial Sales Company to distribute the chapter play via the already-well-established "state rights" system, which allowed for the rental of prints to exhibitors by independent contractors (known as sub-distributors) on a territorial basis.

Released late in 1921, *Adventures of Tarzan* was extremely successful. The Sterns, still having Lincoln under their thumbs, decided they could do their own Tarzan films and bypass the Weiss brothers altogether, now that Numa had shot its bolt. In 1922, with *Adventures* still in theatrical playoff, Julius, Abe and Louis Jacobs paid Burroughs $40,000 for screen rights to *Tarzan and the Jewels of Opar* and *Jungle Tales of Tarzan*, fifth and sixth books in the series.

Then fate stepped in. For reasons not clear today, the Great Western Producing Company dissolved shortly after this transaction. Elmo Lincoln suddenly found himself unemployed and reduced to taking supporting roles in such feature films as *Quincy Adams Sawyer* (1922) and *Rupert of Hentzau* (1923). He returned to the Universal lot, where he had been a star just a few years earlier, to play an unbilled bit part in Lon Chaney's version of *The Hunchback of Notre Dame* (also 1923). The recently acquired Tarzan option went unexercised.

Great Western's unexplained demise must have been a blow to the Sterns, but they still had steady income thanks to their brother-in-law: Carl Laemmle continued to distribute their Century Comedies, which were churned out by the dozen every year. Additionally, Julius returned to the ranks of Universal management and held several executive positions throughout the Twenties.

Movie serials diminished in stature and significance as the decade wore on, and although Universal maintained a healthy market share, its chapter plays rarely proved to be big grossers. (Two exceptions were 1924's *The Riddle Rider* and 1927's *Blake of Scotland Yard*.) But Laemmle, who prided himself on the diversity of Universal's extensive short-subject program, never lost faith in serials. Every season's offerings were announced to the trade with great fanfare and the promise that, in the year to come, chapter plays would be restored to the position of industry importance they had occupied in the halcyon days of *The Perils of Pauline*.

A story in the April 7, 1928 issue of *Universal Weekly* (the company's house organ, circulated to distributors and exhibitors) announced that Universal had "just acquired rights" to ERB's *Jungle Tales of Tarzan*. A follow-up story in the April 28 number stated that *Jungle Tales* would be filmed in 12 chapters and serve as lead-off serial for the 1928-29 season. It's not clear why the Stern brothers waited so long to relinquish their hold on *Jungle Tales*. Possibly they were inspired to dispose of the property in the wake of FBO's poorly reviewed but extensively promoted and generally successful 1927 feature film, *Tarzan and the Golden Lion*. It could also be that the growing popularity of Grosset & Dunlap's inexpensively priced Tarzan reprints, then being issued on a regular basis, further enhanced the character's public profile and earning power. In any case, Laemmle paid his relatives for the motion-picture rights they held to ERB's sixth book. Whether they made a profit, incurred a loss, or simply recouped their investment is anybody's guess.

Naturally, production would be overseen by William Lord Wright, the firm's serial czar. Direction was entrusted to Jack Nelson, who had recently helmed a 10-chapter serial, *Perils of the Jungle*, for none other than the Weiss brothers. Nelson was a newcomer to Universal City; a former actor, he cut his directorial eyeteeth on films made by the Thomas H. Ince organization but spent most of his career working for those independent production companies occupying the lowest links on Hollywood's food chain. Nonetheless, he had done an excellent job on *Perils of the Jungle*, utilizing practically the entire menagerie housed at the Selig Zoo. Each chapter of *Perils* ended with cast members imperiled by wild beasts, and Nelson got the maximum number of thrills obtainable on what must have been a modest budgetary outlay. He was obviously the right man for the job.

The task of adapting Burroughs' book, a collection of short stories set during Tarzan's youth and early adulthood, fell to one Ian McClosky Heath, about whom nothing is known. (Universal's two Tarzan serials are his only screen credits, and his name cannot be found on any roster of fiction writers plying their trade in the 1920s.) Confronted with the impossible task of crafting a suitable serial plot from ERB's unrelated tales, Heath jettisoned the book and devised an original story.

In that same April 28 article designating *Jungle Tales of Tarzan* as the opening act in Universal's 1928-29 serial program, the anonymous scribe reported "a great rush on amongst the mighty men of Los Angeles to play Tarzan." There's no way of knowing how many actors tested for the role, but the casting process could not have been a lengthy one: A squib in the May 19 *Universal Weekly* declared that Frank Merrill had just been signed as the ape-man, and that filming would commence shortly.

A persistent myth about Universal's first Tarzan serial is that the title role was originally awarded to Joe Bonomo, the New York-born strongman who had previously starred in two of the company's 1925 chapter plays, *The Great Circus Mystery* and *Perils of the Wild*. The numerous reports of Bonomo's casting all derive from passages that appeared in two 1968 books: Gabe Essoe's *Tarzan of the Movies* (New York: The Citadel Press) and Joe's self-published autobiography, *The Strongman* (New York: Bonomo Studios Incorporated).

Essoe's account had Bonomo bowing out after fracturing his left leg and injuring his sacroiliac shortly before completing work on *Perils of the Wild*. Inasmuch as *Perils* was shot fully three years before Universal's first Tarzan serial—a fact of which Essoe was apparently unaware—this report is easily discredited.

Bonomo's version of the story seemed more credible but hasn't held up to close scrutiny. While vague as to the exact date, he recalled being cast as Tarzan some six months before the expiration of his Universal contract. The way Bonomo remembered things, he was antsy to freelance but Laemmle wanted him to stay with the studio. In order to keep the stuntman-turned-actor busy pending the negotiation of a mutually acceptable deal, "Uncle Carl" (as he was by then known within the industry) awarded Joe the role of Tarzan, released publicity pegged to his casting, and immediately began shooting the serial. Bonomo claimed he fractured his left leg on the third day of work, falling heavily to the ground after a vine snapped while he was swinging from tree to tree. He added that production came to a screeching halt and only resumed "much later on" with Merrill in the lead.

As proof, Bonomo reprinted in *The Strongman* one small news item, apparently clipped from a newspaper or trade journal. Seen today, it looks convincing enough. The headline proclaims: "Tarzan to Appear on Screen Again; Joe Bonomo Is He!"

Undated and not bylined, the dispatch's first paragraph reads: "Those refreshing stories of jungle life by Edgar Rice Burroughs, which have thrilled children and adults alike, are again to appear pictorially, it was bruited yesterday, with none other than Joe Bonomo, who styles himself as 'the Hercules of the Screen,' in the role of the super-hero, for Universal."

Clipping aside, there are several problems within Bonomo's account. To begin with, his last picture for Universal was an epic Western, *The Flaming Frontier*, released in September 1926. (It was, in fact, the only picture he did for the studio that year.) Assuming his contract had not yet run out, this would indicate that principal photography on *Jungle Tales* commenced nearly two years before it actually did. Secondly, close examination of Universal's yearly program announcements reveals no mention of a Tarzan serial on the 1925-26, 1926-27, or 1927-28 schedules. There's no way that any Hollywood studio would have rushed into production a chapter play featuring as well known a fictional character as Burroughs' ape-man without considerable ballyhoo. Thirdly, even if Bonomo was wrong about the timing of *Jungle Tales*, he couldn't have spent three days shooting it in the spring of 1928, because at that time he was making *The Chinatown Mystery*, a Trem Carr-produced serial released by Syndicate Pictures only two weeks after Universal's first Tarzan opus hit theater screens.

The news clipping reprinted in *The Strongman* seems to lend credence to Bonomo's version of the story, but it hardly supplies conclusive proof. No title is given. No dates are given. And the report maintains that Bonomo has been "bruited" as a possible movie Tarzan. As "bruited" is a synonym for "rumored," one could reasonably assume that, at the time of the article's appearance, Universal had contemplated but not actually scheduled production of a Tarzan serial. Remember, that April 7, 1928 news story reported that the company had "just acquired" rights to *Jungle Tales*.

Finally, there's this: I've yet to see mentioned anywhere in *Universal Weekly* a single mention of Bonomo being cast as

Tarzan. Not in 1926, not in 1927, and certainly not in 1928. Had one of the company's former serial stars even been *considered* for the role, the house organ would surely have reported as much. Long ago I came to the conclusion that, while Joe might have discussed making a Tarzan serial for Laemmle, he was never actually cast—and that the injury he later recalled was actually sustained during production of *Perils of the Wild*, which also took place in a jungle and found Bonomo's character swinging from vines and leaping from tree to tree.

In short, there's a distinct lack of hard evidence to support the assertion that anybody but Frank Merrill was awarded the title role in Universal's first Tarzan serial.

Born in 1893 as Otto Poll, the New Jersey native worked for several years as a police officer in the city of Newark before attempting to parlay his good looks and athletic ability into a movie career. A superb physical specimen who won dozens of gymnastics awards in competition, Poll was cited in a 1918 *New York Times* article as a "champion at flying rings." Not long afterward, he relocated to Los Angeles and became active in West Coast athletic circles. He secured bit roles and performed stunts in motion pictures (including *The Adventures of Tarzan*, in which he played an Arab heavy and doubled Elmo Lincoln in certain shots) but remained an active participant in gymnastic exhibitions. A 1922 *Times* article on upcoming events sponsored by the Amateur Athletic Union referred to him as a "famous gymnast from Los Angeles."

Poll took the name Frank Merrill upon being hired to star in the first of a dozen low-budget feature films for Hercules Film Corporation. Designed for undiscriminating audiences and employing simple, action-oriented plots, such pictures as *A Fighting Heart* (1924) and *Dashing Thru* (1926) gave the star athlete frequent opportunities to show off his impressive physique and gymnastic skills. He had more of the same as the hero of *Perils of the Jungle*, swinging through trees, dangling from gnarled limbs, and climbing vines hand over hand. It's no wonder director Jack Nelson wanted him for the role of Tarzan.

The next casting challenge, not surprisingly, was finding a suitable female lead to appear opposite Merrill. Heath's scenario stuck to ERB's book only to the extent that its action took place before Tarzan met Jane. The necessary heart interest was supplied by Mary Trevor, a young woman shipwrecked off the African coast and held prisoner by a tribe of savage white men descended from pirates. This was a key role; Mary would occupy the screen as much as the ape-man. An experienced actress would be required.

In mid-May, shortly after Merrill was signed, Natalie Kingston was cast as Mary. A lissome, leggy, olive-skinned brunette of Spanish and Hungarian descent, Kingston broke into show business as a dancer and enjoyed a brief, modest Broadway career before entering motion pictures in 1923 at the age of 18. Never really a star, she played leads and supporting roles alike; shortly before accepting the role of Mary Trevor, Kingston finished a character part in Frank Borgaze's *Street Angel* and appeared opposite Western star Tom Mix in *Painted Post*. She had the necessary acting experience and looked fetching in abbreviated jungle garb.

Rounding out the small group of principal players were director Nelson's five-year-old son Bobby, who had appeared opposite Merrill in *Perils of the Jungle*, and Irish actor Al Ferguson, a familiar heavy of Westerns and serials.

With the cast finally in place, principal photography began immediately. *Jungle Tales of Tarzan* was dropped as a title in favor of *Tarzan the Mighty*, and Universal's publicity machine geared up to promote the serial. According to Irwin Porges' definitive biography, *Edgar Rice Burroughs, The Man Who Created Tarzan* (Provo, Utah: Brigham Young University Press, 1975), ERB visited the Universal lot to screen rough footage assemblies on June 14, 1928. Not entirely happy that long-dormant rights assigned to the Stern brothers were finally being exploited with no additional compensation to him, Burroughs chafed at the serial's deviation from the book on which it was ostensibly based. He enumerated his problems with the screened footage in a memorandum quoted by Porges:

> [T]here was only one character that appears in the original work, namely Tarzan, and no suggestion of any episode or action taken from the book.
>
> They have incorporated many characters, including a Lord Greystoke, some pirates, sailors, and castaway girl and her little brother, none of which appears in the original work.
>
> They have incorporated a love interest between Tarzan and the girl, which does not exist in the book.

Burroughs had always been annoyed by Hollywood's treatment of his brainchild, and Universal's incarnation of the ape-man only exacerbated his disenchantment with filmmakers. He did, however, admit that the muscular, fierce-looking Merrill made a good Tarzan. As a good-will gesture, the studio paid ERB $1,000 for newspaper syndication rights to *Jungle Tales*, even though the novelization being circulated was based on Heath's scenario and not the book. It was reportedly written by Craig Kennedy creator Arthur B. Reeve, who had recently scripted *Return of the Riddle Rider* for Universal. But it doesn't read like Reeve's prose, and I suspect the novelization was actually penned by a drone in the studio's publicity department.

(Universal used part of the novelization to good advantage as a promotional tool. A compilation of the first three chapters was made into an eight-page booklet of six by nine inches. Illustrated with stills from the film, this pamphlet was sold for six dollars per thousand copies to exhibitors who distributed it to potential customers. Circulated in advance of the serial's playdate, the eight-page prose "teaser" proved a tremendous drawing card. Since the booklets were giveaways meant to be discarded after reading, very few copies survived. Today they are expensive, highly sought-after collectibles.)

The June 30 *Universal Weekly* carried a news item stating that production of *Tarzan the Mighty* was nearly half-completed. The advance word was good; prominent exhibitors given previews of the first several chapters were uniformly enthusiastic, and even Uncle Carl was impressed. He lauded the serial in one of his avuncular "Straight from the Shoulder" columns written for the house organ. Universal's sales department began taking orders from theater chains, including some that didn't normally run serials. Exhibitors who subscribed to the company's "Complete Service" plan (under which they paid a flat fee for a full annual complement of Universal feature films, short subjects, and serials) got *Tarzan the Mighty* at a bargain price, but those who normally shunned Laemmle product paid excessively for it. The heavily promoted chapter play was booked for big downtown houses in major metropolitan areas—movie palaces that seldom offered such lowbrow fare as serials. The prestigious Loew's chain, allied with no less a studio than Metro-Goldwyn-Mayer, scheduled it for their New York City flagship theater.

Initially skeptical exhibitors changed their minds once the early reviews broke in various trade journals. A mid-July screening of the first three episodes in Universal's New York office wowed even the most jaded critics. Industry veteran William Wilkerson, then editor of *Exhibitors Daily Review*, led the parade:

> We were greatly surprised. This [serial] is different and is going to have a wide appeal, in that it is going to create a new audience for this type of entertainment. . . . [Universal has] taken a story that is plausible, given it excellent direction and a superb cast. But the big kick of the chapters we saw were furnished by the animals. . . . Adults will go for this one with more interest (if possible) than the kids. They will not have to stretch their imagination to be entertained, nor will they snicker at the impossibility of the story or situations. The production values have lifted to the par of feature productions in that the sets and the camera work are superb. Exhibitors would do well to look at this one [at their local Universal exchange office] before booking it. They will forget about the 'for matinees only' and run it all day and maybe more.

Chester J. Smith of *Motion Picture News* was similarly effusive in his praise:

> This gives promise of being one of the most unusual serials yet produced. It is entirely out of the ordinary run of such pictures and should develop some highly interesting highlights before its conclusion. . . . There are some exceptional shots of the jungle and the wild animals, and they add greatly to the general effectiveness of the picture, which gives rare promise of developing into a tremendous thriller.

Over the years, chapter plays had drawn considerable criticism from watchdog groups believing them harmful to the children that comprised the lion's share of their audiences. *Tarzan the Mighty* got a clean bill of health from most of these, and was highly recommended by Mrs. E. H. Florence Jacobs of the California Federation of Women's Clubs:

> *Tarzan the Mighty* is an unusually fine serial, remarkably well told, full of action and exciting sequences, and is superior in direction, continuity, and photography to most serials. While we have only seen three chapters, I feel safe in saying this serial can be highly recommended for junior matinees, and we are looking forward to seeing the rest of it. It is a thrilling story, told in specially commendable titles in their presentation of suspense, which means so much in a serial of this type, and at the same time has no exaggerated criminal characters.

Tarzan the Mighty, like all but a few silent serials made by Universal, is a lost film. But one can reconstruct it, after a fashion, from careful readings of the Arthur B. Reeve novelization and the individual chapter synopses printed in *Universal Weekly*.

Chapter One presents the familiar Tarzan origin story: how his English parents, Lord and Lady Greystoke, were stranded on the African coast and forced to take shelter in a crudely built hut; how his mother and father perished, leaving him to be "adopted" by a she-ape; how he matured among the beasts of the jungle, forced by his savage upbringing to develop uncommon strength and agility; and how he learned rudimentary English by studying the books left behind in his parents' hut, which became a sanctuary to him.

At this point *Tarzan the Mighty* diverges from the canon. Ian McClosky Heath's original screen story shifts focus to a village, deep in the jungle, inhabited by an atavistic tribe of whites descended from pirates marooned on the African coast many generations before. The tribe is ruled by a shifty, opportunistic beachcomber named Black John (Ferguson), who has played on the superstitions of these ignorant people so long that they believe him possessed of near-supernatural powers.

Currently living among the tribe are Mary Trevor (Kingston) and her young brother Bobby (Nelson), castaways rescued by Black John and forced to accept his dubious hospitality. The erstwhile beachcomber has designs on the beautiful girl and hopes to make her his bride. That prospect repulses Mary, but she bides her time, hoping to keep Black John at arm's length long enough to arrange an escape.

The first episode ends on a thrilling note. While bathing in a jungle stream, Mary is imperiled by a monster crocodile. Her screams attract Tarzan, who's been swinging through the trees. The ape-man dives from great height into the water and grapples with the giant reptile as the chapter fades out.

Needless to say, the crocodile never lived that could clamp its jaws around Tarzan of the Apes, and Chapter Two opens with the jungle lord defeating the beast and making Mary's acquaintance. He rushes off to save one of his simian friends and the girl returns to the village, where Black John is already planning to trap her savior. In fact, he promises to give her Tarzan's head as a wedding present.

Hoping to lure the ape-man into his clutches, Black John prepares a trap for Tarzan's elephant friend, Tantor. Little Bobby, learning of the plot, dashes into the jungle to warn his new pal, only to be caught in Tantor's path when the terrified elephant is stampeded toward a spiked pit. Tarzan whisks Bobby into a nearby tree, but the limb snaps beneath their combined weight, plunging man and boy into the pit.

Chapter Three finds Tarzan dazed but unhurt by the fall;

he and Bobby have narrowly missed the spikes embedded in the bottom of the pit. He brings the unconscious boy to his hut and attempts to revive him while Black John, claiming to have spirited Bobby away himself, bluffs Mary into consenting to marriage as a means of having her brother restored to her. That night's wedding ceremony is disrupted by the unexpected arrival of Tarzan, who thrashes Black John in hand-to-hand combat but is surrounded and overcome by tribesmen. The episode draws to a close with the ape-man bound to a stake and Black John hurling a spear at him.

Subsequent chapters repeat the familiar serial pattern of capture and escape; Mary is forced several more times to participate in a marriage ceremony, but Tarzan always manages to rescue her before vows can be exchanged. Eventually, Black John discovers that the ape-man is the scion of an English nobleman, and when the current Lord Greystoke (Lorimer Johnston) shows up looking for his long-lost relative, the crafty tribal chieftain uses papers stolen from Tarzan's hut to palm himself off as the missing heir. From this point forward, things *really* get complicated.

Released nationally on August 13, 1928, *Tarzan the Mighty* was an instantaneous success. It was, in fact, a bonafide sensation. Serials were habitually ballyhooed to such an extent that they couldn't possibly measure up to studio hyperbole, but this one delivered the goods. Exhibitors reported standing-room-only crowds and record-breaking grosses. Having circulated a bare handful of episodes, Universal was besieged with requests to elongate the serial from 12 chapters to 15. This represented a significant change in attitude on the part of theater operators, who had bitterly complained just a few years earlier that Universal chapter plays—which at that time had a standard length of 18 installments—were padded with repetitious situations that bored patrons and caused them to abandon a serial halfway through. In 1926 the company settled on ten chapters as the optimal length; since then only one serial—*Blake of Scotland Yard*—had gone longer, and by just two episodes at that.

Buoyed by exhibitor enthusiasm and thrilled with the prospect of squeezing additional revenue from *Tarzan the Mighty*, Laemmle ordered William Lord Wright to rework the serial's continuity and devise as many new situations as would be necessary to extend the chapter play by three installments. The decision was apparently made in mid-September, with principal photography already completed. It's not immediately clear from a reading of the synopses just where or how the storyline was stretched, although it's likely that Heath's shift of locale from the jungle to the high seas, and thence to England, was made during this chaotic period. Contract director Ray Taylor supervised the shooting of new scenes. By late October all 15 episodes had finally been completed, and the serial's playoff continued to the delight of exhibitors and patrons alike.

Universal was flooded with unsolicited endorsements, many of which made their way to the pages of *Universal Weekly* and into double-page advertisements placed in the leading trade journals. Typical of the raves was this one from Vogel Gettier, manager of the Capitol Theatre in Grand Island, Nebraska: "A box-office attraction and a real tonic for tired patrons. The only serial that has ever been booked in the Capitol, as it is the only one having real feature-picture strength. Pleases 100 percent all ages."

Said Ernest K. Pappas, manager of Copperfield, Utah's Diana Theatre: "Results and comments of patrons seeing *Tarzan the Mighty* were numerous, and all expressed satisfaction together with a promise to follow every episode to be shown. Box-office receipts on [opening day] surpassed every record for more than 16 months past."

"*Tarzan the Mighty* is the biggest attraction of its kind I've ever played," reported Roy W. Adams of Mason, Michigan's Pastime Theatre. "When the first and second episodes packed the house I thought it might be an accident—but it has held up consistently for six weeks now, doing two or three times as much business as any serial ever did in the past for me."

W. T. McEntyre, manager of the Princess Theatre is Enterprise, Alabama, declared: "I ran Chapter Eight last

Saturday and did a *tremendous business*. [emphasis his] My patrons say every episode gets better, and they are tickled to death that it has been extended to 15 episodes. It is the best serial I have ever run." Such comments were printed not only in Universal advertisements but also in the avidly read "What the Picture Did for Me" column in *Exhibitors Herald*, which had recently merged with the venerable *Moving Picture World*.

An acquaintance of mine, the late Harold T. Penney, was nine years old when *Tarzan the Mighty* came to his local theater in Erie, Pennsylvania. Fifty years later, he still remembered it warmly. "Nothing like it ever came to town," he recalled for me in 1979. "You couldn't find an empty seat in the house on Saturday afternoon. We whooped and hollered and carried on something awful when the main title flashed on screen. The noise was so loud you couldn't hardly hear the organ music. And after the show, we'd be walking home and climbing up every tree along the way, beating our chests and hanging off the limbs. We all wanted to be Tarzan. It's a wonder we didn't break our damn necks."

Viewers of all ages thrilled to Frank Merrill's feats of strength and agility. They marveled as he hauled himself up vines, hand over hand; as he swung from trees and darted through the jungle. They goggled at the shots of exotic beasts, some of which attacked each other in close-up while the camera rolled. It didn't seem to matter that the plot was thin and some of the chapter endings pedestrian. Everybody loved the serial; Universal reported that some exhibitors were running chapters two days a week instead of the usual one.

Tarzan the Mighty earned more in film rental—remember, that was the fee exhibitors paid to distributors, having nothing to do with box-office attendance—than any Universal movie released during 1928. That included such prestige feature-length attractions as Paul Fejos' *Lonesome* and Paul Leni's *The Man Who Laughs*, as well as the studio's enormously popular Reginald Denny comedies and Hoot Gibson Westerns. Edgar Rice Burroughs might not have been happy, but he was the only one who wasn't.

And what of Uncle Carl's relatives, the Stern brothers, whose 1922 purchase of the film rights to *Jungle Tales of Tarzan* had made all this possible? They were still gainfully employed at Universal, producing cheap two-reel comedy shorts. They did not participate financially in the serial's success; *Tarzan the Mighty*'s huge profits went straight to Universal's bottom line. Julius and Abe knew they held a trump card, though: Laemmle would certainly want a sequel, but Burroughs was notoriously prickly when it came to dealing with Hollywood producers. And they still held the film rights to *Tarzan and the Jewels of Opar*.

That, however, is another story . . . .

The Last Silent Serial Team: Allan & McConnell

The Tiger's Shadow
(1928, Pathé Exchanges, Inc.)

The Fire Detective
(1929, Pathé Exchanges, Inc.)

by Ed Hulse

The talking-picture revolution of 1928 seriously impacted the movie serial, a storytelling form that had been in decline for several years and was already considered moribund by many within the industry. Although occasional releases such as 1925's *The Green Archer* and 1927's *Blake of Scotland Yard* racked up impressive grosses, serials had lost the prestige they enjoyed in the Teens and early Twenties, with Pearl White, Ruth Roland, Charles Hutchison, Helen Holmes, and Eddie Polo in their respective primes. The chapter play's most profitable days were already behind it, although serial producers opining in trade-magazine articles kept promising that a revival was just around the corner.

Pathé, long known as "the House of Serials," continued to provide serials to the ten thousand or so exhibitors who still played them. For the most part, these were independent theater owners with individual houses or small chains that catered to small-town, suburban, and rural audiences. The grand "downtown" picture palaces—most of them belonging to chains owned by the major production and distribution entities—booked upscale product that appealed to the better classes. The serial's florid melodramatics were best suited to thrill-hungry kids and unsophisticated, undiscriminating adults.

In dire financial straits and without its own theater chain to support more expensively made product, Pathé had little choice but to continue grinding out the newsreels, short subjects, serials, and cheap feature films that supplied its income. A 1927 merger with Cecil B. De Mille's Producers Distributing Corporation had not yielded fruit, and the next year Pathé paid no dividends on its Class A stock.

If contemporary reviews and trade-paper reports are to be believed, the company's 1927 and 1928 serials failed to meet the standards set by earlier releases. Chapter plays produced on the East Coast by Schuyler Grey and E. Oswald Brooks were singled out for harsh criticism, with the Hollywood-based unit headed by director Spencer Bennet attracting fewer and milder complaints. The most popular star duo in serials, Allene Ray and Walter Miller, continued to please audiences, but following the successes of *The Green Archer* and *The House Without a Key* (1926), even their vehicles now reflected carelessness and corner-cutting in scripting and production.

Bennet, who learned the serial business under director George B. Seitz and worked most effectively with writer/producer Frank Leon Smith, hoped to retain the autonomy they had earned with *Green Archer*'s success. But Smith's late-1926 departure from the serial unit left him without a reliable partner, and he was increasingly subjected to interference from Pathé's front office. Loathe to engage in studio politicking, Bennet did what he was told and concentrated on obtaining the best results possible. His 1928 productions were marked by budget cuts and truncated shooting schedules, but Bennet soldiered on.

That year Pathé entrusted its most reliable chapter-play director with a new pair of serial stars. Born on October 22,

1905 in Oklahoma City (at that time was still part of Indian Territory), Gladys McConnell was crowned a teenage beauty queen before heading West to find fame and fortune in Hollywood. She made her film debut in a 1926 comedy short, *Elsie in New York*, and soon thereafter won ingénue roles in inexpensive Westerns, playing opposite actor/stuntman Yakima Canutt in *The Devil Horse* and Buck Jones in *The Flying Horseman* (both 1926). McConnell co-starred with legendary film funnyman Harry Langdon in *The Chaser* (1928), although the poorly received comedy did little to help her career. Just prior to signing with Pathé, she landed a key supporting role in *The Perfect Crime* (also 1928), a part-talkie starring Clive Brook and adapted from Israel Zangwill's novel, *The Big Bow Mystery*.

Hugh Allan was born Allan Abram Hughes on November 5, 1903 in Oakland, California. A handsome, strapping six-footer, he entered pictures in 1925. Generally cast as a secondary male lead, he made his starring debut opposite Priscilla Dean in *Birds of Prey* (1927). Allan appeared in support of future Western stars William Boyd and Johnny Mack Brown in similarly themed films set in West Point and Annapolis Naval Academy respectively: *Dress Parade* (1927) and *Annapolis* (1928). Although he still looked boyish and seemed less virile than such mature serial stars as Walter Miller, Jack Daugherty, and William Desmond, Allan was deemed an acceptable counterpart to the pretty, winsome McConnell.

The first McConnell-Allan chapter play, *The Tiger's Shadow*, went into production late in the summer of 1928. Bennet directed from an original story and screenplay by George Arthur Gray, the former newspaperman and Pathé publicity guru who had replaced Frank Leon Smith as Pathé's foremost serial scribe. Although Gray secured this position on the strength of his scenario for a Ray-Miller Western serial, *Hawk of the Hills* (1927), he preferred to write present-day thrillers with strong mystery elements. *The Tiger's Shadow* was one of these.

The story opens with a daring heist made by "The Tiger," a masked criminal who specializes in outwitting other crooks and making off with their recently stolen swag. Clad in flowing robes and a tiger-head mask outfitted with burning eyes, this flamboyant thief is the terror of the underworld. Shortly after the events pictured in Chapter One's opening moments, The Tiger is said to have perished in a mysterious fire. The yarn jumps ahead two years later, centering audience attention on the lavish estate of Amos Crain (Broderick O'Farrell), a wealthy invalid confined to a wheelchair. His physician, Dr. Sandro (Frank Lackteen), owns a sanitarium adjoining the estate. Crain's secretary Slayton (Edward Cecil) and butler Briggs (F. F. Guenste), suspicious characters both, believe that their employer has concealed a fortune in an old grandfather's clock he will permit no one else to wind.

When the timepiece breaks down, Crain orders Slayton to call Martin Meeker (Paul Weigel), the only clock repairman he trusts. Meeker's lodger, aspiring crime novelist Tony Kent (Allan), comes along for the ride. Meanwhile, Crain has sent for his ward, Jane Barstow (McConnell), who arrives from boarding school that night just as a violent storm breaks. Making her way through the heavily wooded grounds, Jane spies a tiger's head with burning eyes. Terrified, she dashes toward Crain's house just as a bolt of lightning strike a nearby tree, which crashes down on top of her.

That's how Chapter One ends. Needless to say, Jane escapes with only minor scratches and finds herself plunged into mystery. Who is The Tiger? Why is he hanging around Crain's house? What connection, if any, does he have to the sinister Dr. Sandro? These are the questions Jane hopes to answers with the help of Tony Kent.

Crain entrusts his ward with a small steel box, which she is to deliver to his old friend, noted explorer Andre Blanc (Henry Hebert). While attempting to carry out this mission, Jane is kidnapped by thugs in Slayton's employ and taken to Rattler Island, described in an intertitle as "an outlaw rendezvous." Tony eventually rescues her, but the mystery deepens.

In the eerie final episode, "The Sky Clears," Dr. Sandro and Slayton are exposed as thieves on whom The Tiger preyed. After apprehending them, the mystery man unmasks and reveals himself as Amos Crain, who is not an invalid at all. As The Tiger, he operated outside the law to recover stolen loot, which he then secreted in a hidden room behind the grandfather clock. After coming to suspect that Sandro was the criminal mastermind he had thwarted two years before, Amos revived The Tiger to draw this master crook into the open. Blanc aided in the scheme by wearing the Tiger disguise when Crain couldn't slip away. Meeker, too, helped The Tiger by preserving the secret of the clock. With the gang rounded up, the captured swag is turned over to police for return to its rightful owners, while the slightly befuddled but relieved Tony and Jane look forward to a less stressful phase of their relationship.

The Tiger's Shadow, which survives in the form of an old 16mm rental-library print on deposit at the UCLA Film & Television Archives, is the earliest extant serial directed by Spencer Bennet. It was a solidly entertaining effort, inexpensively but sturdily mounted. The days of extravagant action sequences—such as the famous runaway-boxcar sequence that ends Chapter One of *The Timber Queen* (1922)—had long since passed for Pathé serials, but Bennet injected thrills wherever the script called for them. Fights and chases were kept to a minimum, but Allan acquitted himself handily in the scraps in which he participated. The mystery angle always took center stage, and Edward Snyder's cinematography emphasized it with spooky lighting effects. The Tiger never remained on screen for long periods of time, his relatively few appearances being all the more effective for their brevity. It's hard to make authoritative judgments about Pathé serials when so few survive, but based on trade-paper reviews and exhibitor reports, *The Tiger's Shadow* is likely representative of the company's late-Twenties chapter-play output.

McConnell and Allan were rushed into another serial, *The Fire Detective*, which was released on March 3, 1929—immediately following issuance of *The Tiger's Shadow*'s last episode. Previously, Pathé had avoided releasing back-to-back serials with the same stars, so piggybacking *Fire Detective* on top of *Tiger's Shadow* may have been a calculated attempt to create a fan following for McConnell and Allan. Bennet wielded the megaphone once again, but this time he shared director credit with Thomas L. Storey, the younger brother of Pathé vice president John E. Storey (and, reportedly, a talentless oaf who owed his minor career entirely to nepotism).

This chapter play was produced at the tail end of a cycle of movies about metropolitan fire fighting. Serial makers had picked up on the trend early, beginning with Rayart's *The Flame Fighter* (1925), starring Herbert Rawlinson. Universal adapted a ten-chapter opus, *The Fire Fighters* (1927), from John A. Moroso's popular "Cap Fallon" stories in the *Saturday Evening Post*. M-G-M in late 1926 contributed the cycle's most lavish entry, a ten-reel feature film titled *The Fire Brigade*, starring popular leading man Charles Ray.

George Arthur Gray penned the scenario for *The Fire Detective*, adapting an original story supplied by Frank Leon Smith, moonlighting from his job as story editor for Paramount. Although the serial itself is lost (save for a few small fragments and the coming-attractions trailer), a reading of chapter synopses filed with the Library of Congress for copyright purposes indicates that both writers were slumming. The plot is pedestrian, and in place of a strong mystery-man character like The Tiger there is only an arsonist who clomps around in a heavy asbestos suit, his features concealed by a thick hood with a small eye shield.

Chapter One, "The Arson Trail," begins with the release from prison of convict Matt Coston (former Western star Leo Maloney), a master thief who spent seven years behind bars rather than divulge the hiding place of a half-million dollars in stolen loot. Two men are interested to hear that Coston is back on the street: Senator Samuel Faraday (John Cossar), who as District Attorney prosecuted him, and Coston's shady attorney, Richard Hollingsworth (Larry Steers), who has always wondered where the thief cached his swag. Faraday's daughter Helene (McConnell), recently engaged to Hollingsworth over the objections of her father, is a newspaper reporter covering a series of arson cases. In this capacity she becomes acquainted with Jeff Tarrant (Allan), a special investigator in the Fire Marshal's office.

The plot thickens when Coston learns that the hidden half-million has been uncovered and stolen during his stay in prison. He suspects Hollingsworth, who directs the ex-con to Faraday and tells Coston that the Senator carefully guards some shameful secret. Could it be that Helene's father is himself a thief?

The ongoing arson investigation repeatedly puts Helene and Jeff in peril, especially when chemist Leon Zangrados (Frank Lackteen) is implicated. As you might imagine, there's a fire of some sort in nearly every chapter. An odd attempt to inject bizarre menace into the story results in the introduction of an "ape man" who attempts to kidnap Helene at the end of Chapter Seven. This frightening creature turns out to be a disguised thug, however, and he is quickly dispatched by Zangrados.

Eventually—and none too convincingly, judging from the chapter synopses—the arson investigation is linked with the disappearance of Coston's loot and Senator Faraday's secret. It develops that Zangrados, finally identified as a long-time criminal and the instigator of the arson racket, is actually Faraday's half-brother and has been blackmailing the Senator. Hollingsworth loses his life in a valiant attempt to save Helene, but not before confessing that he found and stole Coston's swag. The police eventually nab Coston and Tarrant arrests Zangrados.

The Fire Detective, the third serial in Pathé's 1928-29 schedule, slipped into release largely unheralded. By this time the company had decided to abandon production of chapter plays—which, ironically, had been responsible for its financial success back in the *Perils of Pauline* days—in favor of an ambitious program of newly fashionable talking pictures. Bennet's last two Pathé serials, *Queen of the Northwoods* and *The Black Book*, limped into the marketplace without significant advertising or marketing support, and they performed poorly at the nation's box offices.

Neither Gladys McConnell nor Hugh Allan made much of an impression on moviegoers after starring together in serials. McConnell played the female lead in a few part-talkies, including a 1930 Ken Maynard oater, *Parade of the West*. She married soon thereafter and promptly retired from the screen.

Hugh Allan made only one other film appearance following *Fire Detective*, taking a supporting role in a 1930 comedy two-reeler. He, too, abandoned film acting and married in 1932. That union produced two children. Forgotten for the next six decades, Allan resurfaced briefly in the 1990s when he gave an interview to a fan who had tracked him down. He took his own life in 1997.

Jungle Mystery
(1932, Universal Pictures)

by Brian Taves

In late 1903, Talbot Mundy was in Hobart, Tasmania, with no prospect of employment and his writing career still years in the future. Desperate for money, he sailed on a three-masted vessel "bumping bluey"—carrying a form of Australian eucalyptus known as blue-gum piles for a new pier at Delagoa Bay. This ship was nearly wrecked when the cargo shifted, and the entire crew became ill. They jumped ship at Laurenco Marques, but conditions ashore were even worse. Without a job or money, a man could be jailed, after which he was either shipped back to sea or sent at gunpoint to boss slave labor.

This was the ignominious beginning of Mundy's longest and most confused odyssey, one that would carry him across nearly the entire eastern length of Africa. These were the most tortuous and uncertain years of his life, both physically and morally. His experiences during this period would include big-game hunting, safaris, various financial scams, and an initial probing into indigenous magic. Some of these exploits later wormed their way into his fiction, including one of his very best novels, The *Ivory Trail*. That story proved so rich in character, incident, and exotic appeal that it was later adapted by Hollywood as *Jungle Mystery,* a 1932 movie serial released by Universal, and by Mundy himself as a continuity for the radio adventure show he scripted from 1936 to 1940, *Jack Armstrong, the All-American Boy*. These adaptations of Mundy's classic novel are lost, but evidence indicates that both were extremely popular in their time. It's unlikely, however, that they were any more colorful than the author's real-life adventures on what was then known as "the Dark Continent."

Laurenco Marques was part of Portuguese East Africa in what is today the southernmost part of Mozambique. Mundy later described it as the most lawless place in the world, "where a man was fined only ten pounds for killing a white, and only a pound or two for a black." He was utterly destitute, the climate was dreadful, and in the swamps of the Umbuluzi River he succumbed to fever. A Chinese laundryman nursed him back to health, then directed him to a good job running a big estate up the Limpopo River at Chai-Chai in Gazaland.

The railway to Lake Victoria had just been completed. Mundy heard reports that British East Africa was booming and decided to get his share. He left at the end of January 1904 on the steamer Bundesrath, bound for Zanzibar and Mombasa. The reports turned out to be overstated.

With no jobs to be found, the only money was in illegally shooting elephants. Escaping the government's reach required traveling "up country" and "off the beaten track," at least 60 miles from the Uganda railway. Mundy took a train and hired a native servant-just out of jail-named Kazi Moto ("Work like hell"). They put together a safari and slipped into elephant country. Mundy hoped to find the legendary buried ivory hoard of Tippoo Tib, but the terrain and its inhabitants—from lions to tsetse flies to reported cannibals—proved too formidable.

With his proceeds from the safari, Mundy acquired a herd of 4,000 cattle that bore the brand of an official entitled to own only half that many. With British officials on his trail, he decided to drive the herd across the border into German East Africa. Near Shirati, on the eastern shore of Lake Victoria, a band of fierce Masai fought Mundy and his men, taking the cattle. The wayward Englishman received a wound in the right leg from a spear dipped in gangrene, and later it took seven men to hold him down while the wound was cauterized with stems of grass heated in a fire.

Mundy and Kazi Moto began walking to the nearest doctor, 200 miles away in Muanza, where the Germans were inhospitable. Mundy had developed black-water fever, and upon his arrival he was placed in a rat-filled shed where he was expected to die. Kazi Moto stole food for him, and the doctor made brief visits. After a few days, he heard the doctor order a sergeant to bring the chain gang to dig a grave and bury him. "Up to that time," Mundy wrote in the April 1, 1919 issue of *Adventure,* "I had not particularly wanted to get well; I had neither money nor prospects and was feeling much too ill to care, and I haven't the least doubt that if he had said nothing I would have died either that day or the day following. But I hated the man so, and was so utterly disgusted with his treatment of me, that I made up my mind to disappoint him, and from that minute I began to get better. When the chain gang came with a sack to tie me up in I was sitting up with the aid of Kazi Moto. Two days later I leaned on Kazi Moto's shoulder and walked out to have a look at the grave; I was so weak that I very nearly tumbled into it."

After "trekking about" in German East Africa, Mundy realized he could not make enough to live on and took passage on a dhow for British territory. He did road work and was appointed town clerk of the frontier village of Kisumu, on the northwest shore of Lake Victoria and situated almost exactly on the equator. He saw two campaigns and mastered several of the local languages.

By this time, Mundy's interest in Africans extended beyond his study of their magic. He had affairs with women from various local tribes, causing a scandal that lost him his job. On one safari, he made the acquaintance of rambunctious, quarrelsome Rupert Cecil Craven, formerly of the Royal Navy. Craven and his fellow travelers, known as heavy drinkers and gamblers, entered the ivory trade. His wife, 35-year-old Inez Broom, was regarded as one of the great beauties of the day, her exotic good looks perhaps inherited from her Spanish grandmother. Mundy and Inez became romantically involved, and repercussions from the ensuing scandal drove them out of

Africa and even England; both eventually wound up in the United States.

Mundy's experiences in Africa became the basis for a series that had the most autobiographical tone of any of his writing. "Oakes Respects an Adversary" *(Adventure,* December 3, 1918) introduced the characters that would take center stage in The *Ivory Trail.* "Adversary" begins a saga of fortune hunting set before World War I and written in the first person. Lord Montdidier (pronounced Mundidger), Earl of Kirkudbrightshire, a middle-aged bachelor and unrepentant member of the English old order, seeks to replenish the family treasury. Slightly older is his lifelong friend, Frederick Joliett Oakes, another English bachelor of similar build, weighing some 240 pounds. Oakes is distinguished halfway through the opening series of stories by his occasionally irritating passion for the concertina, which he uses to accompany songs composed on the spot. He is fluent in a dozen languages and full of humor. William Simpson Yerkes, often called "America" by Oakes, is no enthusiast for autocratic government, whether in the colonies or in Africa accompanied by a lord, but he learns to respect "Monty."

Monty, Oakes, and Yerkes are modern-day equivalents of Dumas's three musketeers, with the narrator serving as the initiate d'Artagnan. The three protagonists unite diverse levels of society in a mix that dismisses differences of class and caste. Each individual must prove himself worthy, regardless of birth, with the only distinction based on ability. Adhering to a chivalric sense of honor, they are valorous and humane; fulfilling the obligations of duty and selflessness is as much their objective as searching for wealth.

The African portion of the saga reached its pinnacle in The *Ivory Trail,* originally titled "On the Trail of Tippoo Tib" for its six-part serialization in *Adventure* from May to July 1919. (It also was reprinted in 1953 as *Trek East).* Exciting and well written, with colorful descriptions of the African land and animals, this long, sprawling, hastily composed epic became Mundy's second great success in book form, following *King—of the Khyber Rifles* (Indianapolis: Bobbs-Merrill, 1916).

Today, *The Ivory Trail* is something more than an entertaining adventure: It serves as an autobiographical testament of colonial conditions on the continent at the turn of the century. Most of the characters are based on people Mundy knew. The aging great hunter Frederick Courteney Selous appears under the name of F. Courtney, singled out for his gentleness. He advises that Mount Elgon, with its unmapped caves, some inhabited by cannibals, is just the location Tib would have chosen to hide the ivory. Selous was probably a childhood hero of Mundy's, having also been at Rugby for two years nearly three decades earlier, and was already a legend by the time Mundy arrived in the continent. Mundy saw no need to hide the name of the loyal and courageous guide Kazimoto. One of the novel's villains, Georges Coutlass, was based a foul-mouthed Greek who had accompanied Mundy and Kazi Moto on a safari. In real life this character met a much less merciful death in German East Africa than Mundy provided for his fictional counterpart.

Possibly the beautiful, arrogant temptress and German agent, the treacherous Lady Isobel Saffren Waldon, was inspired by Inez Broom Craven. Just as she and Mundy lived together as husband and wife before the marriage, so does Waldon agree to pose as the wife of the German villain, Professor Schillingschen. Lady Isobel constantly imposes on the chivalry of the Anglos to escape the consequences of her deeds. She is a sad but entirely selfish figure, exploiting others, even to having her Syrian maid appeal to Coutlass's rough affections. She comes to a bad end, being burned to death by the German steamer when she steals the dhow.

The Ivory Trail begins when Monty, Oakes, Yerkes, and the narrator decide to search for the hidden treasure of fabled 19th-century Arab slave trader, Tippoo Tib. Monty travels to Britain to arrange shares with the various European powers that dispute the area; he thus remains absent for most of the novel. Oakes, Yerkes, and the narrator plunge inland, pursued by Germans who believe they have secret information that, in fact, they lack. The adventurers travel to Mombasa, Nairobi,

Kikuyu, Lumbwa, Lake Victoria, Muanza, Ukerewe, and Kisumu before arriving at Mount Elgon. All of these were places Mundy knew personally.

In Chapter Four, they meet Brown of Lumbwa, a settler who becomes their companion, a friend but never an intimate. Brown drinks constantly but he is also a man of courage; assisting him when his cattle are stolen becomes the catalyst for a long detour amidst the blight of German misrule of East Africa. Following the pattern of Mundy's World War I fiction, the book is as much a denunciation of Germany as an adventure in Africa. Certainly the war prompted Mundy to emphasize the German atrocities he had witnessed. A court practicing "good, sound German law that knows no fear or favor, but governs all alike" becomes a mass of bloody beatings, men and women writhing under the whip. As Brown explains, in British courts the blacks are treated with leniency because they often do not understand the law, and both races can be condemned for a crime against the other; in German courts only Africans may be found guilty, with a hanging preferred. The Germans seek to elicit local fear; Oakes and his friends first see such "justice" in the lashing of a black who begged for money after the commandant had made his daughter pregnant.

Even Kazimoto is given 200 lashes and sentenced to the German chain gang, from which Oakes and Yerkes help him escape. They flee in a dhow with Coutlass and Lady Isobel, and traverse regions plagued by hunger and tsetse flies. However, the sudden deaths of Waldon, Coutlass, and Schillingschen, and the heroes' discovery of Tib's ivory, even when it is guarded by cannibals, is almost too much of a contrast to the preceding events, ending the novel on too abrupt and automatic a *deus ex machina*.

A key theme is the nature of friendship and the interaction among Brown, Coutlass, and Lady Isobel: who is an ally, who is an enemy, who is seeks his or her own interest first, who can be trusted? The constant shifting of allegiances of Coutlass, and to a lesser extent the Waldon woman, enhances the novel's episodic quality with a potentially endless series of unfolding incidents. This very structure made The *Ivory Trail* suitable for adaptation as a serial for the motion picture screen and for radio.

By 1932, Mundy's Hollywood agent, I. M. Sackin, had clients only in the second tier of authors, but despite the author's less-than-stellar representation, studios continued to consider many of his stories for screen adaptation. Two of Mundy's early short stories, "The Fire-Cop" and "For Valour" had been filmed in 1912. *King—of the Khyber Rifles* had been filmed in 1929 as The *Black Watch,* with Victor McLaglen as King, but it was largely a World War I regimental chronicle that used little of Mundy's narrative.

In 1930, Metro-Goldwyn-Mayer produced *Trader Horn,* the first major sound film made on location in Africa. The movie proved extremely popular upon release the following year, and studios quickly followed it up with other jungle adventures from best-selling books. These ranged from fictional features like M-G-M's *Tarzan the Ape Man,* (first of a 16-year series starring Johnny Weissmuller as Edgar Rice Burroughs' classic hero), to such documentaries as Frank Buck's *Bring 'Em Back Alive,* produced by The Van Buren Corporation for RKO release and filmed in the jungles around Malaysia. In August 1931, with the jungle-movie cycle in full swing, Universal Pictures Corporation expressed serious interest in filming *The Ivory Trail*. Mundy had recently transferred the film rights to his novels from Bobbs-Merrill to his literary agent, Carl Brandt, who finally sold the novel to Universal on March 3, 1932.

Mundy's bad luck with Hollywood persisted. The *Ivory Trail* adaptation would not be an expensive feature film but a serial, a form considered inherently more juvenile and less respectable. This decision virtually guaranteed that the film would fail to achieve a fraction of the eminence of *Trader Horn* or the Tarzan or Frank Buck movies. Made on relatively low budgets (anywhere from one quarter to one half the cost of the average major-studio feature film of the day), serials of necessity eschewed expensive expeditions undertaken to secure location photography.

After barely two months of preparation, the serial—now titled *Jungle Mystery*—went into production in May of 1932, directed by one of the genre's leading practitioners, Ray Taylor. The "supervisor" (a vintage-film term for what is now called a "line producer") was Henry MacRae, who in one capacity or another had been involved with Universal chapter plays since 1915. Ella O'Neill, George Plympton, Basil Dickey, and George Morgan—all well versed in the rather specialized form of serial writing—adapted Mundy's novel in 12 two-reel installments.

The *Jungle Mystery* cast included erstwhile cowboy star Tom Tyler and perennial sidekick Noah Beery, Jr. as Mundy's heroes Monty (here Kirk Montgomery) and "Fred" Oakes, with Frank Lackteen cast as their servant Kazimoto. Philo McCullough, Carmelita Geraghty, and James A. Marcus played Mundy's villains, George Coutlass, Lady Isobel Saffren Waldon (here renamed Belle Waldron), and Schillingschen (rechristened Boris Shillov), respectively. Newly devised characters included Cecilia Parker as Barbara Morgan, William Desmond as her father John, Sam Baker as Zungu, Peggy Watts as Azu, and Anders Van Haden as Krotsky, Shillov's guard. The nationality of several characters was changed; Will Yerkes and the novel's narrator were eliminated.

As *Jungle Mystery* begins, Monty and Fred are introduced as two Americans flying to Africa in quest of big game and crashing their airplane in the Dark Continent. Shillov, a South African searching for Tippoo Tib's ivory, refuses to aid them. Making their way toward Zanzibar, Monty and Fred encounter a strange creature-half-man, half-monkey known as Zungu.

In Zanzibar, Barbara Morgan induces her former suitor Monty, as well as Fred, to join her father on an expedition in search of her missing brother, Jack, who had also been hunting for the ivory. Prompted by Belle Waldron, a dangerous adventuress and Shillov's agent, the "burly ruffian" Coutlass attempts to become the guide for the expedition.

Because of the well-known interest of Monty and Oakes in Tippoo Tib's ivory, and disbelieving their ostensible purpose, Belle Waldron abducts Barbara. While trying to rescue her,

Fred and Kirk fall into a pool of man-eating sharks. So ends the first episode, "Into the Dark Continent."

Coutlass rescues Fred and Kirk to gain their confidence, but tells Belle of their plans. The Montgomery-Morgan party is led toward Nairobi by Monty's old guide, Kazimoto. *The Ivory Trail*'s German imperialists, all too reminiscent of antagonists in propagandistic World War I films of dubious popularity, undergo convenient transformations to Russians, always reliable as villains in empire-building yarns.

Coutlass, fearful after Shillov has Krotsky (a new character added for the movie) whipped for almost releasing Barbara, directs John Morgan to the Russian's camp. Kazimoto learns that Shillov's man Baganda has been propagandizing on his behalf with the indigenous people under Chief Barzibas, and Monty goes after a dangerous tiger to get them to side with him. Instead, Coutlass shoots the beast, thereby winning the natives' friendship. Morgan questions Baganda, who escapes and informs Shillov of his rivals' whereabouts.

The Prussian-mannered Shillov wants the ivory to finance a Russian colony in Central Africa, just as the novel's Schillingschen wanted for Germany in the novel. By contrast, Monty and Oakes have a government-sanctioned desire for the ivory, and unlike the Russians do not abuse the tribesmen.

Captured once again, Barbara bargains with Shillov to give him the information about the ivory if he will first find her brother Jack. This prompts Belle to grow jealous and arrange for the girl's escape. While searching for Barbara, Kazimoto is captured but solicits the help of a witch doctor.

From Barzibas, the two expeditions race toward Mount Elgon when they learn that natives have found tusks guarded by cannibals and a white man. Morgan encounters Hassan, an agent of Shillov, who gives him misleading directions. Shillov finds a map to the ivory and tries to eliminate Belle, who allies with Krotsky against him. The Waldron woman and Krotsky have known of Jack's whereabouts all along, keeping young Morgan imprisoned because he refused to tell them where the ivory was located.

When Monty attacks, Krotsky is killed and Belle mortally wounded by Coutlass. Before dying, she confesses that Shillov is nearby. Overhearing the revelation of the ivory's whereabouts, Coutlass goes on ahead with Shillov following. Zungu catches up with both, and in the ensuing struggle all three fall to their death. Jack leads his friends to a cave where they find the ivory, which is not the only prize: Monty has won Barbara's love.

Belle Waldron (Carmelita Geraghty) directs her henchmen to attack Monty and Fred.

Although retaining much of Mundy's original plot, *Jungle Mystery* also utilizes the conventions of chapter-play structure. While the narrative still ostensibly concerns a hunt for the legendary ivory cache of Tippoo Tib, *Jungle Mystery* to the motivations and number of characters found in the original. These include the obligatory but muted romantic subplot and a search for a missing fortune hunter, as well as the standard jungle-serial plot device of a woman imperiled at every turn by man and beast. There are many fights and supporting characters, and the indigenous people constantly shift sides, with much treachery on the part of Belle Waldron and Coutlass—which also was a motif of the novel. Nearly every chapter of the serial contains an encounter with a dangerous animal, providing many of the necessary episode-ending cliffhangers showing the heroes in life-threatening situations without any apparent escape.

Shot on a four-week schedule for a "negative cost" (the figure encompassing all production expenses incurred up to preparing a negative from which release prints can be struck) of $157,894, *Jungle Mystery* was released on September 12, 1932. It went on to generate $368,772 in worldwide revenue for Universal. Subtracting the costs of prints and advertising, along with the customary distribution fee of 35 percent, the serial yielded a net profit of $ 17,513—a pittance by today's standards, but a not-inconsiderable amount considering that 1932 was the Depression's worst year.

In 1992, *Jungle Mystery* leading lady Cecilia Parker reminisced about making the serial. "We worked long, long hours," she said. "The unions hadn't really gotten underway, so the producers kept shooting until people started dropping. We would get to the set early in the morning, before the sun rose, and if the day's work took us until nightfall to finish, the director would say, 'Oh, good, now we can take those night scenes we were going to do next week.' It was awfully tiring, but it was fun too."

Interiors for *Jungle Mystery* were shot on the sound stages at Universal City, and numerous facades on the back lot were altered by the studio's art department and dressed with the appropriate props to suggest African dwellings in Zanzibar. Parker recalled the jungle scenes being filmed at a San Fernando Valley ranch with dedicated acreage specially outfitted with dense tropical undergrowth. "It was out in the western end of the Valley," she claimed, "near the Sepulveda Basin. I worked there several times. That's where we shot the jungle scenes for that serial I did with Clyde Beatty [The *Lost Jungle,* 1934 Mascot]. It wasn't far from the studio; we could get there in 15 minutes or so. Now, with the freeway that cuts through the Valley, you could do it a lot quicker, but that ranch is long gone and there are houses where the jungle lot used to be."

During the first half of the 1930s Talbot Mundy continued writing tales of high adventure for pulp magazines, but word-rate cuts fueled by the Depression diminished his earning power, and he found it difficult to modify his style so as to crack the more lucrative "slicks." Therefore, in the spring of 1936, his financial resources at low ebb, Mundy accepted a job writing radio scripts for a children's adventure serial, *Jack Armstrong, the All-American Boy.* Created in 1933 by Robert Hardy Andrews, *Jack Armstrong* initially proved popular with youthful listeners but after three years was getting stale.

For those unfamiliar with the show: Jack (played by Jim Ameche) is a high-school student in the Midwestern town of Hudson. His best friend is the younger Billy Fairfield (John Gannon), whose capable sister, Betty (Sara Jane Wells), is present for female listeners. The siblings' uncle, Jim Fairfield

(James Goss), is a former high-ranking army officer who owns an aircraft factory. A walking cornucopia of knowledge, Uncle Jim frequently brings the teenagers with him on his travels.

Before long Mundy took the opportunity to adapt The *Ivory Trail* in a different serial form. In January of 1937, Jack went to Africa to hunt elephants and search for the fabulous ivory treasure reputedly buried in the legendary Elephants' Graveyard. Although every broadcast in this continuity (broken down into 15-minute episodes heard five days a week) is lost, various sources, when compared to the source novel, allow for reconstruction of the radio version's plot. Mundy's only surviving script from *Jack Armstrong,* published in a 1938 anthology, *Radio Continuity Types,* dates from this period in the show's history.

The new serialized adaptation of *Ivory Trail*—sans any thematic references to a nation's colonial oppression of African natives-opens in Brazil on the plantation of the villainous Alonzo Lopez, who regularly mistreats his servant Ali (taking the place of *Ivory Trail's* Juma). Jim arranges for the servant's freedom, and in gratitude Ali turns over to Jack an ivory ring given him by Tippoo Tib. Ali warns the Fairfields and their friend that Lopez will come after it, and that proves to be the case.

In the radio version, snub-nosed Kazimoto is presented as a loyal friend who provides minor amusement, calling himself a "first-class, top-hole feller." Hardly the pillar of courage presented in the novel, he follows the Fairfield party because he is more afraid to be left behind.

The first native village seen by Jack, Billy, Betty, and Uncle Jim is Matadi, in the Belgian Congo. There they meet the silent magician Booloola, described in the *Radio Continuity Types* script as "the Elephant Man—six feet four inches of magnificent bronze savage. He is clad in a lion-skin apron and a necklace of lions' claws. His dark eyes glow with mystery and his thick African lips smile with proud cunning." Booloola purportedly knew Tippoo Tib and where he buried the map of the place where the elephants go to die.

Flying his speedy "Silver Albatross" up the Congo River, Uncle Jim lands on a placid lake once crowded with hippos and crocodiles. Just as Jim lands, so does a Belgian hydroplane from Senegal, missing them by only a few yards. They are surprised when Lopez emerges from the craft. Jim dispatches Jack, Billy, and Kazimoto to the wharf to fend off the Brazilian plantation owner. With Kazimoto's assistance, Jack tackles Lopez to prevent him from beating Booloola with a stick.

Lopez is taken aboard the Silver Albatross as Uncle Jim navigates by Booloola's directions to a lost city in the jungle where Lopez believes Tib's map has been secreted. Menacing pygmies are turned into friends to help in the search. While searching a cave, Jack and the Fairfields find the map, which shows the Mountains of the Moon, Lake Victoria, and the unknown "Castle That Shouts." Booloola steals the map, but not before Jack makes a mental copy in his mind. Stopping at Kisumu, Lopez disappears during the night, having disabled the Silver Albatross. Jim old friend, Sheik Mohammed, invites him to join them in his camp near Mount Elgon.

Mohammed shows Jim a much more complex parchment map, and when the Sheik is abducted by Lopez, Booloola leads Jack to the Rocks That Shout, so named because of the sounds produced by the wind whipping across their odd shapes. A landslide traps the party and crushes Lopez, and Booloola deliberately blocks the way into the elephant's graveyard to protect it. Mohammed explains that Booloola mistrusts all whites, believing them merciless in their quest for wealth. In that way his switching of sides, a useful serialization device for extending the narrative, is explained altruistically. Booloola meant to keep anyone from finding the map, and joined whoever would advance that purpose of his own.

Jack Armstrong's 1936-37 season lasted 34 weeks, wrapping up on April 23, 1937. During the summer hiatus, Mundy returned to writing short stories, but come fall he was back in harness, and he remained the shows primary scripter until he died in 1940. The sequence adapted from *Ivory Trail* was itself adapted for a 1937 Big Little Book, *Jack Armstrong and the Ivory Treasure,* credited to Leslie J. Daniels, Jr.

Sadly, both The *Jungle Mystery* and the Spring 1937 broadcasts of *Jack Armstrong* are today lost. One can only hope that some collector, having acquired and saved further relics that will shed more light on serial and radio dramatization, comes forward to add to our knowledge of these Talbot Mundy adventures. Until then we'll have to be content with reading *The Ivory Trail* and *Jack Armstrong and the Ivory Treasure.*

The Red Rider
(1934, Universal Pictures)
by Daniel J. Neyer

The Red Rider is yet another wonderful chapter play from the golden age of Universal serials. It's amazing how many gems there are from this period (*Gordon of Ghost City, Pirate Treasure, Rustlers of Red Dog*, etc.), and it's also amazing how little known most of them are. I suppose they've fallen victim to the snobbery of pseudo-critics, those who refuse to believe a simple Western or treasure hunt can be any fun without fantastic gizmos, gadgets, and so forth.

Since the serial takes at least two chapters to set up the basic plot, and since new developments are added throughout, *The Red Rider* is not easy to summarize. Basically, it involves the efforts of former sheriff Red Davidson (Buck Jones) to clear his friend Silent Slade (Grant Withers) of a murder charge. This requires getting the necessary evidence to prove oily villain Jim Breen (Walter Miller) guilty of the killing. There are several subplots that neatly intertwine with the main plot thread: Breen's involvement in a diamond-smuggling operation, Red's efforts to protect rancher Bob Maxwell (Charles French) and his daughter Marie (Marion Shilling) from Breen's machinations, and the scheming of Breen's lieutenant Joe Portos (Richard Cramer) against his boss.

The Red Rider is a fairly conventional Western, but like *Gordon* and *Rustlers* it's done with such style and gusto as to seem fresh and lively throughout. The serial was adapted by George Plympton, Vin Moore, Basil Dickey, and Ella O'Neill from a W. C. Tuttle novel serialized in *Adventure* magazine as "The Red Devil from Sun Dog" (March 1—April 1, 1929) before being published in hard covers the following year by Houghton Mifflin as *The Redhead from Sun Dog*. Subsequently it was reprinted in a popular-priced edition by Grosset & Dunlap, and in a 1949 paperback by Hillman.

The serial's scenario tracks Tuttle's yarn closely, retaining (and in some cases expanding on) every major character and incident presented in the book's first third, straying from the source material only as much as necessary to fill out 15 chapters. With just a couple exceptions the screenwriters keep Tuttle's character names: Brick Davidson is renamed Red—a meaningless change inasmuch as both names suggest the color of his hair—and Joe Pico becomes Joe Portos. The title character is ever so slightly modified to accommodate Buck's well-established screen persona, but the others behave very much in keeping with their print counterparts.

Plympton and company deserve the highest praise for their scriptwriting, a near-perfect example of faithful adaptation that continually sees the development of interesting characters and the weaving of new plot threads before the action can get repetitive—the bane of many serials. The fidelity to Tuttle's novel might have been mandated by producer Henry MacRae, or perhaps by Jones himself, a fan of pulp fiction and a friend of the author's. In any case, *Red Rider* avoids most of the pitfalls of Western serials by hewing closely to its rough-paper source. To see the difference between the styles of the various serial studios, and the influence they obviously had on writers and directors, compare Dickey's no-nonsense Republic scripts and Plympton's lackluster work on Columbia chapter plays to their witty, energetic work here. Miss O'Neill's writing is always of the highest quality, and we probably have her to thank for the well-done bits of romantic comedy featured in this serial and its predecessor, 1933's *Gordon of Ghost City*, another better-than-average Jones serial. Vin Moore was a former comedy director, and I suspect his touches are evident in the characters of the bumbling Mexican henchmen played by

Jim Thorpe and Monte Montague. These two characters, however, manage to be funny without undermining the serial's suspense, unlike the comic heavies of James W. Horne's early-Forties Columbia chapter plays. That's a tough thing to manage, but Moore pulls it off. In short, the script of *Red Rider* represents a fine achievement for all involved—and all due credit going to Tuttle's original story.

The writers' sterling efforts are complemented by the efficient direction of Louis Friedlander, who—under the name of Lew Landers—would go on to direct many good "B" Westerns in the Thirties and Forties before graduating to low- and medium-budgeted "civilian" pictures. He maintains a swiftness of pace equal to or surpassing the pace of fellow serial director Ray Taylor's outings from this period, and his staging of the many horseback chases is particularly exciting. It's the riding sequences and the extensive location shooting that help to give this serial a real "out of doors" feel appropriate for a Western. There are only a handful of extended fistfights throughout the serial but we never notice their absence at all, a sure sign that director and writers are doing their job in maintaining audience interest. In a serial like *Tex Granger* (a 1948 Columbia), everything is so dull and lifeless that the absence of fights sticks out like a sore thumb, but *The Red Rider* doesn't need set-busting tussles to liven things up—it's fun enough already. Serial fans who fear that *Red Rider* is a talk-a-thon (like some Universal chapter plays) needn't worry: There are chases, shootouts, and ambushes aplenty to keep action fans happy.

The cliffhanger endings seem to have been oddly manhandled after the first two or three chapters. Frequently, episodes end just before the peril has materialized or just after it's been resolved. However, since Universal's chapter endings were never their strong point, this oddity doesn't really interfere with appreciation of the serial.

The combined efforts of Friedlander, Plympton, Dickey, O'Neill, and Moore would have been meaningless without a good cast, but *The Red Rider* features a flawless group of players. Buck Jones is provided with opportunities to play serious drama *and* light comedy, both of which he does incredibly well. His resignation as sheriff after allowing Grant Withers to escape jail in Chapter One is a powerful piece of acting, but he does equally well in the serial's many lighter moments, delivering wry quips with youthful energy and good-humor. As in *Gordon of Ghost City*, he manages to be determined, humorous, intelligent, and happy-go-lucky, all at the same time.

Former and future leading man Grant Withers is very good as Silent Slade, conveying real sadness and frustration over his position as a fugitive from justice. His undercover pose as one of Breen's henchmen in the middle section of the serial is very well done: He does such a good job of behaving in typically surly "mug" fashion that you don't blame Breen for being taken in by him for so long. But Silent always remains sympathetic, and we root for Red as he continually tries to clear his wronged friend.

Heroine Marion Shilling doesn't have a huge amount of screen time, but her characterization is far from one-dimensional or dull. Her growing love for Jones' character and her amusement at his complete ignorance of her feelings is well portrayed, and she proves herself helpful and brave in times of danger. Margaret La Marr, as Withers' sweetheart (and daughter of the man Withers is accused of killing) delivers a touching performance, steadfastly sticking by her man even though all the evidence is against him.

Erstwhile silent-serial star Walter Miller is his usual sly, sharp self as Jim Breen, curtly dispatching his men on their errands of nastiness and trying his best to annihilate everyone who stands in his way. And not only is Breen utterly ruthless, he's also extremely untrustworthy, selling out his own partners more than once. His comment of "No friend is worth five thousand dollars" sums up his attitude pretty well. It's a pleasure to watch Red bring down such a despicable miscreant. Joe Portos, played by Richard Cramer, is almost a match for Breen in underhanded villainy and his superior when it comes to outright physical violence. While the sneering, leering Portos is technically Breen's henchman, he's a full-fledged malefactor in his own right and clearly resents having to jump at Breen's command. Cramer's vivid, swaggering performance is a delight to watch; he dominates the screen every time he appears.

Edmund Cobb has one of his best roles as Johnny Snow, a cowboy on the Maxwell ranch who becomes Jones' trusty ally in his quest to bring Breen to justice. Those who have accused Cobb of being a limited or even talentless actor should see him here; he's consistently funny but never becomes a buffoonish sidekick. His raucous attempts to serenade the heroine ("Sweet Marie, come to me . . .") are hilarious, as are many of his lines. Cobb turns in an easy-going "cowpoke" performance that compliment's Jones' similar personality perfectly. Charles K. French, grandfather of Victor French, is a typical serial heroine's father: dignified, likeable, and venerable, but apparently not too bright.

Monte Montague and Jim Thorpe, already mentioned above, are priceless as the dimwitted Abel brothers (named Abelardo in the novel), Joe Portos' cousins and clumsy assistants. Montague's character clearly fancies himself the smarter of the two, repeatedly addressing his brother as "dumb one," but he's hardly any sharper than his sibling. Their bumbling antics liven things up considerably, but they don't diminish in the slightest the menace conveyed by Miller and Cramer's characters. Three old pros—Jim Corey, Al Ferguson, and Bud Osborne—play Miller's principal thugs, and are suitably tough and mean. Chester Gan pops up as Miller's sneaky Chinese cook, who outwits and flabbergasts Jones and Cobb in one hilarious sequence.

Other veteran actors contribute texture and atmosphere in minor roles. Lee Beggs plays the gabby, chatty mayor of Jones' hometown Sun Dog, who tries to prevent Red from handing in his badge in the first chapter. J. Frank Glendon (villain of a 1932 Universal serial, *The Lost Special*, and a one-time chapter-play hero himself) has a small role as Sun Dog's smug prosecuting attorney, and Robert McGowan plays an ill-fated partner of Walter Miller's. John Merton makes his serial debut as the aggressive ranch hand that accuses Grant Withers of murdering Scotty McKee, played by pioneering serial director J. P. McGowan. William Desmond, one of Universal's most popular cliffhanging stars during the Twenties, appears as an intelligent, fair-minded lawman who agrees to hold off arresting Slade in hopes that Red can prove him innocent—a far cry from the irascible, impetuous character he plays in *Gordon of Ghost City*. Speaking of *Gordon*, Tom Ricketts—the heroine's grandfather in that serial—puts in a brief appearance here as a judge. Finally, future leading man Dennis Moore (at this stage of his career known as Denny Meadows) pops up as Slim, another of the Maxwell ranch hands, and lends occasional support to Jones, Withers, and Cobb throughout most of the running time.

The Red Rider, based on a novel as it is, boasts a stronger story than serials that generally involve a tug of war over a treasure map, a secret formula, or some similar MacGuffin. Many Universal Western serials of the Thirties center on a villain who covets land and/or a gold claim and stirs up Indians to make raids on the good guys in chapter after chapter. *The Red Rider*, on the other hand, focuses on solving two mysteries—ferreting out the killer of Scott McKee and thus clearing Silent Slade, and finding what happened to a shipment of smuggled diamonds. The script never loses sight of these objectives (too many other serials allow key plot points to be forgotten for several episodes at a time, only to bring them back onstage in the last chapter) and *Red Rider* is the better for it.

Many chapter plays adapted from books went pretty far astray from the source material. In some cases—as in Republic's 1944 *Haunted Harbor*, based on a novel by Ewart Adamson writing as Dayle Douglas—the deviation didn't hurt the end result. In others, it was nothing short of embarrassing. *The Red Rider*, however, benefits enormously from adhering to W. C. Tuttle's original story. It's one of those happy serials in which effective scripting, direction, and acting combine to make the end result as enjoyable as possible.

The New Adventures of Tarzan
(1935, Burroughs-Tarzan Enterprises)
by Ed Hulse

By 1934, best-selling author Edgar Rice Burroughs was thoroughly disgusted with Hollywood's treatment of his most famous creation, Tarzan of the Apes. A succession of motion-picture producers had signally failed to accord Tarzan the respect Burroughs felt the character deserved. Metro-Goldwyn-Mayer's 1932 smash, *Tarzan, the Ape Man*, made the Jungle Lord an illiterate wild man who spoke in monosyllables—a characterization ERB detested. Sol Lesser's 1933 *Tarzan the Fearless*, a cheaply made serial starring Buster Crabbe, was even worse. So, when approached by his old friend Ashton Dearholt with a proposal for producing Tarzan films faithful to the author's vision, Burroughs jumped at the chance.

ERB and his wife Emma had been acquainted with actor/producer Dearholt and *his* wife, silent-screen actress Florence Gilbert, since the late Twenties. At one time Ashton both produced and starred in Westerns, achieving modest success as a character called "Pinto Pete." Florence was friendly with Edgar's daughter Joan, whose husband was James Pierce, himself a former screen Tarzan. With the advent of sound, Dearholt had chosen to remain behind the camera, working as a freelance production manager for First National Pictures and RKO Radio. While supervising a film for the latter studio—

1934's *Adventure Girl*—he became smitten with a dark, alluring young actress billed as Ula Holt. After divorcing Florence, he wed Ula. The former Mrs. Dearholt took up with (and eventually married) Burroughs, who had just left Emma. Amazingly, she maintained cordial relations with Ashton and his new bride.

Dearholt knew ERB secretly yearned to guide the cinematic destinies of his fictional characters—a desire that only intensified after the April 1934 release of *Tarzan and His Mate*, second in M-G-M's series starring Johnny Weissmuller and Maureen O'Sullivan. Produced on a more lavish scale than Metro's first Tarzan movie, *Mate* garnered uniformly enthusiastic reviews and racked up impressive grosses. The always cash-strapped Burroughs could hardly afford to turn down M-G-M's generous license fees, but he longed to see Tarzan portrayed on screen with at least passing fidelity to the printed-page character.

Partnering with movie-industry veterans George W. Stout and Ben S. Cohen in a company called Romance Productions Inc., Dearholt approached his old friend about letting the new corporation produce a Tarzan serial. At first ERB demurred, but eventually he agreed to license for $20,000 the screen rights to an original Tarzan story to be filmed in "not more than 12 episodes totaling 25 reels."

Shortly thereafter, Burroughs was persuaded to lend his name to the venture and Romance Productions was reconstituted as Burroughs-Tarzan Enterprises. Edgar was granted a 40 percent interest in the new firm while Dearholt (listed on the company letterhead as Vice President in Charge of Production), Stout (President), and Cohen (Vice President) agreed to split the remaining 60 percent evenly. Burroughs had been seduced by Dearholt's promise that Tarzan would be depicted as the educated English lord of the novels, and that his screen adventures would take place "throughout interesting and unusual parts of the world."

Burroughs-Tarzan Enterprises (hereafter referred to as BTE) set up shop in the heart of Hollywood, at 8476 Sunset Boulevard. The company's formation was heralded with great fanfare; movie-industry trade journals ran story after story about BTE's grandiose plans to shoot a Tarzan serial in exotic foreign locations. Dearholt, Stout, and Cohen went about the business of raising funds—which proved to be more difficult than anticipated, glowing publicity notwithstanding.

Although the original deal called for Burroughs to write a story that would be used as the serial's basis, he apparently had nothing to do with its actual composition. That responsibility was delegated to screenwriters Charles F. Royal and Edwin H. Blum. Dearholt had them incorporate the Guatemalan locations he had visited while supervising the production of *Adventure Girl*. According to ERB biographer Irwin Porges, Dearholt urged Edgar to write a book-length novelization of the script to be titled *Tarzan in Guatemala*, but this Burroughs refused to do. He did, however, approve the final script.

(By the way, Dearholt and his partners had trouble assigning a title to the serial. At various times before, during, and after production, it was referred to as *Tarzan in Guatemala*, *Tarzan's New Adventures*, *Tarzan and the Green Goddess*, *Tarzan and the Lost Goddess* and, finally, *New Adventures of Tarzan*.)

In August, BTE launched a highly publicized campaign to find the screen's next Tarzan. The company placed ads in local newspapers, inviting would-be ape-men to strut their stuff in front of Dearholt and his associates. One of these advertisements captured the attention of a man who had nearly been cast as Tarzan by Metro.

Herman Brix (who died earlier this year at the age of 100), a University of Washington football star and silver medalist at the 1928 Olympics, broke his shoulder shortly after testing for the role of Tarzan in 1931. With his first choice out of commission, director W. S. Van Dyke chose another Olympian, champion swimmer Johnny Weissmuller. Still a dedicated athlete and now a bit player as well, Brix was newly married and looking for his big break when he found out about BTE's casting call.

"They held tryouts at the Los Angeles Athletic Club," recalled Brix in an exclusive 2002 interview for *Blood 'n'*

Thunder. "Those of us who answered the ad ran around the track, did some physical things like climbing up ropes and what not, and struck some poses. I didn't know any of the producers, but after I did my bit they called me aside and asked me to stick around for a while. Eventually, they came up to me and said, 'Well, you're it.' Just like that."

Contrary to pre-production publicity (often cited in later books and articles on ERB), Edgar did *not* personally choose the Olympic athlete from a reported one hundred applicants. "He *approved* me," said Brix, "but I was *selected* by Dearholt, Stout, and Cohen. After I got the part, I met Burroughs and we posed together for some pictures. That was the only time I ever saw him." And Brix remembered competing against only "a couple dozen guys" at the Athletic Club tryout.

With his Tarzan in place, Dearholt quickly filled out the supporting cast. Not surprisingly, Ula Holt was given the role of an exotic mystery woman. Frank Baker, an old pal of Dearholt's from the "Pinto Pete" days, signed on to play Major Martling, the archeologist who takes an expedition to Guatemala. The juvenile leads were entrusted to Dale Walsh and Harry Ernest. Silent-era comic and one-time leading man Lewis Sargent was engaged to provide comedy relief.

It's frequently been reported—by film historians and ERB scholars alike—that the villain part was originally given to one "Don Castello," who supposedly took ill during the early days of production and was replaced by Dearholt. "Castello" mysteriously retained his billing on film and in publicity materials. The problem with this story is that no such actor ever existed. There was a character actor named Don *Costello*, but he wasn't working in films when Dearholt's Tarzan serial was cast. Brix confirmed to *Blood 'n' Thunder* that neither a Castello nor a Costello ever worked with the company; Dearholt played the heavy from the beginning. "As I recall, he planned on doing that character all along."

Late in the year, with production finally about to get underway, Dearholt and his partners confessed to Burroughs that they had been unable to secure all the necessary funds. ERB was persuaded to obtain and personally guarantee a $50,000 loan from the Citizens National Bank of Los Angeles. On November 28, just days after this money was received, principal photography on what was then titled *Tarzan in Guatemala* commenced with wild-animal scenes shot at the Selig Zoo in Los Angeles. Colonel William N. Selig, a true movie-industry pioneer, had been producing jungle films since before the World War, and his menagerie was employed by practically every studio in Hollywood at one time or another.

On December 2nd, Dearholt and his company—actors and crew members alike, 29 in all—sailed for Guatemala aboard the steamship *Seattle*. Not wanting to waste time during the expensive trip, directors Edward Kull (who doubled as one of the cinematographers) and Wilbur F. McGaugh (another old crony of Dearholt's) staged and shot scenes for Chapter One taking place on board the Guatemala-bound liner carrying the Martling expedition. In one sequence, Brix appeared in dinner clothes and looked every bit the cultured English lord Tarzan was when away from the jungle. The performances were a little stiff, but the shipboard action scenes were appropriately vigorous. Brix felt the production had gotten off to a good start.

The Dearholt Expedition, as it came to be called, first ran into trouble upon the *Seattle*'s arrival at San Jose, the port of entry in Guatemala. The small, primitive harbor couldn't really accommodate a ship of the *Seattle*'s size, so the anchor was dropped three miles off shore and huge barges dispatched to ferry passengers and equipment to the mainland. The ship's derrick was thought to be of insufficient strength to lower the heavy sound truck, but with no viable alternative Dearholt ordered the crew to proceed. The derrick boom snapped just as the truck was about to touch down on the barge. Fortunately, a quick check of the valuable sound-recording equipment revealed nothing broken except a few easily replaceable tubes.

The next challenge was getting sound truck, lights, and cameras up to Chichicastenango, a picturesque city where numerous scenes were to be shot. The steep, poorly graded roads made speedy progress impossible, and it took nearly 18 hours to travel less than a hundred miles. "In some places," recalled Edward Kull in an article for the March 1935 issue of *International Photographer*, "the roads were so narrow that had we met an oncoming vehicle of any kind, one of us would have had to back up many miles or else—and it would not have been me." He added, "We had to pull [the truck] in low gear most of the way up, nearly 6,000 feet, with many stops to cool the engine, while [second cameraman Ernie] Smith sat inside the truck holding his breath, hoping against hope nothing would be smashed."

Transportation difficulties turned out to be the least of Dearholt's problems. Nearly four months were required to shoot the serial, and before the last scene was taken, nearly every cast and crew member had been sick—some of them more than once. Ticks and sand flies abounded in the jungle, frequently burrowing their way through fine mosquito netting to feast on unsuspecting humans. Tropical storms battered the Guatemalan wilderness with regularity; during these, rain fell in torrents and made travel impossible.

"Oh, it was something," recalled Brix for *BnT*. "We ran out of food, we ran out of water, we ran out of medicine, and we even got stuck in the jungle for a couple days. It was pretty tough on everybody."

The first casualty was co-director Wilbur McGaugh, who clearly wasn't up to the rigors of location shooting and failed to meet his old friend's expectations. "He was a misfit," Brix claimed. "He didn't understand what was going on around us. We weren't there [in Guatemala] more than a few days before Dearholt sent him home. After that, Eddie Kull continued directing in terms of camera placements and lighting, and Dearholt set up the 'mechanics' of each scene."

Nearly 68 years after filming the serial, Brix still admitted a grudging respect for Dearholt, a man he never truly liked. "He was the key to the whole operation. A very capable and resourceful guy. He wasn't a warm or endearing man. I thought he was pretty cold, actually. But he got the film made under very tough conditions. It isn't everybody that could keep a company together [in those circumstances], but he did it."

Shooting progressed slowly, at first because cinematographers Kull and Smith weren't certain they were getting the proper light for their exposures. "In spite of our thorough advance studies of light qualities in tropical lands," Kull explained for *International Photographer*, "we found conditions more tricky than could have been imagined. Our first test stills, though to our estimate under-timed, were over-timed. Then the actinic quality of the light in high places, 6,000 feet up in that clear and rarefied atmosphere, had us constantly guessing, the varying quality being greatly different than conditions met in California in both high and low spots."

The high altitude also affected sound recording, which explains the unusual variability of the serial's audio track. Also, during production two microphone booms were broken and one mike smashed beyond repair. Screeching jungle birds constantly drowned out actors saying their lines. Take after take was required for relatively simple scenes that would have been filmed with no difficulty at all in the controlled environment of a Hollywood-studio back lot.

Through it all, Kull kept his cool and treated both cast and crew with tender loving care. "Eddie Kull was a very capable old cameraman," recalled Brix. "A real old pro. He was partially crippled, but he got the job done. In my opinion, he was one of the best people in the whole company."

The arduous working conditions forced Dearholt to make unanticipated compromises. The complex script written by Royal, Blum, Ben Cohen, and an uncredited Basil Dickey was jettisoned soon after the Expedition started shooting in the jungle. As the delays piled up, the company began taking short cuts and making things up on the fly. "We had a script about [three inches] thick," said Brix, "but once we got down there, really got into things, I don't think I ever looked at it.

"A lot of what we wound up with was governed by where we were shooting that day. If we had a nice looking spot with plenty of light, we'd set up the cameras, discuss the gist of what we were supposed to say and do, and then we'd go ahead and wing it."

Brix's admission explains why there was so much variance between the chapter synopses prepared for exhibitor pressbooks and the serial as released: The pressbook copy was written back in Hollywood, using the original script as source material. In the script, for example, Ula Holt's character was a secret agent pursuing smugglers. That entire subplot fell by the wayside. Also, the script gave prominence throughout to the young lovers—Alice Martling and Gordon Hamilton— played by Dale Walsh and Harry Ernest. In the finished serial, however, they appear only in early episodes; in Chapter Five the lovebirds are shown taking a steamship back to the States. Brix never knew what led to the sudden departure of cast members Walsh and Ernest. "I wasn't a party to that decision," he told *BnT*. "I just knew that, all of a sudden, they weren't there anymore."

No good Tarzan movie is complete without a lost city, and the serial's was a dandy. In fact, it was the real McCoy. Dearholt had shot scenes for *Adventure Girl* in the ruins of Tical, an old Spanish city reportedly built atop the remains of an ancient Mayan village. The climax of *Tarzan*'s Chapter One—arguably the most thrilling sequence in the entire serial, not to mention the feature version edited from it—would also utilize this eye-catching location, which the characters revisited in later episodes.

The Tical sequences, while visually stunning, were particularly tough on Brix. Running back and forth across the ruins *sans* footwear, he cut his feet to ribbons. Local natives were hired to play the lost city's denizens, with most being paid the princely sum of five cents per day. Those who fought Tarzan, however, got twenty cents per day and felt obligated to prove themselves worthy of the higher wages. In every shot calling for hand-to-hand combat, Brix was buried beneath an avalanche of Guatemalan locals and pummeled unmercifully. "I was pretty badly banged up after doing those scenes," he said. "My skin was rubbed raw all over."

The lost city's requisite white goddess, Queen Maya, was portrayed by Jackie Gentry, whose husband was the trainer of Jiggs, the chimpanzee playing N'kima. Suitably leggy for Maya's abbreviated costume but not otherwise prepossessing, Mrs. Gentry passed muster . . . until the camera came in for the obligatory close-ups. Whether she was cast in the role from the start or pressed into service at the last minute is one of the many little mysteries surrounding the making of this film. (Brix couldn't remember one way or the other.)

On February 25, 1935, with another month of principal photography scheduled, the Citizens National Bank note came due. Burroughs got an extension, but BTE scrambled to raise additional funds, only managing to do so after securing payment guarantees from regional distributors. Brix was upset when he learned that his wife back in Hollywood apparently hadn't been receiving his salary checks on a timely basis. Even with the additional financing in place, Dearholt and Kull barely had enough money to complete production and pay their bills.

Finally, in late March, the Dearholt Expedition pulled up stakes and sailed back to the States, exhausted but relieved. The company had exposed more than enough footage to fill the mandated 12 chapters; the real work would commence in a Hollywood cutting room, where Dearholt and his film editor would have to identify all the improvised scenes and insert them at the appropriate places.

By the time he got back to Los Angeles, Brix—who endured incredible hardships to play the role he hoped would catapult him to stardom—was practically a shadow of his former self. Just over 200 pounds when he went away, he weighed 172 upon returning home. He'd contracted fever and sustained innumerable injuries; one of them, which necessitated hospitalization in Guatemala, would continue to plague him for years.

Dearholt and his editors—Harold Minter, Thomas Neff, Edward Schroeder, and Walter Thompson—assembled the serial, chapter by chapter, from countless thousands of feet of film exposed during the four months of principal photography. Adopting a strategy employed by Sol Lesser on his Tarzan serial of 1933, Dearholt and his partners elected to release their epic in both episodic and feature-length form. The eight-reel feature was comprised of all the footage shot for Chapter One, part of Chapter Two, and a few brief scenes specially filmed with it in mind.

The story gets underway when Tarzan decides to search for his old friend D'Arnot, stranded somewhere in Central America's wilderness after crashing his plane. The ape man—or, rather, Lord Greystoke, to begin with—joins the party of Major Martling, an old friend leading an expedition into the Guatemalan jungle. Accompanied by his daughter Alice and her fiancé Gordon Hamilton, Martling hopes to locate the fabled Green Goddess, a priceless Mayan relic said to contain a fortune in jewels—as well as the ancient formula for a powerful explosive.

The Major is followed by Raglan, a treacherous soldier of fortune who covets the Goddess, and Ula Vale, an enigmatic young woman with her own reasons for trailing the Martling expedition. Tarzan foils an attempt on Martling's life during the ocean voyage to Guatemala and secures the Major's promise to help him locate D'Arnot.

In Chichicastenango, Martling learns that his notebook—which contains directions to the lost city where the Goddess is guarded by superstitious natives—has just been stolen from the old priest to whom it had been entrusted. Sensing that Raglan is behind the theft, Tarzan uses his matchless tracking skills to pursue the swarthy villain. About to capture Raglan at the lost city, Tarzan and the Martling party are attacked and captured by savage natives under the control of Queen Maya, who orders the outsiders put to death. Tarzan is shocked to learn that the long-missing D'Arnot is also a prisoner.

The deluxe Chapter One (made available to exhibitors in 43-minute and 67-minute versions) ends with Tarzan tied to a sacrificial altar and Queen Maya plunging a dagger toward his heart. At the beginning of Chapter Two she stops herself in mid-thrust and tries to make the ape man her consort. The feature version goes in a somewhat different direction. Suffice to say that the last-second intervention of George, Martling's generally ineffective assistant, enables Tarzan and his friends to turn the tables.

Upon seeing the "rushes" from Guatemala, Burroughs was enthusiastic and optimistic. But he wasn't sanguine after seeing a rough cut of the eight-reel feature version Dearholt had assembled. In a BTE memo quoted by Porges, Edgar lamented, "... what impressed me last night was the fact that we had sacrificed both the story and the scenic shots in an effort to achieve action that either was not there or not worth while, and what action there *is* is not particularly thrilling."

Burroughs urged his partner to recut the feature version in a way that would stress picturesque views of Chichicastenango and Tical, and include more of Jiggs the chimp, whose scene-stealing antics were, he felt, "far more interesting than a great deal of the stuff we had in."

What especially irked ERB was a "very noticeable weakness" in the feature's climax. He felt the sequence played up George at Tarzan's expense. "[T]he big climax at the end of the picture features the comedian. He is the real hero and the rescuer of the party. I should have caught this in the script months ago, but it did not strike me forcibly until I saw it on the screen last night."

Burroughs wasn't the only one dismayed by the finished product. Dearholt was stunned by audience negativity at an April preview screening of the feature. "The reaction was most unfavorable," he wrote Burroughs in a memo. "It was a body blow." The picture's detractors criticized its highly variable sound and image quality and claimed Tarzan didn't do enough.

There's no denying that *New Adventures of Tarzan* (as both feature and serial were ultimately titled) is inferior in many ways to Metro's Tarzan pictures. But Dearholt's relatively inexpensive effort shouldn't be judged by the same standards applied to a lavish production like *Tarzan and His Mate*, which underwent extensive reshooting and cost well over a million dollars—a vast fortune in those Depression days. Dearholt's serial, for all its faults, has a quality that none of M-G-M's

Tarzans ever achieved: authenticity. The beautiful arch at Chichicastenango, the ruins of Tical, the lush forests lining the Rio Dulce river—these are natural wonders, not back-lot confections. The hundreds of savages gathered in the temple for Tarzan's sacrifice aren't extras from downtown Los Angeles, they're honest-to-goodness Guatemalan natives. The numerous shots of Central American flora and fauna aren't snippets from a stock-footage library, they're the real deal, taken contemporaneously with the serial's other scenes.

The authenticity of Brix's athletic feats is another asset. With the notable exception of a lion-wrestling sequence in the early minutes of Chapter One, the former Olympian performs his own stunts. Lithe and sinewy but not muscle-bound, he's plenty convincing in scenes calling for near-superhuman displays of speed, strength, and coordination. Granted, his acting is stiff, and he's never quite as imposing as you would want the ideal screen Tarzan to be. Nonetheless, he brings dignity and authoritativeness to the role, and it's clear he's playing his part seriously, without the slightest hint of condescension.

Unfortunately, the serial's authenticity and Brix's gravitas weren't enough to make *New Adventures of Tarzan* the smash Burroughs and Dearholt had hoped for. But it wasn't entirely the picture's fault. M-G-M, already preparing a third Tarzan film and thus uneasy about competition from the character's creator, warned owners of the big theater chains that by playing BTE's Tarzan film they would forfeit their rights to Metro's future entries in the series. (Overseas, where ERB was enormously popular and Metro didn't wield as much influence, *New Adventures* was hugely successful, warts and all.) Most trade-paper reviews savaged both feature and serial versions—perhaps honestly, but perhaps also because they relied heavily on M-G-M advertising and were eager to curry favor.

In any case, Brix's hopes of achieving stardom were dashed. He spent years toiling in low-budget features and serials before changing his name to Bruce Bennett and ultimately becoming a Warner Brothers contract player. Burroughs-Tarzan Enterprises limped along for another two years, managing to distribute several low-budget features (including a redubbed version of Dearholt's unreleased 1930 Western, *The Phantom of Santa Fe*) but never generating enough income to satisfy its financial obligations.

In 1937, distributor Jesse J. Goldburg, who represented BTE product in foreign territories, persuaded Edgar to let him cut and release a second feature version of the serial. This film, *Tarzan and the Green Goddess*, did well enough in international markets to enable Burroughs to finally pay off the Citizens Nation Bank loan and get out from under. Having earned Edgar's gratitude, Goldburg was assigned sole rights to both feature versions when BTE finally went belly-up in 1938. Under the auspices of his newly formed company, United Screen Associates, he kept the films in release for years.

Burroughs and Dearholt, once the closest of friends, drifted apart after the dissolution of the corporation for which they once had the highest hopes. The erstwhile Pinto Pete faded into obscurity with his wife, Ula, and passed away in 1942.

For many years Brix was bitter about the serial's failure and its detrimental effect on his fledgling movie career. But until the day he died, nearly 67 years after completing that grueling shoot in the wilds of Guatemala, he was still receiving fan mail from Tarzan aficionados.

Tim Tyler's Luck
(1937, Universal Pictures)
by Daniel J. Neyer

The serials of Universal Pictures couldn't match the competing chapter plays of Republic Pictures when it came to special effects or choreographed action scenes, but Universal frequently surpassed Republic in other departments. The older studio relied less on fights and explosions than on interesting characters and strong casts. In many of Universal's later serials, the actors and their characterizations were the only interesting feature, but during the firm's 1930s heyday, performers were usually backed by fast-moving and involving scripts. The earlier Universals also benefited from budgets that exceeded those of Republic. Whether filming a serial that took place in the depths of the jungle or in outer space, Universal could produce sets that conveyed more atmosphere than the exotic locales in other studios' releases.

In 1937, all these Universal strengths—casting, scripting, and atmospheric locales—came together in one of the studio's best sound serials, *Tim Tyler's Luck*. This chapter play was based on a popular comic strip created in 1928 by Lyman Young, the older brother of Chic Young of *Blondie* fame. The strip's early years, which chronicled the attempts of a plucky young orphan to succeed in the world, were largely cast in a Horatio Alger mold, but *Tim Tyler's Luck* later moved into more exotic territory, taking Tim to Africa and putting him through many adventures there. The serial borrowed several elements from the strip—chief among them the "Ivory Patrol," a remnant of British colonialism—but also changed the source material as the screenwriters saw fit, giving Tim a father that didn't exist in the strip and severely reducing the role of his pal Spud.

Tim Tyler's Luck begins as a steamer is filling its hold at an African river port. The vessel's most important cargo is a load of armaments for the Ivory Patrol, a Mounties-like organization that maintains law and order in the wild jungle region. We're then introduced to youthful stowaway Tim Tyler (played by Frankie Thomas), traveling up river in search of his father, Professor Tyler (Al Shean). It seems the Professor, an expert on gorillas, has been absent too long on an expedition. Gruff Captain Trowbridge (Al Bridge) orders Tim off the boat, explaining that the jungle is too dangerous for a boy. Another passenger, Lora Lacey (Frances Robinson), sympathizes with the lad's plight, since she also is seeking someone in the interior. Though she's ostensibly going up river to hunt big game, Lora—whose real last name is Graham—actually seeks "Spider" Webb (Norman Willis), the poacher, outlaw, and diamond thief who framed her brother Donald for a diamond robbery in Kimberly. Lora hopes to find Spider and force him to clear her sibling, who's currently serving a prison term. Although Lora's attempts at intercession don't stop the Captain from kicking Tim off the steamer, the indefatigable boy stows away a second time just before the riverboat casts off.

Unbeknownst to Captain Trowbridge, several of the crew members belong to Spider Webb's gang, and passenger Garry Drake (Anthony Warde) is actually Spider's lieutenant. Webb's men, determined to grab the arms being shipped to their archenemies, the Ivory Patrol, take over the ship and wipe out Trowbridge and his men. Lora is locked in her cabin, and, after finishing off the crew, Drake prepares to eliminate her as well. Tim, overlooked by the outlaws, helps Lora escape the ship, and soon afterwards they encounter a division of the Ivory Patrol under Sergeant Gates (Jack Mulhall). The Patrol escorts them to headquarters, where Lora begins trying to recruit guides for her "big-game hunting" safari. Tim, having learned that Spider's gang is using his father's tank-like "Jungle Cruiser" exploration vehicle, is more concerned than ever about his dad's safety.

As it turns out, the elder Tyler is not in the hands of Spider's gang, but the gang *does* go after him when Spider learns that the Professor knows the location of the fabled Elephants' Graveyard, where giant pachyderms have been going to die for thousands of years and where a vast treasure of ivory can be found. Spider then begins a relentless pursuit of the Tylers, father and son. If that wasn't bad enough, Tim is forced to cope with a hostile native tribe, a colony of wild gorillas, and assorted lions, leopards and alligators. His titular luck works overtime before the serial's conclusion.

Tim Tyler's Luck, despite a relative absence of the fistfights supposedly so essential to a serial's success, is an exciting adventure from start to finish, thanks to good writing and acting and an incredible array of colorful characters and locales. Veteran director Ford Beebe holds the serial together nicely, aided by Wyndham Gittens (who also worked on the screenplay). The action is backed by a memorable musical score, some of it taken from Universal's *Bride of Frankenstein*. The main-title music, lifted from Universal's 1935 version of E. Phillips Oppenheim's *The Great Impersonation*, oddly seems quite appropriate to this episodic thriller, as do the other borrowed musical cues.

The serial's screenwriters—Gittens, Norman S. Hall, and Ray Trampe—keep the plot developing constantly and move the characters from one interesting location to another. They also give *Tim Tyler's Luck* a real feeling of danger and suspense by dispatching major characters from time to time; while many early Universal serials avoided killing either heroes or villains, in this one both good guys and bad meet violent ends from time to time, which gives the whole adventure a more suspenseful tone—nobody seems altogether safe.

The serial's sphere of action covers a lot of ground, including the riverside, the Ivory Patrol's fort, the caves in Gorilla Canyon, Spider Webb's quicksand-surrounded swamp hideout, and the steam-filled volcanic crater at the Elephants' Burial Ground, with a lot of jungle foliage and rolling rocky hills in between. The jungle area containing all these interesting spots assumes a real sense of geographical place, and the viewer can almost picture it on a map.

The serial's cast does full justice to its script. While most serial juveniles are strictly of the tagalong variety, teenaged Frankie Thomas is called upon to carry *Tim Tyler's Luck* squarely on his slender shoulders. Few other young actors of the period could have done it as well as he does. Thomas' sincere, good-natured acting wins audience sympathy for Tim from the start, so we readily forgive the character's occasional bursts of youthful impetuosity and instead admire his courage and quick thinking. In an informal 1990 interview with *BnT's* editor Ed Hulse, Thomas—the scion of an acting family—recalled the grueling circumstances under which he turned in his likable performance:

"It was exhausting. You know, when you're the lead, you're in most of the footage. A lot of scenes would be grouped together for convenience, so I might spend three days in a row with the Ivory Patrol and then three days in a row with the heavies, who kept capturing me. I remember getting to the studio in the morning when it was dark and going home at night when it was dark. Sunday was the only day I saw the sun while I wasn't working."

Thomas' co-stars deliver equally good performances. The severely underrated actress Frances Robinson brings intelligence, determination, and dignified beauty to her character Lora Graham. Her assumed British Colonial accent is quite convincing, and she drops it for an equally convincing "tough girl" voice when posing a crook in an attempt to win Spider's confidence. Of Robinson, Thomas recalled, "Francie—we all called her Francie—was just a lovely gal. Really lovely, inside and out. Talented, too; I was surprised she didn't go further than she did in the business. . . . Somehow Francie missed out on those couple of juicy parts that might really have elevated her to stardom. It wasn't for lack of talent or personality, I can tell you that."

In Spider Webb, Norman Willis creates one of the meanest, most unpleasant bad guys ever seen on the serial screen. Spider is a truly ruthless villain (he lets one of his own men die in quicksand rather than risk losing some stolen weapons), and Willis makes him even more unpleasant by barking out orders with a dictatorial snarl, sneering sarcastically at both allies and opponents. Willis' metallic voice and hard, cunning face are perfectly suited to the part, and he creates a memorable serial villain without the aid of mask, bizarre costume, or flamboyant death-dealing devices.

Anthony Warde, as Spider's chief henchman, is very nasty himself, though he seems to slightly resent and fear his boss; it adds to Spider's menace to have hard-as-nails Warde behave so circumspectly towards him. Earl Douglas is excellent as Spider's French henchman Lazarre, who begins as a bad guy but is won over to the good guys' side when Tim saves his life. Douglas makes this transformation convincing, and the moment when Lazarre pledges to help Tim escape from Spider's swamp hideout is truly touching. Douglas then functions as a colorful and capable sidekick for the balance of the serial, playing well off Thomas and Robinson. Frankie Thomas also cherished fond memories of Willis, Warde, and Douglas:

"Norman Willis was great. A fun guy to be around . . . he was terrific. That voice of his could really give you the chills down your spine. Tony Warde was another good guy. But I really got along best with Ernie Yaconelli. He played Lazarre, the sympathetic heavy. He's the one who takes a shine to me in the picture. 'Earl Douglas' was just a stage name. He played a couple leads in silent movies. His brother Frank did a lot of sidekicks in Westerns, you know, Mexican guys named Pablo or Pancho. Ernie was a terrific athlete. He was short but wiry, muscles like steel cables. Another good guy to be around."

Al Shean, one-half of the famous vaudeville team of Gallagher and Shean as well as uncle and mentor to the Marx Brothers, is lovable as Tim's slightly absent-minded scientist father. Jack Mulhall is his usual jovial and exuberant self as Sergeant Gates, participating in several running shootouts between the mounted Ivory Patrol and the passengers of the sleek, tank-like Jungle Cruiser. Mulhall, himself a former serial star, even gets his own chapter-ending cliffhanger. The Ivory Patrol comes off as an enthusiastically heroic outfit, charging determinedly after Spider's gang even when the villains are ensconced in the Jungle Cruiser, and Mulhall's cheerfully courageous manner makes him an ideal field commander for the group.

Billy Benedict has surprisingly little to do as Ivory Patrol Corporal Spud, which is odd given the prominence his character had in the *Tim Tyler* comic strip. Lane Chandler, Ethan Laidlaw, Lane Chandler, and Pat J. O'Brien play additional Patrolmen, and serial fans will easily spot Tom Steele (who also handles some of the stunt work) as a trooper. Frequent heavy Stanley Blystone is cast against type as the Patrol's captain. Alan Gregg, Charles Sullivan, Ernie Adams, Charles Murphy, Eddie Parker, Chuck Morrison, and big Everett Brown are members of Spider Webb's gang. Frank Mayo and Kenneth Harlan appear as ivory traders, and Al Bridge is the gruff ship's captain of the first chapter. The stern and dignified William Desmond also pops up in the initial episode, playing a dock official.

In addition to the talented human cast, some good animal performers are on hand. For example, there's Fang, Tim's black-panther friend, who saves him several times after our hero bandages the cat's injured paw. Then there's Ju-Ju, a mischievous but helpful chimpanzee, and Bolo, an elephant that provides Tim with valuable assistance in the later chapters. No other jungle serial of the sound era boasts such a varied ensemble of animal sidekicks.

Tim Tyler's Luck is also replete with unfriendly animals, whose periodic attacks are unusually effective, thanks to the combination of the expected wildlife stock footage with new shots of trained beasts seen interacting with human cast members. A lion attack on Tim and Lora in Chapter Three is particularly memorable, since the lion is clearly in the same shot with the actors as they tear over a hillside with the big cat hot on their heels. The other bits of animal footage are smoothly interspersed, with each animal's appearance (even that of an apparently displaced South American anteater in Chapter Ten) having a bearing on the plot and not being simply thrown in to pad the running time, as in so many jungle-set "B" films.

Unlike the other fauna in the serial, the gorillas of Gorilla Canyon (actually a section of the Universal back lot constructed for 1933's *Nagana* and known, not surprisingly, as Nagana Rocks) aren't genuine animals, but the standard men-in-hairy-suits; they're fun to watch nevertheless. There's a friendly gorilla, a very mean and scary-looking gorilla, and a whole gang of unfriendly gorillas that attack members of a safari by hurling boulders on them in one of the serial's most memorable and offbeat cliffhanger sequences.

Several of *Tim Tyler*'s chapter endings are almost as memorable, including the above-mentioned lion attack in Chapter Three; the climax of Chapter Four, which has Tim and Lazarre (Earl Douglas) racing through the quicksands as Spider's men hurl hand grenades at them; the Chapter Seven finale, with Tim about to be choked to death by the evil gorilla; and the Chapter Eight cliffhanger, in which Tim falls from the top of a riverboat into crocodile-infested waters.

Thomas recalled the latter sequence in a 1981 letter to *BnT*'s Ed Hulse: "The riverboat—I believe it was called 'the Jungle Queen' or something like that—had been built for Universal's production of *Show Boat*. It rested in about two feet of water. [Producer] Henry MacRae explained to me that he had ordered a pit dug, and it was ten feet deep. Now, the top deck of the riverboat was about three stories high, but he assured me that I would be able to spot the hole because it would appear darker than the water surrounding it. You have to remember, the boat was anchored in what was not much deeper than a wading pool. Well, let me tell you, as I went over the rail that was the smallest-looking patch of dark water I ever saw. But I had it square and Ford [Beebe] decided one take was all we needed—thank God!"

Ultimately, Thomas' memories of *Tim Tyler's Luck* were fond ones, despite occasional nerve-wracking moments and a hectic shooting schedule: "If we were driving somewhere to a location, like Vasquez Rocks, where we shot a lot of stuff with the 'Jungle Cruiser,' I'd have to get up at five in the morning. Those were long days. I remember Ford Beebe most. He was a chain smoker. Very good director, though; he knew exactly what he wanted and how to get it. And he moved fast. There wasn't a lot of down time between scenes on that show. It was hard work but a great experience for me."

Tim Tyler's Luck remains a great experience for serial fans as well, thanks to Frankie Thomas' performance, those of his co-stars, and the chapter play's generous amounts of adventure, drama, and exotic atmosphere. Any cliffhanger fan who hasn't seen it should book a riverboat passage without delay and set out for the Elephants' Burial Ground—but they'd better be forewarned and keep an eye out for Spider Webb and company.

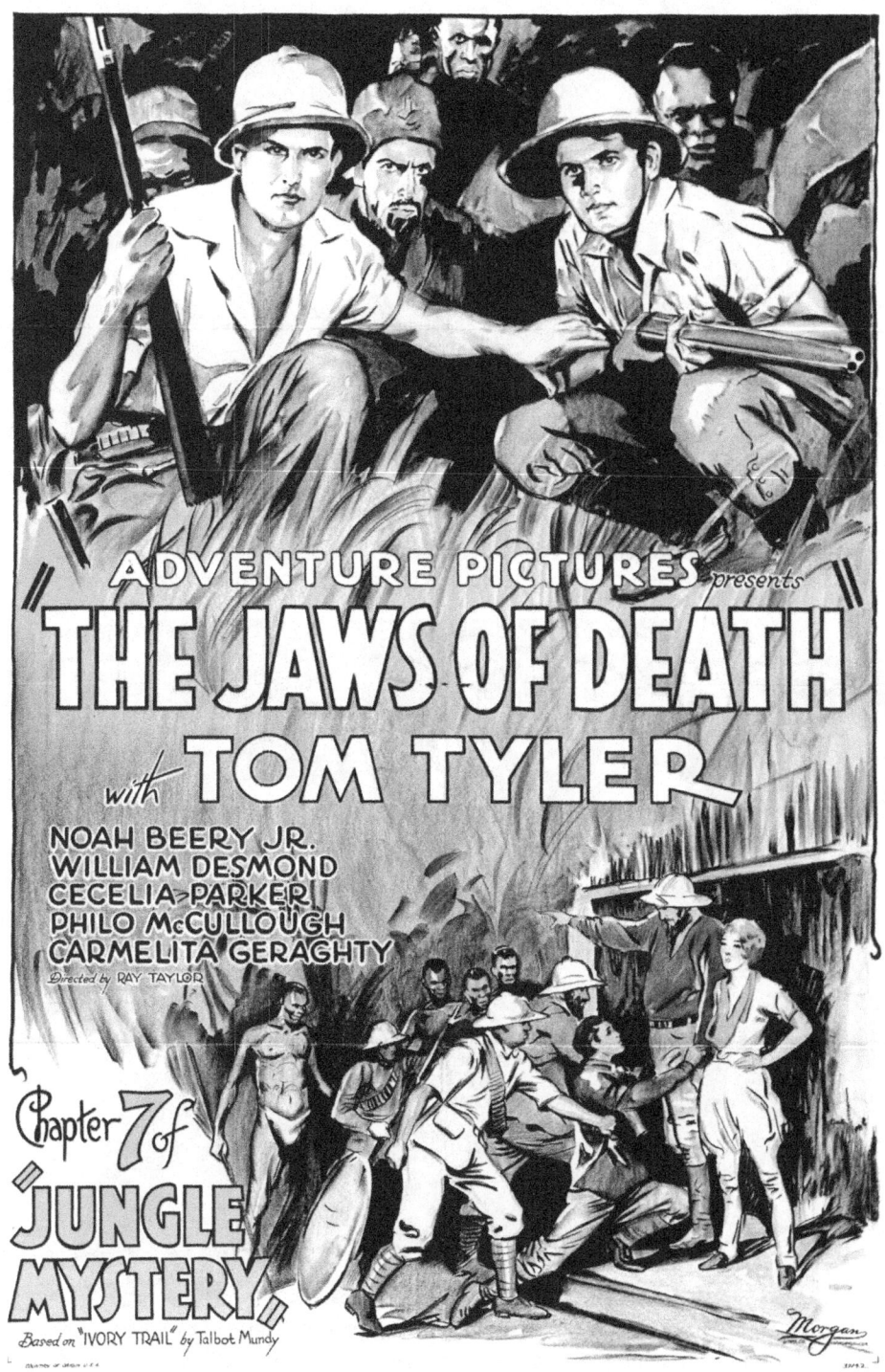

Jungle Mystery's Frank Lackteen, Bill Desmond, Tom Tyler, Noah Beery.

Tyler and Beery getting the worst of it from Carmelita Geraghty's henchmen.

GALLERY

An eerily lit portrait of Buck Jones as he appeared in *The Red Rider* (1934).

L to R: Edmund Cobb, Charles K. French, Marion Shilling, and Buck Jones.

That's Buck behind the serape, trying to intimidate villainous Walter Miller.

GALLERY

New Adventures of Tarzan: George Walsh and Herman Brix help Merrill McCormick.

While shooting this scene Brix was actually pummeled by Guatemalan extras.

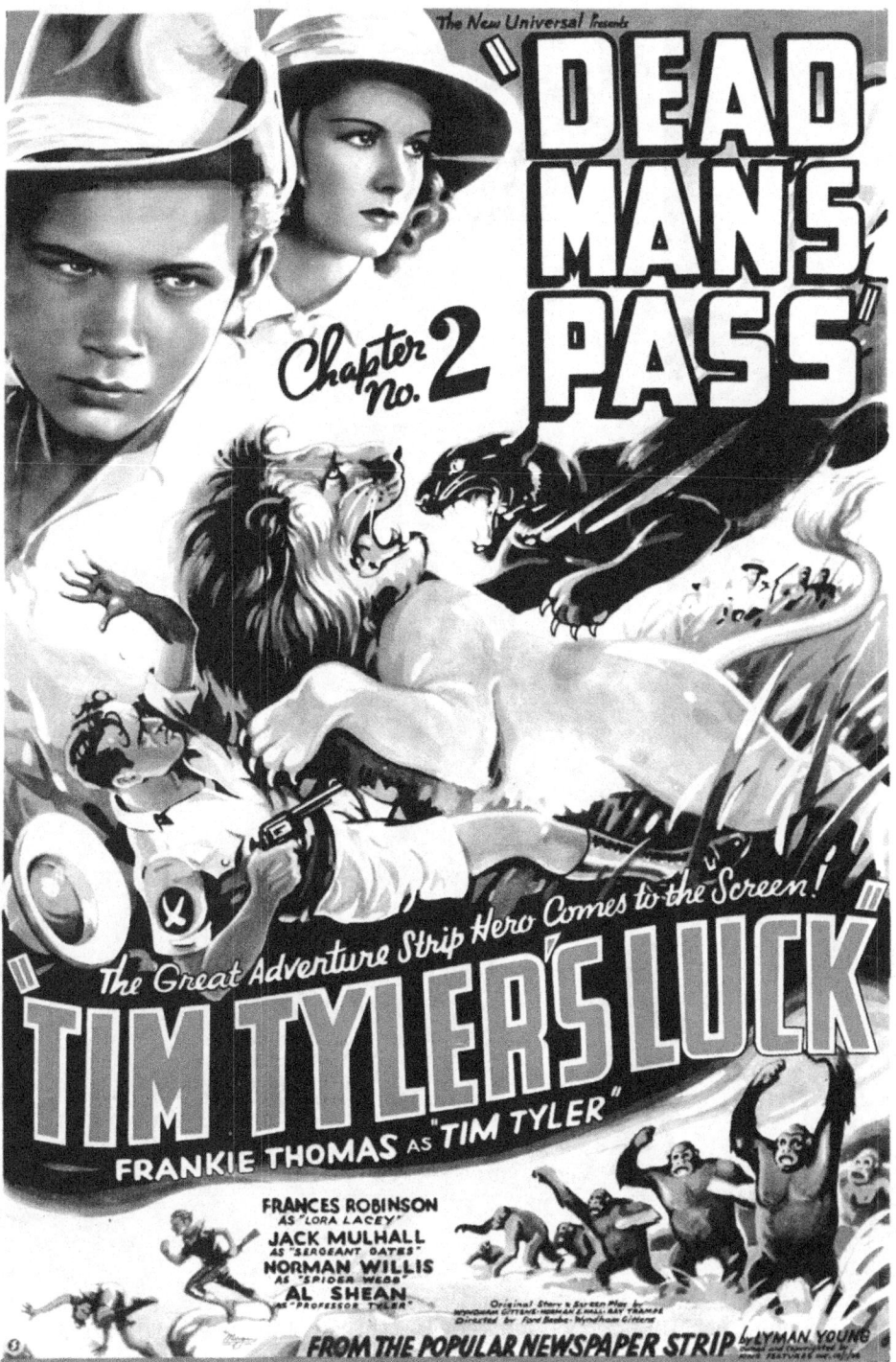

Lee Powell and Chief Thundercloud in early publicity shot for *The Lone Ranger*.

GALLERY 201

L to R: Lone Ranger "suspects" Chandler, Powell, Brix, Letz, and Taliaferro.

The Lone Ranger battles one of Jeffries' spies in the cave hideout.

Don Terry battles a pretty lively ghost in *Secret of Treasure Island* (1938).

Don Terry and Gwen Gaze in a publicity shot for *Secret of Treasure Island*.

The Shadow (Victor Jory) comes to the aid of Margot Lane (Veda Ann Borg).

Sound serials were especially popular in small-town theaters like this one.

Fu Manchu (Henry Brandon) convenes a meeting of his organization, the Si-Fan.

Nayland Smith (William Royle, R) has Fu Manchu in his power—but not for long.

Daredevils of the West (1943): Renegade redskins attack Kay Aldridge.

Tom London makes things hot for Allan Lane in *Daredevils of the West*.

This long shot from *Daredevils of the West* shows off the Lone Pine location.

Tom Brown (with rope) essayed the title role in *Adventures of Smilin' Jack*.

Rose Hobart (center) played the Nazi spy Fraulein von Teufel in *Smilin' Jack*.

Fraulein von Teufel instructs a henchman to try the voice-distortion device.

A member of the Black Samurai gets the drop on Smilin' Jack.

GALLERY

Gilbert Roland (center) is taken prisoner in this scene from *The Desert Hawk*.

Dick Foran (second from left) headed a large cast in *Riders of Death Valley*.

A crook is surprised by the Green Hornet (Gordon Jones) and Kato (Keye Luke).

Kioga (Herman Brix) menaced by Yellow Weasel in *Hawk of the Wilderness* (1938).

The Lone Ranger
(1938, Republic Pictures)

by Ed Hulse

Republic Pictures Corporation began as a conglomeration of independent producers who had one thing in common: They depended on Consolidated Film Industries, a corporation founded by former tobacco-industry executive Herbert J. Yates to supply film processing services and manufacture release prints for Poverty Row companies. One of Consolidated's biggest, and most stable, clients was Nat Levine, whose Mascot Pictures turned out serials and grade "B" feature films from the former Mack Sennett studio in Southern California's San Fernando Valley.

In June 1935 Levine officially joined the newly formed Republic, which sublet Mascot's plant. He was given the responsibility of overseeing some of the company's "B" Westerns and all four of the serials it promised for release during the 1935-36 season. The legendarily shrewd Levine had never licensed existing characters for his serials; Mascot chapter plays were based either on original stories or properties in the public domain. The initial Republic serial was to have been an adaptation of Daniel Defoe's *Robinson Crusoe*, but the first to actually reach theater screens was *Darkest Africa* (1936), a jungle adventure starring wild-animal trainer Clyde Beatty. Plans to film the Defoe novel were scrapped, but having already announced the title Levine ordered his writers to develop a story titled *Robinson Crusoe of Clipper Island*, a modern-day take that ignored the 1719 yarn.

Republic's early serials achieved modest success, but Yates and his underlings realized that they were not competitive with the chapter plays made by Universal, which had struck box-office gold by licensing popular characters from comic strips and radio programs. The ever-parsimonious Levine couldn't see shelling out thousands of dollars for movie rights to characters from the funny papers, but Yates and his second-in-command, Moe Siegel, felt otherwise. In late 1936 Republic cut a deal for rights to Chester Gould's wildly popular comic strip, *Dick Tracy*. Originally announced as a starring vehicle for former real-life G-man Melvin Purvis, the 15-chapter serial starred little-known Ralph Byrd, who became identified with the character for the remainder of his career.

The initial episode of *Dick Tracy* was just being shipped to exhibitors when, on February 23, 1937, Republic secretary-treasurer Emanuel Goldstein received word that one of the country's hottest radio characters, the Lone Ranger, was available for motion pictures. Goldstein had previously met George W. Trendle, owner of Detroit's WXYZ radio station, from which the Lone Ranger program emanated. Trendle, a former exhibitor who had sold his chain of theaters to get into radio, was a canny businessman and very protective of his properties, which also included the Green Hornet program. Whether he felt obligated to offer Goldstein first dibs on the Ranger or simply saw Republic as the likeliest buyer, given the studio's reputation for quality serials and "B" Westerns, is not known. But negotiations ensued in earnest, and Trendle quickly demonstrated that he was no pushover.

Film historian Jack Mathis, whose *Valley of the Cliffhangers* remains the ultimate reference book on Republic serials, had unfettered access to the company's records and carefully sifted through the mountain of correspondence relating to the Lone Ranger. He uncovered the very specific requirements the WXYZ owner had with regard to the character's appearance:

> Heretofore concerned only with a voice over the airwaves, Trendle envisioned his creation in real-life form as

following the mold of such contemporary Western stars as Tom Mix, William S. Hart, and Richard Dix. Specified to be a clean-shaven, rugged outdoors type of a height not less than 5-foot-11 and a weight of approximately 170 pounds, the white-Stetsoned, boot-shod, but chaps-less Lone Ranger was not to swear or drink and could only smoke if the plot demanded. . . . Trendle delineated Tonto in the same general terms save that he was to be several inches shorter than the Lone Ranger, then meticulously described Silver as approximating the characteristics of an Arabian stallion not less than 15 1/2 hands high and White Fella—Tonto's steed in the pre-Scout days—as a pinto or paint breed of Indian pony.

Although Trendle was aware that Republic was interested in obtaining the Lone Ranger for a serial, he suggested—but did not insist—that Yates' studio utilize the character in a feature-length Western prior to making a chapter play. This, he felt, would introduce moviegoers to the character and stimulate interest in the serial to follow. Manny Goldstein broached the idea to Armand Schafer, a Mascot serial alumnus who by 1937 had assumed responsibility for the "B" Westerns starring Gene Autry, Republic's top star. Schafer rejected a Lone Ranger feature as a vehicle for Autry and opined that the property was much better suited to chapter plays.

George Trendle and Republic Pictures Corporation finally came to an agreement on June 22, 1937. The contract signed that day called for a licensing fee of $18,750, payable to The Lone Ranger, Inc., and ten percent of Republic's rental revenue above $390,000. By this time Nat Levine had been replaced as chapter-play production chief (and was, in fact, about to leave the studio altogether). Sol C. Siegel, Moe's brother, was assigned to oversee production of a 15-episode serial titled *The Lone Ranger*. Day-to-day supervision was entrusted to Robert Beche, who had performed the same task on Republic's previous two serials, *S.O.S. Coast Guard* and *Zorro Rides Again*.

In July, upon receiving from WXYZ some 66 carefully chosen scripts from the Lone Ranger radio program, the members of Republic's serial-writing department—headed by Barry Shipman, son of silent-screen star Nell Shipman—poured over the material to see what could be gleaned from it for motion pictures. For several weeks the staff debated various concepts, but always the writers returned to what Shipman later described to me as the central problem: "There was no indication as to where this guy had come from. You were just supposed to believe that the Lone Ranger had always been there, riding around with a mask on."

It was a fair observation. Up to this point the radio program had never presented an origin story for the Lone Ranger. Shipman believed that, given the character's enigmatic nature, a back-story of some sort was essential to audience acceptance. Then again, by mid-1937 some 20 million people had already heard episodes of the radio show, and there's no evidence they were clamoring for an explanation.

By early September the screenwriters had come up with a variation on the mystery-man motif found in serials going back to Pearl White and *The Exploits of Elaine*. The Lone Ranger would be identified as being one of five Texans—all physically similar—united for a common purpose. This gambit would allow for a handful of subplots by pointing the finger of suspicion at each man over the course of the story. But that still didn't explain from whence the Ranger had come.

Oliver Drake, a prolific scripter of Westerns going back to the silent era, was assigned to lend a hand to Shipman and his staff, which included Franklyn Adreon and Ronald Davidson. In mid October he wrote a "treatment"—an extended synopsis that the screenwriter fleshed out into a detailed shooting script—depicting the cold-blooded killing of a squad of Texas Rangers by outlaw troopers commanded by a dictatorial commissioner. Drake wrote it as the climax of Chapter One's third sequence:

> We DISSOLVE to the Rangers making camp and preparing to spend the night.

THE LONE RANGER   217

> They are suddenly attacked by the troups [sic] who, firing from ambush, completely wipe out the entire group. Satisfied that the last of the Rangers is dead, Snead starts back toward Pecos with his troup [sic].
>
> The ambush and massacre has been witnessed by Tonto, an old Indian.
>
> SEQUENCE #4:
>
> That night we find Tonto at the scene of the massacre. He searches among the bodies for a sign of life and at least bends over one of the Rangers and discovers that the man is still breathing . . .

In Drake's treatment, Tonto brings the severely wounded Ranger to a cave and nurses him back to health, whereupon this survivor—the *lone* Ranger—swears to bring the crooked official to justice.

Nearly four years later, when the Lone Ranger radio program finally got around to presenting an origin, series scribe Fran Striker drew heavily on Oliver Drake's idea, identifying the ambushers as Butch Cavendish and his gang but otherwise hewing closely to the sequence that ultimately appeared in Chapter One of Republic's serial.

The story begins in 1865, shortly after the end of the Civil War, with a group of Confederate renegades (modeled on Quantrill's Raiders) stranded in Texas. They intercept a stagecoach carrying Colonel Marcus Jeffries, newly appointed Commissioner of Finance, whom President Lincoln has sent to enforce tax collections for the Federal government. The renegade leader, Smith, has Jeffries murdered but steals his credentials and assumes his identity. Then, with his fellow outlaws garbed as "troopers," the imposter sets himself up as dictator of Texas, financing his empire with tax money coerced from the local ranchers and shopkeepers, who naturally believe the Yankee government responsible for their oppression.

The Lone Ranger appears from nowhere and foils the plans of the phony Jeffries whenever possible, but even this mysterious masked man and his faithful Indian companion can't be everywhere. A small group of Texans begins forming organized opposition to Jeffries. They include Allan King, Bert Rogers, Jim Clark, Dick Forrest, and Bob Stuart. A Jeffries spy, Snead (the same villain responsible for ambushing the Texas Rangers detailed to challenge his boss), believes that one of them is the Lone Ranger and has all five imprisoned.

Jeffries visits the jailed quintet and promises that if the Ranger reveals himself, the other four conspirators will be permitted to go free. The Texans turn him down flat, but after the furious Colonel leaves, in their darkened cell, a shadowy figure admits that *he* is the Lone Ranger. "I can't let you die on my account," he says. "Texas needs loyal fighters."

"But she needs the Lone Ranger most of all," says one of his fellow prisoners.

"Jeffries won't keep his word anyway," says another. "We're in this thing together."

"If we die," a third chimes in, "it'll be together . . . and for Texas."

Fortunately, it doesn't come to that. Just as Jeffries gets all five men in front of a firing squad, Tonto commandeers a stagecoach and boldly spurs it past the troopers, giving the Texans a chance to hop aboard and speed off. The four brave men agree to work with the Lone Ranger and Tonto, with their first task to foil an attack by Jeffries' troopers on settlers holed up in an old adobe fort.

Among the interesting ideas written out for Chapter One but ultimately discarded was a series of scenes that would have given each of the five Texans a special skill. Dick Forrest, for example, was to be revealed as an expert with the lariat. Bert Rogers was an amazing horseman. Jim Clark was deadly with a Bowie knife. Bob Stuart was an unparalleled marksman. And Allan King was a superbly trained athlete capable of amazing leaps and other physical feats. According to the jettisoned treatment, at various points the Lone Ranger would exhibit one of these skills, thereby planting seeds of suspicion among audience members playing the which-one-is-he guessing game.

As the episode shooting scripts took form they were sent

to WXYZ for Trendle's approval. He was initially unhappy with their deviation from the canon, and on November 18 Barry Shipman flew to Detroit with instructions to mollify the executive. "It called for a little diplomacy more than anything else," Shipman told me in 1992. "I think he had gotten the idea that Republic's attitude was, 'We paid you for the property so we don't care what you think.' My job was to smooth things over by explaining why we did such-and-such, and why it would make for a better picture."

Trendle softened his opposition to Republic's interpretation of the character. Which was fortunate, because directors William Witney and John English (who had worked together for the first time on *Zorro Rides Again*) were casting the five Texans the very day Shipman went to Detroit. Western and serial veterans Lane Chandler and Hal Taliaferro were signed as Dick Forrest and Bob Stuart, respectively. Herman Brix, a former screen Tarzan, was hired for Bert Rogers. Republic contract player George Letz, at 21 the youngest of the quintet, was assigned to play Jim Clark. Screen newcomer Lee Powell, with just a couple bit parts to his credit, rounded out the group as Allan King.

The key supporting role, that of Tonto, was awarded to Victor Daniels, whose screen name was Chief Thundercloud. The Oklahoma-born Daniels actually was half Native American, but he had a mixture of Irish, German, and Scottish blood as well, and his "Chief" title was strictly an honorary one. Thundercloud's casting was important, though, because it gave Tonto a look that the character retained for decades in comic strips, comic books, TV shows, and licensed products. The early radio scripts described him as a small, aged Indian, but Republic's screenwriters clearly needed to portray him as more youthful and virile, so that he would be convincing alongside the Ranger in numerous action sequences they shared.

The faux Jeffries was portrayed by Stanley Andrews, and perennial heavy Allen Sears was contracted to play Kester, captain of the Colonel's private army. Also in support were

George Cleveland (as government official George Blanchard, sent to investigate complaints against Jeffries), Lynn Roberts (then just 16 years old, as Blanchard's daughter Joan), and William Farnum (playing a kindly cleric, Father McKim).

Possibly the most important hire, however, was ace stuntman Yakima Canutt, who would double the masked hero. He had performed the same function on *Zorro Rides Again* and was in large part responsible for that serial's success. For his services on *The Lone Ranger* Yak was paid $500 per week—more than any of the five Ranger "suspects."

Sol Siegel okayed a budget of $160,000, slightly more than the average for a 15-chapter Western serial. With such a well-known property to exploit, the studio wanted a chapter play with good production values. Rather than rely entirely on typical, familiar locations in the San Fernando Valley, Bob Beche sent Witney and English on an excursion to scout picturesque locales where exterior scenes could be shot. In his 1996 memoir, *In a Door, Into a Fight, Out a Door, Into a Chase* (Jefferson, North Carolina: McFarland & Company, Inc.), Witney recalled that trip:

> Jack English and I spent two weeks looking for locations and finally settled on Lone Pine, California, with Mount Whitney in the background. Covered with snow and the brown, odd-shaped rocks of the Alabama Hills jutting out like lone sentinels, it was beautiful. I had worked there when I was keeping script and knew it was a very workable location. The ride from Lone Pine to the location was only about 10 minutes. For a commercial picture, it was perfect—no lost time coming to work or getting a tired crew back to the hotel without a long ride. It would give Jack and me more shooting time and maybe a better picture.

Cast and crew were dispatched to Lone Pine right after the Thanksgiving holiday, with shooting scheduled to begin that Sunday, November 28. They stayed at the Dow Villa Hotel (still in business, by the way), just a few minutes' drive from the Alabama Hills. The main horses—including the Arabian stallion playing Silver and the paint ridden by Tonto—were stabled at the nearby Spainhower ranch, which was hired to supply extra mounts needed for townspeople, Indians, and Jeffries' troopers. Russ Spainhower had been working with Hollywood producers for many years and was the go-to guy for livestock used in films shot at Lone Pine.

Typically, Witney and English shot on alternate days, one directing the unit while the other planned the next day's work. But *The Lone Ranger* got off to a rocky start, according to Witney:

> Jack was going to be the director on the first day. It was 2:00 in the morning and the sound of someone retching in the bathroom woke me up. I sat up in bed and turned on the light. I looked over in the other twin bed and found it empty. I knocked on the bathroom door and asked Jack if I could help him. The door opened and Jack shook his head. He was as white as a sheet. I helped him back to bed and threw the covers over him. I went back to bed, but there was no sleep for the rest of the night.
>
> We had a 6:00 call for breakfast. Jack tried to get out of bed. "Stay put, Jack. I'll take over today. I'll send the first-aid man in to see you as soon as I can find him." I found him at breakfast and told Bob Beche I was taking over for the day, had breakfast and took off for the location.
>
> [Photographer] Billy Nobles rode out to location in the same car that I was in. He was surprised to see me. When I told him about Jack he laughed. . . . Over the next week almost everyone of the crew came down sick. It hit the town locals just as hard. We called it the "Lone Pine Pip." There was a headline in the trade papers and a swarm of government health people invaded Lone Pine trying to find out the cause. To my knowledge, it's still a mystery.
>
> Billy Nobles and I were among the lucky ones who stood by and watched everyone head for the nearest

bathroom, bush or tree—whatever was closest. We attributed our survival to being smart enough to drink the right booze and plenty of it.

Another first-day casualty of the Pip was Allan Sears, who was scheduled to play Kester and was replaced by John Merton.

Garbed in light shirt (colored yellow in posters and lobby cards for the serial), dark trousers, white Stetson, and a leather half-mask with mesh netting covering the bottom half of his face, the Lone Ranger came to breathtaking life in those Alabama Hills, with Nobles filming Yakima Canutt's daredevil riding from Republic's camera truck, which glided along the aptly named Movie Road while Silver galloped across the sage-covered sands. Witney later recalled the taking of these memorable scenes:

> As a film editor I realized the importance of the scenes shot from the camera car. They were called running inserts and could be cut into any chase at any point in the chase. You could work on the same mile strip of insert road and shoot a 10-minute chase with the same background because it was always moving.
>
> Red O'Hare had a camera-car rental business and had taken an old Simplex truck, cut it down, built low platforms in the front and the back, medium in the middle, and a high one over the cab. These were big lumbering machines, but steady, with no vibration even over rough roads. They were underpowered, to make a running shot of someone riding a horse. The horseman sat his horse alongside the road. The old Simplex started a mile back to get up to 30 miles an hour. When it roared past the horseman, he took off and rode alongside of the camera car at the distance that the director wanted.
>
> It sounds simple, but it took an expert horseman to put the animal where it was supposed to be. After a couple of runs the horses knew from the sound of the roaring engine that they

were going to get to run. They'd spin, rear, back up, spin again. It made putting an actor on the horse who didn't ride well downright dangerous. That is one reason we had tested the leading men in The Lone Ranger. The insert road in the Alabama Hills rocks was long and smooth and the path that ran alongside had sagebrush on both sides so it didn't look like a road. With the snowcapped peaks of Mount Whitney in the background and the big white horse the Lone Ranger rode, it made a beautiful picture, running alongside at racehorse speeds with the long mane and tail flying in the wind.

I loved the low setup with the horse running directly in front of the camera, coming at you. The action of the legs churning and the dust billowing behind seemed to bring the whole outdoors into the theater. This was a Western picture at its best. I always tried to use the running insert on a transfer from a horse to a wagon. It let the camera get close to the action and the fast-moving ground going by led the audience feel the danger of a misstep. I found that dropping down the camera speed from the usual 24 frames a second to 22 frames when the horse was running at you or away from you gave a little more speed and didn't get jerky. If you dropped the speed any lower, it looked like an old silent movie.

Illnesses aside, the Lone Pine location work proceeded on schedule, if not without the mishaps common to the fast-paced production of serials. In his exclusive 2002 interview for *Blood 'n' Thunder*, Herman Brix recalled: "We did lots of shots riding back and forth, here and there, with those mountains in the background." Brix was making his first Western, and though a superb athlete he was a novice horseman. "I remember they assigned me a horse named Blackjack. Now, he had a tough mouth. You really had to jerk the reins back hard to get him to respond. One day I was doing an insert shot, a running insert, and Blackjack got the bit in his teeth and wouldn't stop. He jumped on top of a boulder—I swear, it looked as big as a house to me—and I fell off backward, and he fell down as well. And that was the last day I rode Blackjack."

Horse trouble of a more serious nature threatened to delay completion of the Lone Pine phase of production, as Witney related in his memoir:

> We usually carried an SPCA (Society for the Prevention of Cruelty to Animals) representative on our locations. It was always the same old man who had once been a cowboy. The studio paid him on a daily basis. I was surprised when a new man [Fred Wilson] introduced himself to me on the Lone Pine location. Our old friend was ill and he was replacing him for the picture. He was about the same age as our friend, and new to the picture business, but had been in charge of a dog pound.
>
> Our old friend had a way of disappearing when a "Running W" horse fall or any specialized horse action was about to take place. He'd go to the phone or bathroom. On this day we had a Running W on the schedule. Bob Beche, Yak, Kenny [Cooper, another veteran Western stuntman] and I had a conference. We weren't sure just how this man would react to seeing a running horse go down end over end. I'd never seen a horse injured in the probably 20 such stunts I'd seen performed, but there was always the possibility. Kenny was doubling for one of the leads and was going to do the stunt. He had done at least a hundred of them. He wasn't worried about himself. He was worried about the SPCA man.
>
> Yak went out of his way to heckle him. He told Kenny that the SPCA had told him if there was anything he didn't like or there was any cruelty to the horses, the man responsible could go to jail, something we all had known for the last few years, but Yak just happened to bring it up as a reminder. He also told Kenny that he was glad he wasn't the one doing the stunt because no one knew just how the new man would react to the horse fall.
>
> The Running W had not been banned by the SPCA, but it was frowned on. Bob Beche came up with an idea. He'd ask the SPCA man to get into the back seat of one of the cars with him and go over the action in the script to see if he had any

objections to anything he read that seemed cruel to the horses. He picked an episode that had a stagecoach chase with a six-horse team. The car was parked so that Bob and the SPCA man had their backs to the horse fall location.

We carefully dug up a spot for the horse to fall on. Yak had previously had the stakes that the cable was attached to driven where he and Kenny wanted them and covered with brush. Bob and the man got into the back seat of the car. Yak and Kenny attached the hobbles to the horse's legs. We rolled the camera and Kenny spurred the horse to the dug up spot. The horse went down in a cloud of dust. Kenny rolled free, got up and ran to some rocks as previously planned. It was done.

I always let the camera roll until the horse got up to prove we hadn't hurt him. Usually they hit the ground and were back on their feet shaking the dust off almost instantly. The camera was still rolling. Kenny had run behind the rock and still the horse was down flat on his back with all four feet in the air. His neck was at an odd angle. The camera was still running when Yak ran to the horse and grabbed one of his legs and pulled him over on his side. The horse immediately got to his feet and shook himself. I said cut and thanks at the same time, as I looked up to heaven.

A wrangler ran in and took the horse's reins. Yak walked around on the other side of the horse like he was looking him over. It looked to me like he was checking the cinch on the saddle, and was looking at something over my shoulder. I turned to see what he was looking at and bumped into the SPCA man who brushed past me and went to the horse. I looked at Bob, who was following him. He gave me a little grin and shrugged his shoulders as if to say, "I tried."

I have never seen a Running W performed where the cable didn't break at the point that it is tied to the ring at the bottom of the cinch. When the running horse's momentum plus the weight of the horse come to a stop, the cable snaps and comes singing back in a high arc. Anyone riding behind or even the camera crew is on the alert for the flying cable.

Now Kenny came from behind the rock and joined the circle surrounding the horse.

The SPCA man looked at the hobbles on the horse's front legs, then walked around the horse kicking in the dirt. He looked at Kenny. "Where's the cable?" Kenny spit a long stream of tobacco juice. "What cable?" The man hadn't noticed the small frayed ends left on the cinch ring. Now he looked at the wrangler holding the horse. "Walk him." The wrangler looked at Yak. "You heard the man," Yak told him. The wrangler walked the horse about ten feet. He showed no signs of being hurt. He turned him and walked him back.

The SPCA man's face clouded. He walked up to the horse on the side Yak had been standing on and pointed to the cinch. There was a three-foot stick protruding from under the cinch. He pulled the stick out and looked at it. "So that's the way you do it." He waved the stick at Kenny. Kenny said, "Do what?" We were all as puzzled as Kenny. He said, "Make the horse fall. You jam this stick down between his legs and trip him." I almost laughed out loud. Can you imagine a faster way to get yourself killed, being on top of a horse and jamming a stick between his legs? He wouldn't go down, but you sure as hell would.

I looked at Yak. He was nodding like, "That's right." I turned to look at Bob. He was coughing, trying to keep from laughing. The crew thought it was funny. Me too, until I thought about it a moment. That wiped the smile off my face. The SPCA man took hold of Kenny's arm. "You're under arrest for cruelty to animals," he said. He pulled Kenny toward the car he and Bob had been sitting in. Kenny looked at Yak, Bob, and me in disbelief. He turned to the SPCA man. "Listen, I . . ." The SPCA man said, "You can tell it to the judge in Lone Pine." He pushed Kenny into the car. I turned on Yak. "Damn it to hell, Yak, if you don't clear this up with this dumb bastard, we might not get Kenny out of jail for a couple of days. We need him."

Yak grinned, spat a six-foot stream of tobacco juice and walked to the car as it started to pull out. We couldn't hear what he was saying, but in a couple of minutes Kenny got out of the car and walked to me. "I knew it was a gag. You all knew it was a gag, but did he know it was a gag?" The joke was later turned on us. The SPCA man wouldn't give us a seal of approval on the picture when it was released.

The *Lone Ranger* unit couldn't afford to shoot all the exteriors at Lone Pine and returned to Hollywood after ten days. Some outdoors sequences, including a spectacular mass chase in the last chapter, were shot at Iverson's Ranch, a favorite location of Republic producers because it was less than an hour from the studio. The back lot's Western Street, Cantina Street, and Hacienda Square stood in for the town of Pecos. The cave where Tonto nursed the Lone Ranger after the ambush, which became the secret hideout of the five Ranger suspects, was a plaster-of-Paris structure housed in a large tin shed at the end of Western Street.

Interior scenes were filmed on a variety of standing sets, including adobe-walled rooms that matched the buildings on Cantina Street and Hacienda Square.

Although Bill Witney had worked for Republic since its founding in 1935 (and for Mascot before that), he didn't meet studio president Herbert Yates until Christmas Eve of 1937:

> Republic had always given a party for the entire studio on Christmas Eve. We were still in production on The Lone Ranger on a stage next to where the party was being held. It was around 7:00 at night and the party had been in progress since 5:00. We had to ask the orchestra to stop playing when we rolled the camera because the music filtered through the stage walls.
>
> Visitors had come in and out watching us shoot. The crew didn't pay any attention to them. A group of men came through the door and stood in the back of the stage. The stage became so quiet that I turned to find out why. Moe Siegel and Sol, his brother, were standing on either side of a small baldheaded man. I recognized him as Herb Yates. I'd never met

him. He stayed mostly in New York and ran the studio and Consolidated Laboratories from his office at 1776 Broadway.

Sol walked over to see me. "The dailies were good—no problems." He indicated Moe and Yates with his thumb. "Mister Yates wants to meet you," and led the way. Mr. Yates put his hand out to me. As I shook it he said, "Glad to meet you, kid." I said, "I'm glad to meet you." He waved his hand toward the set. "Why don't you quit shooting and come join the party?" I laughed. "I should have finished an hour ago, but the music has held us up." He turned to Sol. "Go tell the orchestra to go have a drink until he finishes shooting." He slapped me on the back. "I'll save you a drink." Moe followed him out the door. Bob Beche came up to me, and I told him, "I like him." Bob said, "I do too. Now come on, kid, get this set rolling."

Principal photography of *The Lone Ranger* finally wrapped on New Year's Eve, and the editors worked feverishly to assemble the early chapters in time to make the scheduled national release date of February 12, 1938.

Visually, the Lone Ranger, Tonto, and their respective steeds left nothing to be desired. Although George W. Trendle expressed displeasure with certain aspects of the serial, he admitted to being thrilled with the physical interpretations of the radio show's hero. Of course, the Ranger's most important characteristic was his voice. During filming, either the actor under the mask or Yakima Canutt delivered the scripted dialogue. In post-production, their voices would have to be replaced by one more closely resembling that of Earle Graser, who was then playing the Ranger on radio.

It's not known why Republic didn't simply hire Graser and fly him to Hollywood to record the lines for dubbing, but they did the next best thing by matching his voice as best as possible with local talent. Bill Witney was in on the decision:

> One day when we were shooting on location at the Iverson Ranch, Bob told me that they were sending out some actors for

me to test for the voice of the Lone Ranger.... Yak, who doubled him throughout the serial, had a terrible time with the mask. Yak always had a chaw of tobacco tucked in one cheek, and at odd times had to get rid of it in the usual five-foot stream. He got so used to wearing the mask that he'd forget to lift the bottom half before ejecting the five-foot stream. It would stop when it hit the mask. When this happened we were glad that the censorship board wasn't on the set.

Late that afternoon five actors got out of a car and the casting director was with them. Each one had a page of dialogue, starting with five yells of "Hi-Yo, Silver . . . away!" One by one I stood them up among the rocks, so the sound man could give them a little reverberation or echo. Then they read the dialogue to me. When the casting director introduced me to the last one, whose name was Billy Bletcher, I did a double take. Billy was about five-foot-two and probably topped 200 pounds. I looked at the sound man. He wouldn't look at me, and I knew why: to keep from laughing. When Billy cut loose with "Hi-Yo, Silver . . . away!" it practically lifted off his headset and echoed across the valley for what seemed like five minutes. He had a deep voice that was just what we were looking for. Later, whenever the Lone Ranger had something to say on the screen, I looked at the tall handsome actor playing the part, but my mind would picture little fat Billy.

Nonetheless, Bletcher's deep, booming tones were perfect. In my opinion, he was a better-sounding Ranger than Earle Graser. More importantly, Bletcher's voice matched the larger-than-life Lone Ranger that 1938 moviegoers would see on screens 30 feet tall.

By the time post-production work had been completed and the final negatives readied for printing, *The Lone Ranger* had cost Republic $168,117—just five percent over budget.

Republic's home-office Screening Committee, which passed judgment on all the studio's releases, was enthusiastic about *The Lone Ranger*'s prospects after viewing Chapter One on January 20. A memo to the studio stated: "Episode #1 *Lone*

Ranger was very satisfactorily received by the Committee. The consensus of opinion of the Committee is that *The Lone Ranger* promises to be Republic's top serial, and that episode #1 has many thrills, lots of action, and suspense. The Lone Ranger's voice is exactly the same as the voice on the radio broadcasts, and Tonto's excellent performance is convincing."

Individual comments from Committee members included the following: "Magnificent" . . . "This looks like a smash serial" . . . "Believe everybody feels we have a big winner in *Lone Ranger*" . . . "*Lone Ranger* should far exceed anything made in the serial field by any producer."

These predictions turned out to be accurate. *The Lone Ranger* was Republic's highest-grossing chapter play ever, commanding rental prices far in excess of the customary five dollars per episode. During its two-year playoff period, the serial had over 2500 bookings in the United States and generated more than $576,000 in domestic film rental. *The Lone Ranger* performed equally well internationally and eventually earned a total of one million dollars in worldwide film rentals. It won Republic's second consecutive Grand Shorts Award (previously awarded to *Dick Tracy*) from Jay Emanuel's prestigious trade journal, *The Motion Picture Herald*, following a vote by the magazine's readers.

Rather remarkably, the inevitable sequel, *The Lone Ranger Rides Again* (1939), was a near total misfire and easily the weakest of Republic's "Golden Age" serials. (But that, dear reader, is a story for another time.) Some time after the 1940 release of *Hi-Yo Silver*, a 69-minute feature version edited from the first serial, Republic's rights reverted to Trendle, who flirted with licensing the character to Universal for a third serial. He wanted more money and more control; Universal was not willing to give him either.

Trendle buried the two Republic serials—whose negatives he reportedly secured—and they were unseen for decades. In the early 1970s, an enterprising film collector located 16mm prints with Spanish subtitles. While incomplete and of less than stellar pictorial quality, they eventually made their way into the hands of other aficionados, first as 16mm dupe prints and later as bootleg VHS tapes.

The Lone Ranger turned out to be every bit as satisfying as its near-mythic reputation had indicated. The struggle for Reconstruction-era Texas gave scope to the serial, with the dictatorial fraud Jeffries calling to mind James Addison Reavis, the self-styled Baron of Arizona, who forged old Spanish land grants to claim ownership of a huge swath of that territory. And while differing from the radio show in many ways—not the least of which was establishing the Ranger's true identity, something radio writer Fran Striker had not yet done—the chapter play skillfully exploited most of the program's popular elements. Tulsa-based VCI Entertainment markets a licensed DVD version of Hi-Yo Silver, an extremely well-done distillation of the serial. *BnT* readers with an interest in Republic's *Lone Ranger* are encouraged to see that film, which was mastered from original 35mm film elements and thus possesses considerably better picture and sound quality than bootleg versions of the Spanish-subtitled prints.

William Witney went on to direct or co-direct 20 more serials, and more than a hundred feature films and TV episodes. But *The Lone Ranger* always held a special place in his heart. After Bill died in 2002, his son fulfilled the old director's wish by cremating him and spreading his ashes in Lone Pine's Potsagawa Canyon, where his crew had shot the ambush of the Texas Rangers on a cold December day in 1937.

The Secret of Treasure Island
(1938, Columbia Pictures)
by Rex W. Layton

At the time of its release in 1938, The *Secret of Treasure Island* was Columbia Pictures' most expensive serial to date, a hit both with the critics and at the nation's box offices, breaking many house records for chapter play grosses. Today, more than seven decades later, *Secret of Treasure Island*—referred to hereafter in these pages as *SoTI*—is of interest not only to film historians and serial buffs, but also to fans of pulp legend L. Ron Hubbard, upon which unpublished novel, "Murder at Pirate Castle," the serial was based.

In the 1930s, Hollywood was well into its Golden Age, with film production in Los Angeles at an all-time high. Millions of moviegoers flocked into the nation's movie palaces each week, hoping to escape the ongoing Depression by way of a couple of hours of on-screen thrills, romance, or adventure. At the same time an estimated 30,000,000 readers nationwide were snatching up the many pulp-fiction magazines from newsstands every month, in hopes of obtaining similar escape. It's little wonder, therefore, that with such demand for new story material the Hollywood studios sought talent from among the hundreds of high-production wordsmiths who filled the pulpwood pages of these magazines each month. Little wonder, too, that by 1937 L. Ron Hubbard would be among those elite pulpsters summoned to Filmland.

Just over three years earlier, Hubbard's first published pulp story, "The Green God," an adventure yarn set in China, had appeared in *Thrilling Adventures* (February 1934). Throughout 1935 and 1936, with an average of three to four stories appearing each month (and often cover-featured) in such leading magazines as *Adventure, Argosy, Top-Notch,* and *Five Novels Monthly,* Hubbard was firmly established as one of the industry's most popular authors. By early 1937 he'd placed over 1,500,000 words into print, making a meteoric rise into the top ranks of pulp professionals.

On top of this, according to A. B. Dick, the company whose market research helped determine advertising rates of publishing firms (similar to what today's Nielsen ratings do for television), Hubbard's name on the cover would send a magazine's circulation soaring. It's likely that this popularity, along with the efforts of Hubbard's then-agent, Ed Bodin, brought the young author to the Hollywood's attention.

Hubbard met Bodin in New York City in May 1934, just after becoming a member of the American Fiction Guild. The A. F. G. had been founded by prolific pulp author Arthur J. Burks in March of the previous year to organize and promote the interests of its membership. Burks, Hubbard, and Bodin were among the most active and tireless members, with Burks running the national office. Hubbard, all of 25 years old, was elected president of the New York City Chapter in May 1936, presiding over the Guild's weekly luncheons at Rosoff's restaurant (a legendary literary hang-out in Manhattan) until late June, when he resigned to return to his home near Seattle and resume writing full-time. Bodin, meanwhile, continued to sell the output of his many clients to the booming magazine field while also networking to promote his writers to the lucrative Hollywood markets.

Columbia Pictures Corporation purchased the film rights to "Murder at Pirate Castle" in December 1936. The property was subsequently assigned to the Adventure Serials Company, an independent production unit owned by brothers Louis and Adolph Weiss, which had been hired by Columbia to supply four 15-episode chapter plays for release during the 1937-38 season. According to surviving documents, Louis Weiss then personally contracted Hubbard to write the shooting script.

Arriving in Hollywood in April 1937, Hubbard checked into the St. Francis Hotel at 5533 Hollywood Boulevard, where he soon learned to write fully dialogued continuities for the big screen. (The form would not have been totally foreign to him, as Hubbard had earlier written radio scripts for local stations while a student at George Washington University in 1930.) Shortly thereafter, he shared his first impressions of Tinseltown within a letter to his *Five Novels Monthly* editor, Florence McChesney. "This burg is a hysterical place," he wrote, "and I can't say that my first glimpse has done much to impress me about it. What writers I have met here, usually staid chaps, are all gone goofy with the dollar marks. They call anything under five hundred a week 'buttons.'"

Hubbard would soon be living up to his legendary reputation within the pulp community as a fast-production writer, cranking out the screen adaptation for "Murder at Pirate Castle" while continuing to supply his New York editors with stories. As he related years later: "Any writer loves glamour-town. I used to sit in my penthouse apartment on Sunset Boulevard [where Hubbard had relocated from the St. Francis, apparently to be nearer his Columbia office at Gower and Sunset after Weiss extended his contract in mid-June] and write stories for New York and then go to my office in the studio and have my secretary tell everybody I was in conference while I caught up on my sleep because they couldn't believe anybody could write 136 scenes a day. The Screen Writers Guild would have killed me. Their quota was eight."

It is appropriate at this point to relate the story behind "Murder at Pirate Castle" as told approximately one year after Hubbard's arrival in Hollywood, over the airwaves of radio station KVOO of Tulsa, Oklahoma. KVOO broadcast a weekly program called *Writers and Readers*, hosted by one Bob De Haven and including a department called "The Story Behind the Story." In a February 21, 1938 letter to Hubbard, De Haven requested the "inside" story behind the writing of one of Hubbard's latest pulp yarns, along with the publication date so that De Haven could publicize same on his show. Hubbard immediately responded to this generous offer, sending in the details behind his Western tale, "Six-Gun Caballero" (*Western Story Magazine*, March 12, 1938) and including some information about "Murder at Pirate Castle" as well. De Haven's show aired on March 10, 1938. Luckily, a transcript survives, from which the following excerpt is taken.

> One character haunted [Hubbard] for four and a half years and made his life miserable. In truth, he was a ghost, this character. He was an ugly fellow who had a habit of vanishing in a puff of smoke and shooting men in the back. This character was developed about five years ago when Hubbard sat down to see if he could write a story in ten days, a full book of 60,000 words. He made it in 11 days and called the book "Pirate Castle." In it was a pirate's ghost called the Shark of the Caribbean, the villain of the piece, and it was the Shark who haunted the author.
>
> And it was annoying in more ways than one to Hubbard— the novel started to collect rejections in wholesale lots. It went to every magazine that ever printed such stories. It went to every publishing house. It went over the Atlantic and had tiffin with London publishers, and even said skoal with the Scandinavians. But to no avail. Nobody wanted that book, and the ghost kept coming back to bother Hubbard in his sleep.
>
> Well, finally one of the Hollywood studios bought it and hired the author to write the [screen]play, and even then, he wasn't through with it. Argosy asked for a rewrite of the novel, a change of editors and another request for a rewrite. Finally, the story was buried with honors and lives . . . on the screen.

The above paragraphs supply answers to questions Hubbard fans have pondered for years. First, they confirm that Hubbard did, in fact, write the complete, original scenario for *SoTI*. This had previously been unclear, as Hubbard is given story credit on the finished film, while George Rosener, George Merrick, and Elmer Clifton share the screenplay credit. In fact, Hubbard's original script still survives, and reportedly consists of over 2,000 individual scenes.

Many key elements from what would become *SoTI* were drawn from the author's real-life experiences during two early seafaring expeditions conducted in the time period cited in De Haven's program when Hubbard had first been inspired to write "Pirate Castle."

In 1932, while still a student at G. W. U., Hubbard led a group of 50 college students aboard the Doris Hamlin, a 250-foot schooner out of Baltimore, on a "Caribbean Motion Picture Expedition," to film newsreels of old pirate haunts. On Martinique, he scaled and photographed the active volcano, Mount Pelee, a feat he described in a 1935 radio interview.

During his West Indies Mineralogical Expedition of 1932-33, Hubbard explored and photographed the ruins of Citadel de Christophe, an ancient Spanish fortress in Haiti and most likely the inspiration of the "Big House" used as a headquarters by *SoTI*'s villain, The Shark. Later, in Puerto Rico, Hubbard and a companion narrowly escaped a mine collapse, described in harrowing detail in his article, "I Was Buried Alive!" (*Personal Adventure Stories*, September 1937). This probably inspired the tunnel cave-in pictured in one of the chapter play's cliffhanger endings.

The other question answered by the De Haven broadcast has to do with the planned *Argosy* serialization of "Murder at Pirate Castle" prominently featured in Columbia's initial publicity materials and on the pre-release poster: "To Appear in *Argosy Magazine*! Every week—every installment will be serialized in big-circulation Argosy. L. Ron Hubbard—famous action writer—stunt pilot—world adventurer—wrote the thrilling story!"

Apparently, per the KVOO radio broadcast, Hubbard had rewritten the "Pirate Castle" manuscript for *Argosy* editor Jack Byrne, replaced in late 1937 by Chandler Whipple, who requested additional revision. Whipple did, in fact, reference the scheduled serialization within editorial commentary published in *Argosy* in early November of 1937, several months after Hubbard had completed his Hollywood contract. "Next to exorcise the Hollywood virus from his veins was L. Ron Hubbard," wrote Whipple. "He headed straight for the pine forests of Washington—and there, ensconced in a cabin overlooking the Pacific, he set to work to give *Argosy* some more of his rousing yarns. The first, "Cargo of Coffins," is due to appear in the November 13th issue, and *a serial is likely to follow*." (Emphasis added.)

Most likely, Hubbard balked at doing another rewrite, and so the much-publicized weekly magazine serialization was canceled. This might explain why Hubbard wrote only one additional story for *Argosy* under Whipple's editorship, "Orders Is Orders" (December 18, 1937), thus ending his long-term and very successful association with this top general-fiction magazine.

Hubbard's move to Hollywood created quite a stir within the pulp-fiction community, with numerous mentions appearing in writers magazines—including *Writer's Digest* and *The Author & Journalist*—during his extended stay. This was encouraging news for those hoping to break into the movies. One such hopeful was James F. Ayres, who wrote the following in a June 15, 1937 letter to Hubbard:

> I suppose you're wondering of all things, how in the dickens did I ever get hold of your address. Well, it's all pretty simple. . . . I had occasion to drop in on Ed Bodin, your agent. Naturally, we drifted into conversation. . . . "What's become of Ron Hubbard?" I said. "Ron Hubbard?" he smiled back at me. "Why, haven't you heard? Hubbard's out in Hollywood."
>
> "Out in Hollywood!" I exclaimed. "This is the first time I've heard of that."
>
> "Why, sure," he went on. "Hubbard's got a ten-week contract with the Columbia Pictures people. He's doing the continuity of a serial for them."

Hubbard's June 28 reply to Ayres was typical of his generosity towards novice writers for whom he often served as a corresponding mentor, and also provides more details about his time in Hollywood:

> Your letter was quite a pleasing surprise. . . . I have finished my original job and now I'm waiting for a report and filling in the time turning out some other stories and getting them into the studios. In addition to this work I have managed to write several novelettes in the past six weeks and as a consequence my energy is at a very low ebb.
>
> Art Burks and [noted aviation writer] George Bruce are out here but I see very little of Bruce. Art and I get together two or three times a week and swear at the movies.

Hubbard's other screen work during this incredibly prolific period, as referenced in the above letter, included uncredited contributions to two other Columbia chapter plays, *The Mysterious Pilot* (1937) and *The Great Adventures of Wild Bill Hickok* (1938), which bookended *SoTI* on the studio's serial release schedule. Hubbard also worked uncredited at Paramount on Cecil B. De Mille's Western epic, *The Plainsman* (1937)—which, coincidentally, featured Gary Cooper as Wild Bill Hickok. (Hubbard's work on the latter film is documented in a June 28, 1937 letter from Hubbard's father, Harry Ross Hubbard, to Cooper's father, Judge Charlie Cooper. The two families had been neighbors in Helena, Montana, from approximately 1913 to 1930.)

On July 1, 1937, having worked himself to a frazzle with his attempts to please his Hollywood bosses, Hubbard wrote the following to one of his fiction editors back East:

> I am turning down all contracts [in Hollywood] and pulling my freight. I like to write for men like you and books like you print and I guess I'm somewhat unbalanced in that direction. I like my freedom. I fight hard for independent individualism. I love to tie into a yarn and try to make it blaze in print. The magazines will never lose me to the movies. Never. At any salary.

L. Ron Hubbard's return home from Hollywood was duly heralded in his hometown newspaper, *The Bremerton Searchlight*, within a July 15, 1937 story headlined, "Northwest Writer Escapes."

> Worn and haggard by 12 weeks of writing in Filmland, L. Ron Hubbard, magazine fictioneer and novelist, finally returned to his home here today.
>
> Mr. Hubbard, son of Lieut. Comdr. and Mrs. H. R. Hubbard, who makes his home on a farm he purchased last fall in Port Orchard, was called to Hollywood in the spring to adapt one of his novels to the screen for Columbia Pictures.
>
> "After several weeks of unusual weather," said Hubbard, speaking of his trip, "I tried very hard to finish my work hurriedly so that I could leave California.
>
> "Tortured by dreams of a bass in Lake Tanwax I failed to hook last summer and working with a minimum of clothes because of the extreme heat, I worried through the second job, writing my wife every few days that I would start home presently.
>
> "My producer, however, could not be convinced that bass were important. My wife did not agree with the producer that movies were important as my repeated delays in returning home must have been most annoying to her.
>
> "After two or three minor nervous breakdowns brought upon by the trials which make up pictures, I finally got out of Hollywood. Working for the pictures is not as easy as it is generally supposed."

Hubbard offered a few more specifics about his Hollywood "breakdowns" a few days later within an interview that appeared in the *Bremerton Daily News*:

> "There is nothing very difficult about the labor [of writing in Hollywood]," he related, "except that a man has so many bosses who change their minds so often that he is constantly called upon to change his script. The terrific salaries paid do

not compensate for the stress and strain on a writer's consequent less of markets in his own field."

Any losses Hubbard incurred from his fiction markets during the months in California were soon compensated, however; his first hardcover novel, *Buckskin Brigades* (Macaulay), appeared on July 30, 1937, garnering uniformly favorable reviews, most notably in the *New York Times*. Hubbard continued as one of the most prolific writers for the pulps.

Columbia released *SoTI* to the nation's movie theaters on May 6, 1938, to great reviews and ongoing box-office success. "A rousing thriller with all the sensational elements to satisfy the thrill fans who like their excitement in weekly chapter doses," wrote *Film Daily*'s critic, while *Variety* described the 15-part serial as being "stuffed with fist-fighting, rough and tumble action, and enough fright ingredients to keep the kids coming back for each episode." As one Iowa theater owner proclaimed: "Looks like Columbia has figured out how to make serials."

In a prologue, 16th-century pirates hide a fabulous treasure of gold and gems in the caverns of a volcanic island off the coast of Mexico. The volcano erupts, and both pirates and treasure are buried. The story proper opens in the present day (1938), when the island is ruled by ruthless Carter Collins, also known as The Shark (Walter Miller). Collins, who owns half of an old treasure map and is obsessed with finding the pirate gold, lives in the island's medieval fortress and commands Dr. X, a physician (Hobart Bosworth); Zanya, his nurse (Sandra Karina); Professor Gault, a scientist (Patrick J. Kelly); and Hawkins, a servant (Colin Campbell). In underground tunnels that honeycomb the island, The Shark's enslaved diggers—cowled, robed workers known as "Mole Men"—tirelessly search for the treasure.

In California, Collins' henchman Grindley (Grant Withers) learns that Toni Morrell (Gwen Gaze) has the missing half of the map, left to her by the father she never knew. Reporter Larry Kent (Don Terry), assigned by newspaper editor Westmore (William Farnum) to locate their missing colleague

Thorndyke (William Royle), agrees to accompany Toni on a boat trip to the Mexican coastal town of Cortez, the port nearest Treasure Island. She has reason to believe that her father's long-ago disappearance is tied to his visit to the island. While en route, Toni is accosted by Grindley, who wants her portion of the map. Larry intervenes and fights off The Shark's lackey.

After landing at Cortez, Larry and Toni commandeer a small boat that carried a dying escapee from Treasure Island. Unbeknownst to them, Grindley is a stowaway. Upon reaching the shore Larry and Toni are attacked, and while the reporter battles The Shark's men, the girl escapes to a nearby shack. Taking refuge inside, she falls through a trap door and plunges into the subterranean tunnels, where she is confronted by the terrifying Mole Men.

Captain Cuttle (George Rosener), the eccentric seafarer who inhabits the cabin, rescues Toni from the Mole Men and reveals a secret passage that takes her to the Big House. Larry escapes his assailants, enters the shack and falls through the trap door. In the tunnels he encounters Hawkins, who ushers him to the Big House's great hall, where Toni is now dining with Collins and his staff. Below, the rebellious Mole Men attempt to blow up the fortress, but the explosion is insufficiently powerful. Collins orders Larry and Toni to rooms upstairs and leaves to investigate the blast. The visitors from the mainland are confronted by the Ghost of the Black Pirate, who demands Toni's half of the map. Larry draws a gun and repeatedly fires at the phantom who, laughing maniacally, advances with drawn cutlass—and then vanishes into thin air.

After much traversing of the island, the plot is resolved and all questions answered. The ghostly pirate is explained as an image thrown by cleverly concealed movie projectors. Collins and most of his minions are killed when the island is torn asunder by a powerful volcanic eruption. Larry, Toni, and their friends narrowly escape.

Hubbard's first science-fiction story, "The Dangerous Dimension" (*Astounding Science Fiction*, July 1938), which appeared while *SoTI* was still unreeling in movie houses, immediately catapulted him into the top rank of an entirely new writing genre that carries forward his influence to this day.

Many years later—on December 16, 1952, to be exact—during a lecture to Scientology students in Philadelphia, L. Ron Hubbard talked about his early days in Hollywood and *SoTI* in particular. Hubbard's humorous commentary also gave an explanation for various flaws in the serial's plotting, logic, continuity, and character names. The riff on *SoTI* immediately followed his contention that people generally like some "randomity"—an equal balance between predictable and unpredictable action—in their lives. To illustrate his point, Hubbard commented as follows:

> I wrote a serial one time that made history. It made history because it only cost $200,000 to make, and it made $1,750,000 at the box office. [Editor's Note: This is rank exaggeration.] And it was the worst serial ever made, but it didn't lack in randomity. Because after I put the plot together—it had a lot of randomity in it—they decided that the last half of each of the reels, or something like that, ought to be rewritten by somebody else—who needed a screen credit. And, without reading my script, he rewrote it. It was really random.
>
> And then they had a couple of extra stuntmen they didn't know what to do with, so they just threw these stuntmen into various places in the picture.
>
> To this day, if I walk into Hollywood, I could walk into so-and-so's office down there, an agent. And they'd look at me blankly for a little while; I have worked on fairly decent things once in a while. Look blankly for a while, and so on. . . . "Yeah, that's right. I know, yeah—yeah! One million seven-hundred-fifty thousand box office! That's right—yeah! We could put you to work. Let's go over to Paramount and see what they've got to say. . . ."
>
> That's a fact. Just the box office. They never looked at the film. Nobody's ever analyzed that film to find out why it did that. It defies analysis! It has no plot. It doesn't even end with the same characters it begins with!

Its confusion was so wonderful [that] people had to keep coming back to the theater to see it time after time, because they couldn't believe it!

The Secret of Treasure Island, which was theatrically re-released many years later and subsequently included in a television syndication package, technically can't be considered a "lost" film, but it *is* extremely rare. It has been available for many years in poor-quality video copies amateurishly mastered by hobbyists from battered 16mm prints. L. Ron Hubbard's original manuscript of "Murder at Pirate Castle" still exists as well, and it would be great to see the novel finally published—ideally, packaged with a sparkling DVD copy of the fully restored serial!

The Shadow
(1940, Columbia Pictures)
by Ed Hulse

Harry Cohn's Columbia Pictures Corporation was a late player in the serial game, coming to bat in 1937 after various independent producers had departed the field for good. With only Universal and Republic as competition, the studio initially outsourced chapter-play production to the father-son team of Louis and Adrian Weiss, whose Artclass Pictures had long been a mainstay of Poverty Row. Of their three serials for Columbia—*Jungle Menace, The Mysterious Pilot,* and *The Secret of Treasure Island*—the first two were lackluster efforts that underperformed in the marketplace. Only the last-named could be considered an unqualified success, but even *Secret of Treasure Island* failed to live up to the studio's expectations. Cohn summarily dismissed Weiss *pere et fils*, assigning newly hired producer Jack Fier to oversee *The Great Adventures of Wild Bill Hickok*, previously announced as the fourth Weiss/Columbia serial of the 1937-38 season.

Fier determined that the only effective way to seize serial market share was to keep Columbia's chapter-play production in house and make the studio's episodic epics on a slightly grander scale than originally contemplated. This, presumably, would make them more appealing to exhibitors previously reliant on Universal and Republic product.

Columbia's four 1938-39 serials—led by *The Spider's Web,* an action-packed adaptation of the Popular Publications hero pulp that was *The Shadow Magazine*'s most serious competitor—enjoyed considerable box-office success but failed to return the expected margin of profit because their production costs were so high. At a time when the average Republic and Universal serial cost $150,000 to $175,000, Fier was spending well over $200,000 for each of his. Since exhibitor rentals averaged five dollars per chapter at this time, the extra expenditures cut into Columbia's revenues.

The somewhat more lavishly appointed Fier-produced chapter plays did, however, secure enough bookings and generate enough favorable publicity to solidify the studio's position in this niche market. But, having accomplished this aim, Harry Cohn retrenched by once again outsourcing serial production, this time to Larry Darmour, who for some years had been supplying Columbia with short subjects and "B" Westerns on an independent basis. Cohn and Fier were gambling that serial production quality was secondary to promotional value: With an exhibitor client base established, it would be just as easy to sell the studio's chapter plays based on the presence of marketable stars or popular characters licensed from other mediums.

It fell to Jack Fier to select properties with appeal to the generally youthful audience that patronized serials. This meant securing screen rights to characters from pulps, comics, and radio shows. With Darmour hired to produce four chapter plays per "season" (in those days, a movie "season" began sometime after Labor Day and extended through Spring to the beginning of Summer, which typically saw a reduction in theatergoing), Fier commenced his licensing efforts.

The all-important season-opening slot had been reserved for a serial built around some popular fictional character. Following negotiations with Street & Smith, Columbia on May 26, 1939 paid $7000 for the right to produce one motion picture, either a 15-episode serial or a long feature film, based on The Shadow. Surviving documents reveal that the publishing company's vp/general manager Henry W. "Bill" Ralston and licensing director William de Grouchy exercised great care in crafting the agreement and insisted the filmmakers maintain fidelity to Street & Smith's most profitable pulp hero.

Significantly, however, the deal permitted Columbia to adapt episodes of the radio show as well as novels printed in the magazine. This was a potentially risky concession because the two versions of The Shadow were fundamentally incompatible. In a July 19 letter to the publishing company, Columbia vice president B. B. Kahane informed Street & Smith that the studio had decided to use as source material "The Green Hoods" (published in the August 15, 1938 issue), "Silver Skull" (January 1, 1939), and "The Lone Tiger" (February 15, 1939). He also requested a copy of the script to one of the radio episodes, "Prelude to Terror" (broadcast January 29, 1939).

Apparently, Fier at first intended to produce the Shadow serial in house. Brief news items published in movie-industry trade papers during the early part of summer reported that Lorna Gray would take the female lead, and that Norman Deming and D. Ross Lederman would direct in tandem. As all were under contract to Columbia, these accounts lend credence to the supposition that the chapter play was initially slated for more extravagant production mounting along the lines of *The Spider's Web*. But when Larry Darmour signed on to supply serials for Columbia distribution the property was assigned to him.

Writers Joseph F. Poland and Ned Dandy, who had collaborated on the previous two Fier-produced serials, teamed with accomplished scripter Joseph O'Donnell to devise a story containing 15 episodes of thrills that could be realized cinematically on short money. (They were assisted by Charles Condon and John Thomas Neville, whose contributions could not have been substantial as they did not receive screen credit.) Reportedly, Darmour's Columbia chapter plays were budgeted at $100,000—less than half what Fier had been spending. Speed and economy became the new watchwords of Columbia's serial unit. Sound-stage scenes would be shot at Larry Darmour's studio on Santa Monica Boulevard in Hollywood. Exterior street scenes would be taken in Burbank at what was called the Columbia Ranch, or on the adjoining

Warner Brothers back lot, access to which was available for a modest rental fee. The screenwriters kept cost limitations very much in mind as they concocted the scenario, and by mid-July a first draft had already been completed.

Of course, helming production of action-packed, highly melodramatic serials required a master's touch, so at Fier's suggestion Darmour hired James W. Horne, who had co-directed *The Spider's Web* and *Flying G-Men*. Although Horne was best known for his comedies, including many shorts and features starring Laurel & Hardy, he directed numerous chapter plays in the silent era, among them *Bull's Eye* (1917) and *Hands Up!* (1918), which had made top box-office stars of their respective stars, Eddie Polo and Ruth Roland.

The casting process yielded mixed results, although Darmour scored a coup by landing highly regarded major-studio player Victor Jory for the lead role. Actually, Darmour didn't make the deal himself. Canadian-born Jory had been working for Columbia off and on since 1934, and he enjoyed a good relationship with the notoriously irascible Harry Cohn. Even though the darkly handsome, vaguely sinister-looking actor had played leads before, he found steadier work in character parts and in 1939 was considered one of Hollywood's top heavies. His film work that year had already included high-profile villain portrayals in *Dodge City* and *Gone with the Wind*.

"My agent told me he'd made a two-picture deal for me at Columbia," Jory recalled to me in a 1980 interview. "Harry Cohn threw me into [the serial]. He said, 'Vic, you're going to be The Shadow.' It was as simple as that."

The serial's storyline combined elements of both pulp magazine and radio show, although it naturally leaned toward the former, as contractually obligated. The chief element borrowed from The Shadow's airwave adventures was Margot Lane, played by blonde, brassy Veda Ann Borg, a former Warner Brothers starlet most frequently seen as a gangster's moll or wisecracking showgirl. Borg lost her berth at Warners following a serious car accident in which she suffered serious facial injuries after being thrown through the windshield.

Darmour had used her previously in a Bill Elliott Western, *The Law Comes to Texas* (1939), and she agreed to do the Shadow serial while waiting for another round of plastic surgery. Since she still bore facial scars Veda had to be made up, lit and photographed carefully, so she received very few close-ups. A talented actress, Borg was nonetheless ill suited to play the glamorous, sophisticated Margot depicted in the radio series.

Rounding out the starring trio was one Roger Moore, cast as The Shadow's chief aide, Harry Vincent. Moore was in fact Joe Young, the older brother of second-tier movie star and TV's future Marcus Welby, Robert Young. Joe's career had never really taken off, and the role of Vincent was the last sizable one he got. Although he continued to work well into the Fifties, after *The Shadow* the elder Young most frequently appeared in uncredited bit parts. Also seen as familiar figures from the pulp magazine were veteran character actors Frank LaRue, playing Commissioner Ralph Weston, and Edward Peil, as Inspector Joe Cardona.

Principal photography began in the fall of 1939—the exact date is unknown—and proceeded at a rapid clip. "We did 15 episodes in 30 days," said Jory years later. "Less, actually, because we didn't shoot on Sundays. It was hard work—early mornings, late nights, a lot of rushing around." The Fier-produced serials, by contrast, had consumed six to eight weeks of shooting time.

Horne impressed upon his actors a need for speed and didn't waste any time on the niceties of staging scenes. "He instructed us very quickly," Jory remembered. "No real direction in terms of performances, except that we had to take everything 'big' [with exaggerated reactions]. He'd sketch the where and how of a scene, and give us the basic attitude of it, but mostly it was a question of hitting the marks and delivering the lines on cue. We did damn few retakes, and only then if there had been a problem with camera or sound. On serials you didn't get multiple takes to experiment with different line readings."

While shooting *The Shadow*, Horne introduced another time-saving innovation to shave hours off the schedule. In those days, fight scenes were always shot twice—once in a "master" shot that took in the whole set and covered the melee from beginning to end, then with a series of shorter, closer shots that sometimes showed the principals throwing punches, rather than their stunt doubles. These "insert" shots would be cut into the masters to quicken the scene's pace and further the illusion that the actors were doing their own fighting.

George DeNormand, an experienced stuntman who doubled Victor Jory in *The Shadow*, explained to me in 1973 that Horne came up with a way to avoid the time-consuming process of relighting the set for close-ups and refitting it with duplicates of props that had been damaged or destroyed in the first take. "Instead of shooting the scene twice," said DeNormand, "[Horne] got actors who could do their own fights and used them as the heavies. Then he set up two cameras, side by side. One camera took the master shot from a fixed position. The other was tricked out with a special lens that would give you a closer view. The second operator was told to follow me around the set [by swiveling the camera]. This way, the director could chop up the second-unit footage to get those quick, close cuts he needed to edit into the master shot, without having to set everything up a second time. There was never a worry I'd be recognized in the closer view because I was wearing the hat and the cape and a little strip mask that covered the bottom half of my face."

Horne used this technique sparingly in *The Shadow* but more extensively in the following nine Columbia chapter plays he directed for Larry Darmour. (For the subsequent serials DeNormand was replaced as lead double by Eddie Parker and, in the Western cliffhangers, by Cliff Lyons.) Cinematographer James S. Brown Jr. and his assistant "undercranked" fight scenes to speed up the action, making the brawls seem more furious but also giving them a Keystone Kops aspect that latter-day viewers find risible. In a way, though, that was intentional. While directing his Darmour serials Horne never fully sublimated his comedic leanings.

The Shadow had a national release date of January 5, 1940, several months later than the typical season-opening serial. Street & Smith promoted the film extensively, mentioning it several times in the magazine's "Highlights on The Shadow" department and some of the company's other pulps. The chapter play's theatrical playoff period coincided with an increased effort to market the character; 1940 saw the marketing of numerous licensed products and multi-media spin-offs. Fans could buy Shadow hats, masks, cloaks, board games, make-up kits, gun-and-holster sets, and other paraphernalia tangentially connected to the Master of Darkness. Street & Smith launched a *Shadow* comic book in March of 1940, and a newspaper strip syndicated by the Ledger Syndicate followed shortly thereafter.

Of course, buying a comic book or board game wasn't nearly as exciting as seeing one's favorite character live on the big screen, and Columbia's *Shadow* packed houses with devotees of radio show and pulp magazine alike. Serial fans huddled in darkened theaters all across the country learned in Chapter One, "The Doomed City," that the economic life of a great metropolis was being threatened by a well-organized criminal body headed by a mysterious figure known as the Black Tiger, whose mad ambition was to acquire "supreme financial power." To this end he waged a systematic campaign of terrorization and destruction—blowing up factories, crashing trains and planes, extorting money from fear-paralyzed tycoons.

The city's captains of industry prevailed upon Lamont Cranston (described as a "noted scientist and criminologist") to help combat the Tiger and his minions. Unbeknownst to them, Cranston had created two separate personalities to further his fight against crime: Lin Chang, a shifty Chinese merchant with underworld ties, and The Shadow, a mystery man whose hat, cloak, and sinister laugh were trademarks instantly recognizable to evildoers everywhere.

The Black Tiger's identity was a closely guarded secret: Not even his own men know who the Tiger really was, because he possessed the power of invisibility and transmitted instructions to the gang, sight unseen, through a wood-mounted tiger head outfitted with glowing eyes and radio speaker. But as the serial progressed it became apparent that he was one of the industrialists who met regularly with Cranston and Commissioner Weston at the Cobalt Club.

Week after week, The Shadow fought the Black Tiger to a standstill, nearly losing his life at the close of each episode only to escape miraculously at the beginning of the next. The chapter-ending perils lacked ingenuity; an inordinate number of installments closed with a ceiling collapsing on the fallen, unconscious Shadow—who groggily disengaged himself from the wreckage and staggered away the following week.

Truth be told, *The Shadow* didn't follow the pulp magazine or radio show as closely as it did *The Spider's Web*. In fact, it's fair to assume that screenwriters Dandy, Poland, and O'Donnell were instructed to copy the earlier serial, a box-office smash that single-handedly made Columbia a force to reckon with in the chapter-play market. The similarities are marked: *The Shadow*'s Lamont Cranston, like *Web*'s Richard Wentworth, is identified as a scientific criminologist rather than as the wealthy dilettante and world traveler he is in Walter Gibson's stories. The Lin Chang identity corresponds with no character in the Shadow saga but performs the same narrative function as Wentworth's Blinky McQuade persona. Likewise, the serial's Harry Vincent doesn't act independently, as he generally does in the pulp yarns; he stays close to The Shadow in the manner of Wentworth's aides Jackson and Ram Singh.

Moreover, *The Shadow* utilizes the same plot as *The Spider's Web*. Both serials posit the existence of a deranged mastermind who employs an army of henchmen to terrorize industrial leaders in a bid for economic control of a major city. Both show the police powerless to stem the tide of terror resulting from heedless destruction of life and property, concentrated on modes of transportation and newly invented devices.

The writers didn't entirely ignore the Shadow of pulp and radio. The serial is littered with bits and pieces of the licensed material. For example, the master villain's name and a courtroom scene in Chapter One are clearly inspired by "The Lone

Tiger." The opening installment's climax, in which exploding light bulbs (!) are set off by a sudden surge of current, is adapted from "Prelude to Terror." A Chapter Two sequence, in which a disguised Shadow enters the Black Tiger's lair by donning one of the full-face masks worn by the villain's henchmen during meetings with their leader, was clearly inspired by a similar episode in "The Green Hoods."

The chapter play's scripters mined several plot nuggets from "Silver Skull." For example, one scene from that novel finds The Shadow trapped in an underground chamber and taunted by the mystery villain, who speaks through a life-sized mechanical skull outfitted with a radio speaker. While taunting his enemy, Silver Skull fills the room with gas—which, ignited by sparks, causes an explosion that brings the roof crashing down on The Shadow, who narrowly escapes. Poland, Dandy, and O'Donnell got *two* cliffhanger endings out of that one Walter Gibson-devised incident. Other "Silver Skull" elements employed in *The Shadow* include the systematic kidnapping of wealthy and powerful men and the repeated destruction of airplanes by mysterious means.

Aside from Margot's presence and the aforementioned bit with the exploding light bulbs, the serial took nothing from the Shadow radio show. Darmour and company made a reasonable effort to ensure that followers of the pulp Shadow would recognize their hero on screen. (In this respect, it should be noted, the serial improved on *The Shadow Strikes* and *International Crime*, those dismal 1937-38 feature films starring Rod La Rocque.) However, several minor but jarring differences could be noted. Harry Vincent shuttles The Shadow to and from most of his confrontations with the Black Tiger's men. Sometimes, however, he is shown driving a taxicab and wearing a hack's cap. This suggests that the pulp Shadow's usual driver, cabbie Moe Shrevnitz, was originally included in the script, only to have his character combined with that of Vincent for cost-cutting purposes. Also, despite Street & Smith's insistence that the serial Shadow deploy his trademark automatic pistols, he uses automatics and .38-caliber revolvers interchangeably.

These inconsistencies are puzzling because Street & Smith had specifically requested changes to the first-draft script forwarded to them by Columbia. A July 21 letter from the studio's F. L. Weber to Bill Ralston acknowledged receipt of a Street & Smith memo expressing concerns about some scenario deviations from Shadow lore. After expressing gratitude for cooperation extended to the serial's writers by Walter Gibson and *Shadow Magazine* editor John Nanovic, Weber assured Ralston that numerous minor but significant corrections would be made based on their input. "The Shadow's guns will definitely be two .45 automatics, as requested," wrote the Columbia executive. That promise went unfulfilled.

Weber also addressed the fact that Harry Vincent was occasionally seen driving a cab in usurpation of Moe Shrevnitz's function in the novels. "As regards Harry Vincent," he explained, "we are not using the character of Moe Shrevnitz. We will place a line in the first episode stating that Harry is filling in for Shrevnitz, due to his illness." Another note stated: "As regards Burbank, we are changing this character, so it will be Richards playing the role of the manservant." Both characters were regulars in the pulp yarns, but neither turned up in the Columbia chapter play, suggesting that cost-conscious Darmour had second thoughts about including them after script revisions had been made. Other changes requested by Street & Smith including changing the screenwriters' Metropolitan Club to the Cobalt Club and making Cranston an independent research scientist with his own lab, rather than an employee of Stanford Marshall, one of the industrialists targeted by the Black Tiger.

Nonetheless, The Shadow fared better in his one and only chapter play than many characters adapted from other media. Spy Smasher, for example, gained a twin brother. Blackhawk lost two of his subordinates. And Captain Marvel suffered the ignominious loss of his powers in the final chapter of *his* serial. All things considered, the Master of Darkness could have done a lot worse.

Victor Jory deserves the lion's share of credit for the serial's effectiveness. His features don't exactly match those described by Gibson as belonging to Cranston, but they come pretty close. He projects confidence and authority in the role, and it's hard not to appreciate his approximation of The Shadow's trademark laugh. "Oh, I *had* to get that right," Jory recalled in 1980. "Everybody knew that laugh, even people who didn't listen to the radio show every Sunday afternoon. It was a thing, you know, kind of like a catch phrase. 'The Shadow knows' was a popular saying. Comedians on the radio joked about it. So I practiced that chuckle until I felt I had it right. You wanted it to give the kids goose bumps; that was the idea."

James W. Horne's deliberately arch directorial style makes it difficult for today's viewers to appreciate *The Shadow*, which Columbia TriStar Home Video released on VHS cassettes in 1997. The combination of overacting, undercranking, and what film historian William K. Everson called "moments of truly lunatic comedy involving the villains" irritates serial buffs used to the more serious chapter plays of other studios. (Hard-core devotees take particular umbrage at a scene in which one of the Tiger's henchmen implores another, "Tell me the story of Red Riding Hood again. I *like* that one.") But Everson, in his introduction to Alan G. Barbour's 1970 history of serials, *Days of Thrills and Adventure*, probably got it right: "[Horne] was too good a director, too much a past master of great silent and sound comedy, not to know precisely what he was doing. Undoubtedly he reasoned that to play the scripts straight, with their stereotyped stories and meager budgets, could only result in serials spectacular inferior to the competitive ones issued by Republic and Universal. Playing them for comedy didn't make them better, but it did keep them lively, distinctive, and different."

Actually, of the ten Columbia chapter plays James Horne made for producer Larry Darmour before dying in 1942, *The Shadow* contains the fewest cringeworthy moments of campy humor. Unlike *The Green Archer* (1940) and *The Iron Claw* (1941), to name just two, the serial generally preserves its main character's dignity. It surely could have been more faithful to the source material, but *The Shadow* has a lot more going for it than the character's other big-screen incarnations: the two Rod La Rocques, the three 1946 Kane Richmonds produced by Monogram, and the awful 1959 compilation of busted Shadow TV pilots starring Richard Derr.

In his 1980 interview with me, Victor Jory stated: "I've been in a lot of good films and worked with many of the best stars, writers and directors in the business. But, you know, I'd have to say that more people know me from *The Shadow* than anything else I've done. I still get fan mail mentioning it. Here [at the Charlotte Western Film Fair] I've probably had a dozen people come up to me and ask me to do the laugh. It's the damnedest thing."

The Shadow was followed by three more 1940 Columbia serials adapted from properties created for other media: *Terry and the Pirates* (based on Milton Caniff's popular comic strip), *Deadwood Dick* (updating a venerable character of late-19th century dime novels), and *The Green Archer* (from Edgar Wallace's celebrated mystery novel, previously turned into a wildly successful serial by Pathé in 1925). If one is to believe exhibitor reports published in the trade journal *Motion Picture Herald*, the Shadow serial was the most popular of the quartet. But apparently not so much as to induce Columbia to produce a sequel, especially since the contract with Street & Smith called for a bump in the licensing fee to $8500 should the studio want to revisit the character.

It still remains to be seen whether Hollywood will ever produce a Shadow movie that does full justice to the pulp-magazine version of the character as developed by Walter B. Gibson so long ago. For several years now it's been rumored that another feature film was being developed. Perhaps there's a future director out there, reading Anthony Tollin's Sanctum Books reprints and envisioning a faithful Shadow screen story as I write these words.

Drums of Fu Manchu
(1940, Republic Pictures)
by Daniel J. Neyer

In reviewing *Drums of Fu Manchu*, I face the same problem that a movie critic might face reviewing, say, John Ford's *Stagecoach*. *Drums* is such a classic of the form that anything I can say about it will most probably sound just like the reviews of this chapter play by almost every other serial aficionado I know—it will mainly consist of lavish praise. But some serials deserve lavish praise, and *Drums of Fu Manchu* is one of them.

This 1940 Republic Pictures chapter play begins with British secret service agent Sir Denis Nayland Smith (William Royle) being pursued through the rainy streets of San Francisco by mysterious, skulking figures (the "dacoit" henchmen of Doctor Fu Manchu, as we learn later). He arrives at the home of his friend Dr. Petrie (Olaf Hytten) just as one of the sinister henchmen hurls a lethal-looking knife in his direction. Smith dodges the dagger and explains to the astonished Petrie that he has just returned from Asia, where, disguised as a "holy man" among the hill tribes, he has discovered that his old enemy, the insidious Doctor Fu Manchu, plots to lead the tribes in revolt against British occupiers and make himself tyrant of all Asia. All the evil Doctor needs to rally the natives and unite them in a bloody sweep to victory is the Lost Scepter of Genghis Khan—which, once obtained by the Doctor, will enable him to claim that he is the heir of the great conqueror and thus win the loyalty of the disparate tribes.

At this point we are introduced to Fu Manchu himself (Henry Brandon), as he meets with the council of the Si-Fan, a secret order of Eastern thieves and cutthroats. The Doctor plots to obtain the Dalai Plaque, an ancient Asian relic that holds a secret key to the location of Genghis Khan's tomb. As part of his plan to obtain the plaque, Fu Manchu kidnaps its current owners, Dr. James Parker (George Cleveland) and Professor Edward Randolph (Tom Chatterton), which brings Dr. Parker's son Allan (Robert Kellard) into the fight. Smith, Petrie, and young Parker manage to rescue Randolph from Fu Manchu, but Allan's father is killed by one of Fu Manchu's men in the struggle.

From that point on, it falls to Smith and Allan, with help from Petrie, Randolph, and Randolph's daughter Mary (Luana Walters) to block Fu Manchu's attempts to obtain the various clues he needs to discover the lost tomb of Genghis Khan. Since Fu Manchu possesses a sinister array of fiendish weapons, among them his faithful Dacoits, murderous lobotomized slaves who obey his every word, and is aided by his sly daughter Fah Lo Suee (Gloria Franklin), our heroes have their work cut out for them.

The Doctor obtains the Dalai Scroll, translation of which directs him to the Kardac Segment, a fragment of the stone tomb that will identify its bearer as a follower of the great Khan. Smith, Parker, and their friends pursue the Si-Fan's leader to Asia, where they fight against his machinations—as the clock ticks slowly towards the hour of the prophesized uprising that will fulfill Fu Manchu's mad dreams of power. . . .

Drums of Fu Manchu was the great William Witney's favorite among all the serials he directed, and the added care and interest he, his co-director John English, producer Hiram Brown Jr., and the screenwriters took with it is evident in every episode. The whole chapter play is admirably faithful—in small details as well as big ones—to the general flavor of Sax Rohmer's books. Fu Manchu's fiendish torture device, "The Seven Gates to Paradise," is based directly on the "Six Gates of Joyful Wisdom" from the book *The Return of Doctor Fu Manchu*, as one example. The poisonous lizard that is attracted to Smith's pillow by a sprinkled perfume, the noose a Dacoit uses to strangle a policeman from a rooftop, Smith's admission in Chapter Three that Fu Manchu never fails to keep his word—all of these ideas are taken in whole or part from various Rohmer books.

These borrowings are complemented by a pervading atmosphere of ominous menace, achieved through some use of close-ups, lighting, and other cinematic tricks. The scene in Chapter Five, in which Smith tries to convince crotchety and reclusive scientist Ezra Howard (John Dilson) that Fu Manchu is after Howard's Kardac Segment, as Fu Manchu and his minions silently sneak up on the eccentric's isolated house during a raging thunderstorm, is perhaps the highlight of the serial in terms of sheer Rohmer-like eeriness. A sequence in the same chapter, with Fu Manchu's Dacoits posing as wax dummies in a museum right under the noses of the curator and Allan Parker, is also highly suspenseful, and Fu Manchu's attempted brain surgery on Smith in Chapter Fourteen is so creepily filmed that it almost seems to have been taken out of a Universal horror film.

A frequent observation about *Drums of Fu Manchu*, made by its majority of fans and the minority who dislike it, is that it stints on the elaborately staged fistfights that were the trademark of Republic's serials. This, I find, is an exaggeration, but the fact that this impression is left means that Witney and English apparently succeeded in making this serial "different" in flavor from their usual action fests. The serial contains a generous helping of fisticuffs handled with typical Republic professionalism and feature some great acrobatics from Dave Sharpe, who doubles Robert Kellard. The battle in Chapter Seven between Sharpe and Duke Green (doubling villain George Pembroke) is particularly good. But one never gets the feeling that the plot of *Drums of Fu Manchu* is only a framework on which to hang fistic battles, but rather that the fights are organic to the overall plot; plot development never stands still in order to let the heroes and villains slug it out for five minutes at a time, as in some Republic chapter plays. The tussles are often brief.

Another favorite comment by reviewers of *Drums of Fu Manchu* is that it "goes downhill" in the second half, when the scene of conflict relocates to Asia. Again, I really can't go along with this. It's the serial's change of location, I think, that helps give it a more exotic flavor; the shift of the action from San Francisco to the Asian city of Branapuhr to the nearby British fort to the untamed hill country allows for interesting variety in the serial, and keeps it from seeming repetitive. The sequences set in the Temple of the Sun and in the tomb of Genghis Khan are fully as intriguing as anything in the first half, and, of course, the above-mentioned brain-surgery scene takes place in the "weaker" second half as well.

It's true that the actual geographic location of Branapuhr seems a sort of Fantasyland, with Afghanistan-like place names and Caucasian natives, some of whom dress like Persian/Afghan North Indians but others of whom dress like Mongols or Tartars. The tribesmen also talk like Moslems (mentioning Holy Years, Holy Men, etc.), yet worship Genghis Khan as though he were a religious rather than secular figure. But who cares about this kind of thing in a serial? In any case, the setting and native costuming allows Republic to use stock footage from their 1938 adventure film *Storm Over Bengal*. The borrowed scenes from *Storm* figure in two chapter endings and as part of the last-chapter battle sequence. Being cleverly blended, this footage gives the serial more of a larger scope than usual at Republic, and really makes Fu Manchu's uprising seem like more than just two or three tribesmen shooting at two or three soldiers from behind a rock.

While some of the cliffhanger endings are standard Republic issue—plane crashes, train crashes, car crashes, all handled in miniature by the studio's resident special-effects wizards, Howard and Theodore Lydecker—others are as unique as other aspects of the serial. My favorite is the Chapter Two climax, in which Allan Parker is dropped through a trap door into a pool containing a man-eating octopus that has already claimed one victim. The Chapter Four sequence in which Parker is subjected to a pit-and-the-pendulum style treatment is also memorable (Fu Manchu even references the famous Poe story, a nice and unusually literate touch for a serial). Some of the perils occurring mid-chapter are also worthy of mention, and serve to illustrate the writers' big stock of imagination in these Golden Days of Republic. The poisonous lizard scene is one example of this, as is the arrow trap that guards the tomb of Genghis Khan, and another arrow trap that Fu Manchu sets for Smith and Parker in Chapter Four.

The serial's performers are all up to the mark set by the directors and writers. Henry Brandon is wonderful as Fu Manchu, giving the character a sibilant, slightly high-pitched voice, devoid of accent except for the occasional odd inflection (which, incidentally, is quite close to the way Fu's voice is described in the Rohmer novels). Brandon also gives the character an air of slightly mocking condescension towards his enemies, tempered with a steely, white-hot rage that flares up when his plans are thwarted. His "devil doctor" is brave and always keeps his word, another trait shared with the printed-page character. Brandon even imitates Fu Manchu's "cat-like yet awkward gait," hunching his shoulders in the fashion described by Rohmer, leading me to believe the actor must have read the books or at least been coached by Witney or English on such points.

William Royle's Sir Denis Nayland Smith (his first name is only mentioned once in the serial, actually) is not the jumpy, sharp-tongued, nervous-energy-filled character of Rohmer's books; he's more avuncular and good-natured. One can understand why this change was made, since a depiction of Smith as a crank in a serial, with no spare time to show the kindly side of his personality as it is shown in the books, would probably have made the character seem unlikable. Royle is very good in his part, conveying unflappable British determination and considerable sleuthing ability. His British accent is letter-perfect, and amazing when you consider that he was born in Rochester, New York. Royle, a great heavy in serials like

Flaming Frontiers and *Hawk of the Wilderness*, is probably the last person I would have thought of to play Sir Denis Nayland Smith, but we owe a debt of gratitude to whoever came up with this offbeat but effective casting.

It was nice to have my faith in Robert Kellard's talent restored after suffering through his performance in *Perils of the Royal Mounted*, a mediocre 1942 Columbia serial; in *Drums of Fu Manchu*, he makes a fine action hero. He's convincingly tough and courageous, and, what's more, delivers his dialogue with energy and intelligence, as if he actually knows what he's saying—a talent not shared by all serial heroes. The sequence at the beginning of Chapter Fifteen, in which he bluffs Fu Manchu into releasing Smith by pretending that a bottle of quinine is really a bottle of nitroglycerin, could easily have come off as unbelievable but is carried off successfully by Kellard's firm and decisive delivery: You don't blame Fu Manchu at all for falling for Allan's bluff.

These three men—Brandon, Royle, and Kellard—largely carry the serial, and do a fine job of it. The lovely Luana Walters has very little to do as the heroine except participate in three cliffhanger endings. Olaf Hytten doesn't fare much better as Doctor Petrie; he only has about a half-dozen lines throughout the entire serial. Gloria Franklin, as Fu Manchu's daughter Fah Lo Suee, has a bigger part, and does pretty well with it, coming off as almost as slick and fiendish as her father. John Merton is positively scary as the mute, hulking Loki, Fu Manchu's lead Dacoit; he never says a word, and his sinister presence is felt throughout the serial. The other Dacoits (played by stuntmen Augie Gomez, Joe Yrigoyen, Duke Green, Jimmy Fawcett, Duke Taylor, and Ken Terrell, or by all-purpose actors like Alan Gregg, Al Taylor, or Budd Buster) also have a certain sinister presence to them, as they sneak silently about, obeying their master's orders and tossing their deadly knives into any number of victims. The Dacoits' robot-like nature helps to make Fu Manchu's organization seem more formidable, as the Dacoits seem far less human—and therefore less fallible—than the typical Republic pack of "action heavies."

The supporting cast is full of professional character actors—which is unusual for Republic; the studio generally filled bit roles with their many stuntmen—and as a result we get some interesting little character vignettes. Evan Thomas is very good as the dignified Major Carleton, commander of Fort Branapuhr, while Phillip Ahn is memorable as the cultured and heroic Doctor Chang. Tom Chatterton gives his Doctor Randolph character a scholarly, endearingly absent-minded personality, and George Cleveland is very good in his brief turn as the feisty Professor Parker. John Dilson is most amusing and rather frustrating—in his stubborn refusal to believe what Smith tells him—as Ezra Howard, and John Picorri turns in a brief but interesting performance as a villainous plastic surgeon. Hindu actor Lal Chand Mehra is the high priest at the temple of Kardac, and George Pembroke does an excellent turn as the nasty, sneeringly cold-blooded Crawford, English member of Fu Manchu's Si-Fan. Pembroke does a most memorable death scene in Chapter Eight; his facial expressions of fear and sheer terror as he crashes to his death in a booby-trapped plane are most impressive. That great bug-eyed loony of a character actor, Dwight Frye, is wasted as a museum curator but squeezes every ounce of juice out of his limited part. Frye would have been better suited for the part of Doctor Humphrey, a scientist who is hypnotized into becoming a stooge of Fu Manchu's and briefly goes insane as he hears the pounding of the devil doctor's drums inside his brain. Similarly, Wheaton Chambers, who plays Humphrey, would probably have been better as the museum curator, as he's a bit mild-mannered in a part that calls for more over-the-top delivery. John Bagni and Paul Marion play non-Dacoit henchmen of Fu Manchu's, and Norman Nesbitt's voice is heard as a radio announcer murdered by Fu Manchu.

I shall conclude by giving a big hand for Witney, English, producer Hiram S. Brown Jr., and writers Franklin Adreon, Morgan Cox, Ronald Davidson, Norman S. Hall, Barney A. Sarecky, and Sol Shor. I can't neglect to mention Cy Feuer's music score, which, using an Oriental motif, provides perfect accompaniment to the serial's action, in creepy moment or during action scenes. *Drums of Fu Manchu* is a masterful chapter play, and one that William Witney certainly had a right to be proud of.

Daredevils of the West
(1943, Republic Pictures)
by Ed Hulse

Decades ago, when geographically and chronologically disparate film buffs and collectors coalesced to form what today is known as organized serial fandom, group conversations frequently revolved around the fabled "lost" chapter plays: those cliffhanging classics of the Thirties and Forties that had not seen the light of a projector lamp since their theatrical playoffs many years before.

Most of these long-unseen jewels were never released to television or licensed for non-theatrical exhibition due to underlying copyright issues relating to characters adapted from other media, such as the Lone Ranger, the Green Hornet, Jungle Jim, Red Ryder, Secret Agent X-9, and King of the Royal Mounted. In some cases, the respective rights holders had subsequently licensed their valuable properties to different studios and producers. In others, the characters in question—no longer thought to be commercially viable—languished in cinematic limbo, their shadow images eventually fading from sight and memory both.

One particularly tantalizing film, however, evaded serial fans for reasons that remain unknown even today, nearly seven decades after it was made and released. *Daredevils of the West*, a 12-chapter opus produced by Republic Pictures in 1943, didn't have any rights issues; its characters, settings, and situations were dreamed up by the company's screenwriters. In 1951, when the independent studio began marketing to a new medium via its Hollywood Television Service subsidiary, most of the serials not built around licensed characters were made available in reconfigured versions consisting of six half-hour episodes. *Daredevils*, a perfect candidate for such treatment, was nowhere to be found in this group.

What made the omission especially puzzling was that the serial's leading man, Allan Lane, enjoyed tremendous popularity as the star of Republic-made Western feature films geared for the Saturday-matinee market. As "Rocky" Lane, he routinely rated high on exhibitors' lists of the top ten movie cowboys. It seems odd that Republic missed such an obvious bet: *Daredevils of the West* would undoubtedly have been successful in TV syndication.

Even more frustrating to chapter-play aficionados too young to have seen *Daredevils* during its 1943 theatrical run were the appraisals of older fans who had been more fortunate. The dean of the first-generation serial buffs, Alan G. Barbour, lavished praise on *Daredevils* in his books *Days of Thrills and Adventure* (New York: The Macmillan Company, 1970) and *Cliffhanger* (Secaucus, NJ: The Citadel Press, 1977), calling it "a perfect serial" and "the most action-packed of all Republic's Western serial adventures." Alan had seen *Daredevils of the West* as a breathless 11-year-old boy in Oakland, CA's Broadway Theatre, and it so impressed him that, 30 years later, he could still remember specific sequences from individual episodes. His recollections alternately enthralled and frustrated younger devotees convinced that this legendary Western would never be screened again.

The twenty-ninth of Republic's 66 serials, *Daredevils of the West* was the sixth produced by William J. O'Sullivan, a dapper Irishman who has never been recognized for his contributions to that exacting cinematic form known as the chapter play. It's not just coincidence that, under his stewardship, the company's episodic epics settled into the fast-action format for which they are best remembered. His serials ushered in the era of the lengthy, set-demolishing fistfight and the reliance on exploding miniatures (painstakingly crafted by special-effects wizards Howard and Theodore Lydecker) for chapter-ending thrills. He refined a long-established but malleable formula, compressing it as one would compress a lump of coal into a diamond—a hard, smooth, glittering thing, perfect in its own way but limited in functionality. Before O'Sullivan assumed control of Republic's serial unit in 1941, the company's chapter-play producers sought, and generally obtained, variety in the scope and style of their to-be-continued thrillers. They employed ingenious methods to imbue serials with production values that belied their relatively meager budgets. They pushed writers to devise inventive cliffhangers and staged major sequences in unusual real-life locations—gas plants, electric plants, brick factories, lumber yards, and the like. They took the form seriously and never allowed any hint of condescension to creep into the final product.

O'Sullivan took the unit on location when scripts demanded, but on his watch Republic serials increasingly were made on studio sound stages and around the back lot. The chapter endings became repetitious, their resolutions predictable: sprint out of the warehouse before it blows up, jump from the speeding car before it plunges over the cliff, wake up and roll away before the heavy object pins your unconscious form to the floor. The perils always looked real, thanks to careful staging, daring stunt work, and skillful editing, but after a while they only evoked feelings of *déjà vu*.

Perhaps I quibble. It can be argued that the effectiveness of any chapter play depends upon the willingness of its viewers—young or old—to suspend disbelief and accept the dubious proposition that the world being portrayed on screen functions not according to natural law, but to that vague, amorphous system of governance known to the form's True Believers as "serial logic." On that basis, O'Sullivan's ten thrillers—which include *Dick Tracy vs. Crime Inc.*, *Spy Smasher*, *Perils of Nyoka*, *King of the Mounties*, *G-Men vs. the Black Dragon*, *Secret Service in Darkest Africa*, *The Masked Marvel*, *Captain America*, and *The Tiger Woman*, in addition to *Daredevils of the West*—must be judged wildly and joyously successful. They were extremely popular with the predominantly youthful audiences for which they were originally intended, and they have remained popular with fans who discovered them later via TV exposure and home-video availability.

Daredevils was scheduled for production during the 1942-43 theatrical season. (At that time, movie seasons began around Labor Day and continued through the late spring.) It was touted as a Western serial with a historical theme; early promotional pieces carried the legend, "Their bravery welded America together!" Originally Republic may have intended to imbue this serial with the flavor of such frontier epics as *The Iron Horse* or *Union Pacific*, but instead of chronicling the construction of the transcontinental railroad, *Daredevils* dealt with the expansion of a stagecoach line and the building of a road traversing the lawless Comanche Strip.

O'Sullivan's crack writing team—Ronald Davidson, Basil Dickey, William Lively, Joseph O'Donnell, and Joseph Poland, veteran serial scribes all—was instructed to cram the planned 12 episodes with action while avoiding the interpolation of sequences whose realization would call for extravagant expenditures. Production costs were escalating, and the serials immediately preceding *Daredevils* on the 1942-43 slate had gone considerably over budget. Davidson and his fellow scenarists devised a straightforward plot devoid of any mystery element or narrative complexity. They came up with simple situations linking one action sequence to the next—chases followed by fights followed by shootouts, and so forth.

Calculating production costs based on the first-draft "estimating" script prepared especially for that purpose, O'Sullivan and the front-office bean counters arrived at a projected budget of $140,000—quite a modest sum for a serial whose total running time would exceed three hours, and less than the major studios were spending on 70-minute "B" pictures.

In the interest of giving the serial some production value that would suggest a more expensive film, O'Sullivan was allowed to bring his cast and crew up to Lone Pine for location shooting. The picturesque Alabama Hills, with the High Sierras for background, would make a fine backdrop for chase scenes and pitched battles between good guys and bad guys. Republic relied heavily on Iverson's Ranch for exterior work on its Westerns and serials. So did other studios. As a result, that San Fernando Valley property had become overly familiar to audiences. Shooting at Lone Pine would be a welcome change of pace; Republic hadn't used the location in a serial since late 1937, when chapter-play directors William Witney and John English filmed most of the exteriors for *The Lone Ranger*, released early the following year.

Witney, who had helmed all the O'Sullivan-produced serials to date, had just entered the Marine Corps and would be gone for the duration of World War II. English had quit making chapter plays in 1941 after completing *Dick Tracy vs. Crime Inc.* and was cranking out "B" Westerns and melodramas when O'Sullivan had him temporarily reassigned to the serial unit. Since he had already worked in Lone Pine, English was the logical choice to direct *Daredevils of the West*.

The leading roles were given to Allan Lane, who had previously starred in two Republic serials based on Zane Grey's *King of the Royal Mounted*, and Kay Aldridge, who had recently assayed the title role in *Perils of Nyoka*, one of the studio's most fondly remembered chapter plays. As a freelance actor, Lane hadn't been getting much work. Nor had Aldridge, a former model and 20th Century-Fox contract player. But they rated high with serial audiences and, as it turned out, made an attractive screen team—so much so that, in promoting *Daredevils*, Republic referred to them as "their majesties, the King and Queen of serials."

Villain roles went to accomplished character actors. Former silent-screen star Robert Frazer and perennial Western heavy Ted Adams played the master schemers determined to sabotage the stagecoach line. Doing their dirty work were William Haade, a native New Yorker normally seen as a gangster or some other urban dweller, and George J. Lewis, one-time serial star and juvenile leading man of the late silent era. Rounding out the principal players were Eddie Acuff, a breezy sidekick type, and sagebrush stalwart Budd Buster, cast as an old-time frontiersman.

The larger supporting parts went to such veteran actors as Kenneth Harlan, Rex Lease, Edmund Cobb, and Herbert Rawlinson—each of whom, by the way, was a former serial star. Many of the bit roles were taken by members of Republic's stunt crew, headed by Tom Steele, who doubled for Lane. Duke Green, Ken Terrell, Eddie Parker, Allen Pomeroy, Duke Taylor, and the Yrigoyen brothers, Joe and Bill, made multiple on-screen appearances over the course of the 12 chapters. Even Thelma "Babe" DeFreest, Aldridge's double, was pressed into service as an extra.

Principal photography got underway on January 9, 1943. Producer O'Sullivan had worked closely with Republic's various department heads to outfit the production as handsomely as possible while remaining within the confines of a tight budget. As they typically did, the writers crafted each individual episode economically, setting major sequences in and around the studio. Canyon City, a bustling frontier town, was represented by Western Street, the back-lot stretch most frequently employed in horse-opera production. Standing in for Red Gulch, the lawless community to which the heavies frequently retreated, was the assortment of rustic houses and cabins known as Brazos Street (constructed for the 1939 Sam Houston biopic, *Man of Conquest*). An entire sound stage was outfitted to resemble a massive distillery, which would be the scene of a lengthy fistfight and a memorable cliffhanger ending. The familiar ranch house and barn built for a 1940 Gene Autry starrer, *Melody Ranch*, figured prominently in the thrilling conclusion of Chapter Ten. The modular network of man-made caves and tunnels, which stood at the northernmost end of the back lot, underwent reconfiguring to provide settings for several major sequences.

Serial makers naturally preferred to stage elaborate action scenes in the controlled environment of a studio lot, where contingencies could be anticipated and more easily planned for. But even the most rigorous preparations sometimes weren't sufficient. In a 1989 interview, stunt ramrod Tom Steele recalled that a jailhouse fire, shot for the Chapter Two climax, blazed faster than expected and very nearly trapped him when it got out of control.

The location phase of production offered plenty of logistical challenges, but what bothered cast and crew most was the weather. Reminiscing about *Daredevils of the West* in a 1979 interview with this writer, Kay Aldridge said of her sojourn in Lone Pine: "It was beautiful country but, Lord, was it *cold*! To get a full day's shooting in, you see, we had to get up very early in the morning—while it was still dark—and be out in the hills ready to go when the sun came up over the mountains.

"My costume included a light cotton blouse and sleeveless fringed vest, but that wasn't nearly enough up there in January! I can still remember being outside, shivering, all bundled up in a coat, and then having Jack [English] put me on a stagecoach or a horse or something, and then shoot the scene. Well, just as soon as he said 'cut,' I would jump off the wagon or whatever and wrap myself up in that coat again. Sometimes I would ruin the take because my teeth were chattering so, I could hardly get my lines out. Of course, it would warm up during the day as the sun got higher in the sky, but, oh, those mornings! I remember some of the cowboys, they would disappear around the far side of one of those big rocks, and then come back a minute later wiping their mouths. I think they had a little something in some flasks to make them warm, you know?"

On screen there was scant evidence to suggest that the high-desert country wasn't fiery hot. Keen-eyed viewers might see snowcaps on some Sierra peaks far in the background, but otherwise the winter weather remained undetectable. And, of course, midday warming took enough chill out of the air to enable actors to deliver their lines without the frosty breath that signaled cool temperatures.

Climatic challenges didn't hinder the crew from getting spectacular scenic effects. Thanks to Jack English's direction, *Daredevils of the West* boasted some of the most exciting outdoor action ever lensed for a Republic serial. Chapter One gets the chapter play off to a rousing start with an eight-minute *tour de force* that begins with a wild wagon chase, continues with a lengthy shootout at the stagecoach line's road camp, and culminates in a pitched hand-to-hand battle between the heroes and their Indian attackers.

This breathtaking sequence contains a shot that, to the best of this fan's knowledge, is unique in serial history. It begins as a "running insert" that has Republic's camera car racing along the speeding wagon containing stunters Bill Yrigoyen and Babe DeFreest (doubling Eddie Acuff and Kay Aldridge, respectively). We can see the girl in the back of the wagon, firing at unseen pursuers. The camera car pulls ahead, allowing us a view of Indians galloping full tilt and gaining rapidly on the pair. Then the car zooms forward and cuts across the road *directly in front of the wagon*, while the camera swivels to face the onrushing team, which appears to be only a few feet behind. One can only imagine how thrilling this shot must have seemed to howling Saturday-matinee audiences, viewing it on a 40-foot theater screen.

That initial stanza ends with another, slightly less lengthy chase, this time involving an explosives-laden stagecoach on which Aldridge's character is a prisoner. Lane's character, in hot pursuit, manages to shoot the driver from his perch but apparently fails to catch the out-of-control stage before it careens into a mountainside and explodes. Crystal-clear photography, expert stunt work, and mathematically precise editing make this sequence particularly memorable.

Despite O'Sullivan's careful planning, *Daredevils* turned out to be a more expensive proposition than originally envisioned. English finished the final scene on February 13, by which time the serial had been in production for six weeks, more than a week longer than estimated. Its negative cost ended up being $167,000, nearly 20 percent over budget.

Released on May 1, 1943, *Daredevils of the West* opened to favorable if unenthusiastic reviews. Critics for the movie-industry trade journals noted that the surfeit of action would likely make it a favorite of regular serial attendees but lamented the chapter play's paucity of plot. More than one mentioned that *Daredevils* barely had enough story for one of Republic's six-reel "B" Westerns. It was a fair criticism.

Chapter One, "Valley of Death," finds Canyon City in the 1880s bustling with activity. Having been awarded a grant from the Federal Franchise Commission to expand his stagecoach line, Ezra Foster (Charles Miller), is hustling to complete a new road through the lawless Comanche Strip so that he can make the regular runs for which his contract calls. Failure to do so by the deadline will result in a forfeit of the franchise. Foster has capable assistants in his daughter, June (Kay Aldridge), and his foreman, Red Kelly (Eddie Acuff).

Unbeknownst to the Fosters, their supposed friend, local cattle baron Martin Dexter (Robert Frazer), wants them to fail. He is intent on owning the 500,000 acres that will be up for grabs if the stage line loses its franchise. To this end he conspires with lawyer Silas Higby (Ted Adams) and henchmen Ward (William Haade) and Turner (George J. Lewis), who hire renegade Indians to attack the road crew. Foster loses his life during one such raid despite assistance from U. S. Cavalry Captain Duke Cameron, soon detailed to Canyon City to work undercover, helping June and Red complete the road while trying to find out who is behind the outrages.

The opening episode draws to a close with the aforementioned chase and explosion, which results from Duke's attempt to recover stolen payroll money. Subsequent chapters revolve around the efforts of the Foster faction to remove obstacles tossed in their way by the Dexter faction. Finally, the crooked financier and his cronies are revealed as malefactors and killed off. Duke's last-minute efforts enable June and Red to complete their trial run along the finished road, meeting the deadline with barely a second to spare.

Daredevils made the rounds of the nation's movie theaters throughout the remainder of 1943 and most of 1944. There's no evidence to suggest that it was any less profitable than the other Republic serials of the period, yet it disappeared from view and remained unseen for decades. Well, mostly unseen: Chunks of it were appropriated for use as stock footage in Republic's 1949 serial, *Ghost of Zorro*.

In the mid-Seventies, record producer Snuff Garrett founded the Nostalgia Merchant to market 16mm prints of classic Westerns and serials he licensed from Republic. *Daredevils of the West* was high on the list of films he planned to offer, but an extensive search of Republic's vaults failed to yield a complete print. Ultimately, Garrett made available a brace of chapters, Two and Five. He struck prints of Four and Twelve but decided against offering them. Word spread like wildfire through serial fandom: *Daredevils* would remain a lost serial.

Further investigation revealed the fact that in 1946, Republic Pictures sold a 35mm negative (picture only) to William Boyd, who had just acquired the rights to Hopalong Cassidy, the character he introduced to the screen a decade earlier in films produced by Harry "Pop" Sherman for distribution by Paramount. Typecast as Hoppy, Boyd decided to make his own Cassidy films after Sherman lost interest. He planned to shoot most series entries in Lone Pine, and presumably thought that *Daredevils* would provide reels of stock footage he could shoehorn into the new Hoppy Westerns to give them added production value. Strangely, he never used so much as a single frame from the serial in any of the 12 feature films he produced over the next two years.

A successor-in-interest to the Hopalong Cassidy character unearthed the *Daredevils* negative some years ago while inspecting his film holdings. He generously made available a mute print of Chapter One to the Lone Pine Film Festival, which screened it in 1999.

It was long assumed that Illinois advertising executive Jack Mathis, official chronicler of all things Republic, owned a complete print of *Daredevils of the West*. In the early Seventies he had covered it in his series of "Cliffhanger Ending and Escape Pictorial" booklets, reproducing frames from all 11 chapter endings. But Mathis resisted entreaties from serial fans to make *Daredevils* available for screening or purchase. After Jack's death in 2005, his entire collection of Republic memorabilia—including 16mm prints of many of the studio's rarest films, which he acquired only after spending considerable time and expense—was donated to Brigham Young University in Provo, Utah. Its preservation has been championed by BYU's Professor of American Studies, James D'Arc, who arranged to screen *Daredevils* in 2008 at the annual meeting of a serial-fan group. Those aficionados immediately proclaimed it one of the best sound-era chapter plays ever made.

The next year, attendees of the Lone Pine Film Festival had the opportunity to render their own judgments: D'Arc graciously consented to let the serial be screened where it was made, more than 65 years before. The *Daredevils* had finally come home. And that's where I caught up with the serial.

Daredevils of the West is indisputably the most action-packed chapter play Republic ever produced. It brims with Indian attacks, lethal shootouts, breathtaking leaps, Cossack-like riding, and set-leveling brawls. If anything, there's *too* much action. The storyline is anemic, the subplots little more than narrative pegs on which to hang fights and chases. The first three episodes—consuming more than an hour of footage—revolve solely around the theft and recovery of the Foster payroll money. Chapters Four or Five are animated by the theft and recovery of horses rented from Dexter to help with road grading. The next two installments concern the theft and recovery of guns needed to arm a mounted patrol. Indian incitement and the arrival of the Territorial Commissioner carry the plot into Chapter Ten, the end of which finds Duke exposing Higby as one of the villains. The final two episodes see Dexter unmasked as the chief conspirator and Duke back in uniform, leading a cavalry detail to protect June and Red while they make the trial run on which the continuance of their franchise depends.

Some of the cliffhanger endings are unusual. Chapter Five climaxes with a lengthy fight in the Red Gulch distillery and June's immersion in an alcohol vat that catches fire at the installment's fade-out. In Chapter Eight, vengeful Indians subject June and Red to torture by tying them back to back and dumping them in a supply wagon, under which they light a fire while the helpless victims writhe in terror. But lazy scripting results in stock situations being repeated promiscuously: Explosions figure in more than half the episodes, either in the middle or at the end, and nearly every time one faction gets the drop on the other, somebody moves in too close and gets the gun knocked out of his hand, precipitating a donnybrook. Of course, this sort of thing is common in serials—especially Republic serials—and not to be taken seriously. But *Daredevils* really pushes its luck, occasionally dipping a toe into the waters of self-parody but withdrawing it quickly and moving to drier ground.

The stars are major assets, although Lane is typically wooden. (Years later, Aldridge called him "the most conceited man I ever worked with" and confessed that she was relived when the serial wrapped.) His career was just getting underway; following his fourth and last serial, *The Tiger Woman* (1944), Lane won his own series of "B" Westerns, spending a year as Red Ryder before being rechristened "Rocky" Lane. He made several dozen low-budget horse operas between 1947 and 1953, alienating so many people that, his reputation in tatters, he found precious little work after being dropped by Republic. He finished his career, rather ignominiously, as the voice of Mr. Ed.

Kay Aldridge was nearly cast as the eponymous heroine of *Tiger Woman*, but Republic spared her the aggravation of working with Lane again and shunted her into *Haunted Harbor*, the next serial on the studio's 1944 schedule. After completing that episodic opus she took roles in two quickies for PRC, got married, and exited the picture business for good. In the late 1970s, very much aware of her cult status, a still youthful-looking Aldridge had a duplicate of her Nyoka costume made and wore it during personal appearances at film-fan conventions, much to the delight of attendees.

The Adventures of Smilin' Jack
(1943, Universal Pictures)
by Ed Hulse

One of the pioneering producers of serial films, Universal Pictures released chapter plays in a steady stream from 1914 to 1946, when the newly reorganized company—now called Universal-International—disbanded the "B" picture and serial units in a move to upgrade its product and secure better bookings from the major theater chains. Although Universal had supplied exhibitors with low-budget films for most of its existence, the market for such product was beginning to dwindle and the company's owners decided to make a dramatic break with the past by ceasing production of the cheap Westerns, musicals, melodramas, and serials that had been the backbone of its yearly schedule for several decades.

Actually, the chapter play had been losing favor with audiences for many years. Throughout the sound era, serials were primarily relegated to Saturday-afternoon programs geared toward youthful moviegoers. Occasionally, episodic epics featuring popular characters from other media—such as Flash Gordon, Dick Tracy, and the Lone Ranger—played the better picture houses in weekday engagements, but for the most part chapter plays remained a staple of the Saturday matinee. During the mid Thirties, Universal maintained its competitive edge over other serial producers by licensing screen rights to a slew of popular comic-strip characters; bringing four-color favorites to the big screen guaranteed a ready-made audience. Later in the decade, Republic Pictures achieved market dominance by turning out superior serials, both with and without previously established characters.

By the Forties, with Columbia Pictures Corporation also getting more aggressive about marketing serials, Universal decided to jettison its approach to chapter-play production—which, with only minor and occasional variation—it had employed since the silent era. The influence of veteran producer Henry MacRae, whose involvement with Universal serials dated back to 1916's *Liberty, a Daughter of the U. S. A.*, gradually diminished as the front office demanded changes in the way chapter plays were conceived and produced. With film-rental income from serials more or less fixed at a predictable level, monetary outlays (which had been creeping up) couldn't be increased. Anything that could be done to make Universal's serials distinctive, while remaining within current budgetary guidelines, would be much appreciated.

In an attempt to make chapter plays more palatable to adult audiences and possibly secure better bookings for them, the studio's writers and directors began emphasizing complex plotting over fast action and daredevil stunt work. In many cases this took the form of having two villainous factions competing for the same prize, or making it appear as though certain supporting characters were working for good guys and bad guys simultaneously. The unfortunate by-product of the added intrigue was a surfeit of talk, much of it repetitive. The pacing problem this created was only exacerbated by another Universal innovation in serial scripting: doing away with title-card recaps and repeat footage at the beginning of each new episode. Instead, viewers listened to characters telling each other what had transpired in the previous chapter leading up to the cliffhanger ending. All too frequently, the "takeout" (that brief sequence removing the hero or heroine from last week's jeopardy) would be followed by more talk, as the good guys discussed what they planned to do *this* week.

Most Universal serials of the mid Forties, therefore, were torpid affairs, dependent for box-office success on the popularity and their stars or licensed properties. Occasionally, however, a glittering gem emerged. In 1943 it was *The Adventures of Smilin' Jack*, which I believe to be the studio's last great chapter play.

Smilin' Jack Martin, an intrepid airplane pilot with a weakness for trouble-prone women, was a comic-strip character created by artist Zack Mosley in 1933. Marketed to newspapers by the powerful Chicago Tribune—New York News Syndicate, the strip, originally titled *On the Wing*, was running in hundreds of daily and Sunday sheets around the country when Universal licensed it in 1942. Likely influenced by Chester Gould's *Dick Tracy* (another Trib-News strip), Mosley peopled *Smilin' Jack* with oddball characters. Jack's pals, for example, included Downwind Johnson, a skirt-chasing pilot whose face was never seen, and Fat Stuff, an obese Polynesian native whom Jack brought to America and put to work. Nearly every panel in which Fat Stuff appeared showed a button popping off his shirt. Mosley's villains included the Head, a vicious crook who vaguely resembled the movies' Peter Lorre; Baron Bloodsoe, a one-armed miscreant with a sadistic streak; and Toemain the Terrible, who raised piranhas with an appetite for human flesh. Jack's girl friends—at least a couple of whom actually got him to the altar but didn't survive long enough to set up housekeeping—were leggy, buxom beauties with tempestuous natures.

Although most of Universal's comic-strip adaptations maintained some fidelity to their sources, *The Adventures of Smilin' Jack* bore absolutely no relation to the strip, taking nothing from it save the hero's name. Producer Ford Beebe allowed screenwriter Morgan B. Cox to create new characters, settings, and situations out of whole cloth.

Cox devised a high-adventure plot that bore a closer resemblance to a Talbot Mundy novel than anything Mosley wrote for the strip. It hopscotched all over the Orient, beginning in Chungking, moving from there to a mythical mountainous province named Mandon, next to Hong Kong, and then across the Pacific to Honolulu before returning to China. Although the script had some juvenile aspects (particularly the credulity-straining nature of a few takeouts), it maintained a surprisingly mature tone and eschewed the so-called comic relief that makes some serials difficult to watch today.

Beebe assembled a solid cast, filling key roles with well-established actors known for their work in feature films produced at major studios. This was not an insignificant accomplishment; MacRae had always relied heavily on a stock company of players drawn from the ranks of silent-era Westerns, serials, and low-budget program pictures. Their ubiquity may have reassured youthful fans, but it signaled to exhibitors that the latest Universal chapter play would probably be the Same Old Thing. New faces and better actors could only be an improvement.

Cast as Jack Martin was 29-year-old Tom Brown, a silent-era child actor who had no problem transitioning into talkies. Throughout the Thirties and early Forties he worked steadily, making films at every major studio and some of the minor ones as well. Boyish-looking and naturally exuberant, Brown had most often been cast as an excitable kid brother, but the early Forties saw him playing leads in low-budget pictures. He couldn't have been less suited for the role of Smilin' Jack: Mosley's pilot was tall, dark, and lean, with wavy black hair and a neatly trimmed mustache, while Brown was short and stocky, with straight hair and no mustache. But he played the part so earnestly that it was impossible not to like him.

Beebe's real casting coup was the signing of Rose Hobart as the serial's villain, the treacherous Fraulein Von Teufel. Hobart, 36, was a well-respected theatrical actress who bounced from stage to screen during the Thirties, making strong impressions on film fans early on with her appearances in *Liliom* (1930), *East of Borneo* (1931), and *Dr. Jekyll and Mr. Hyde* (1932). The Forties found Hobart settling in Hollywood, where she specialized in playing sophisticated, scheming wives. Still a beautiful woman, she nonetheless had about her a hardness that, along with her outstanding acting ability, made her a particularly effective menace.

Other *Smilin' Jack* cast members probably got their roles simply because they lacked for better-paying, more prestigious assignments. Sidney Toler, having recently wrapped up his Charlie Chan stint at Twentieth Century-Fox, signed on to play a Chinese general. Had the serial been shot just a few months later, he would have been unavailable: By that time Monogram had launched its own Chan series and re-signed Toler to the role for which he was most famous. Austrian-born Turhan Bey, having apprenticed in Universal "B" pictures, had just made a strong impression in Walter Wanger's Technicolored swashbuckler Arabian Nights and would shortly be loaned to Warners for *Background to Danger* and to M-G-M for *Dragon Seed*. Distinguished actor Edgar Barrier, a member of Orson Welles' Mercury Theatre company and more recently an M-G-M player, appeared as Jack's Australian friend, Tommy Thompson.

Wartime material shortages and travel restrictions, coupled with the studio's mandate to keep serial budgets low to offset rising production costs due largely to unionization, forced Beebe to shoot *Smilin' Jack* almost entirely in and around the Universal lot, and Cox's imagination was probably restricted by the necessity of using standing sets. A fair amount of stock footage was worked into the script, in at least one case to highly dramatic effect.

Set in 1941, days before the bombing of Pearl Harbor, the story establishes Jack Martin as a former barnstormer and racing pilot now flying for the Chinese Air Force in its efforts to repulse the Japanese invaders. He's called to the Chungking headquarters of General Kai Ling (Toler) and assigned to carry out a vitally important mission. With Japanese invaders pressing their advantage on the mainland, it will be imperative to open the heretofore secret road linking China and India. The secret of this long-unused route is held by Mah Ling (Cyril Delevanti), elderly governor of Mandon, a remote province nestled at the foot of a Himalayan sub-range. Jack and the

General's adjutant, Captain Wing (Keye Luke), are to fly to Mandon and persuade Mah Ling to entrust them with the secret.

Also desirous of learning the route between China and India is Fraulein Von Teufel, the ruthless Nazi directing the activities of the Black Samurai, a network of Japanese spies and saboteurs. Posing as foreign correspondent Trudy Miller, she has wormed her way into the confidences of Jack's Australian friends, Tommy Thompson (Barrier) and his sister Janet (Marjorie Lord). Von Teufel's Japanese subordinate, Kageyama (Bey), details Black Samurai members to do most of the dirty work to keep suspicion from falling on his mistress.

Mah Ling is loyal to his nation but reluctant to divulge the Mandon secret, fearing that widespread use of the route between China and India could eventually disrupt his peaceful province. He wants assurances that the road will be closed after the war. To this end the governor agrees to return to Chungking with Jack and Wing, accompanied by his friend and protector Wu Tan (Philip Ahn).

As the serial progresses, Mah Ling keep renegotiating the deal, first requiring that British officials in Hong Kong co-sign the agreement, then demanding the same of American officials in Honolulu. Attempting to fulfill the latter condition finds Jack and his friends prisoners aboard a Jap sub tender when Pearl Harbor is attacked.

Screenwriter Cox, apparently having run out of excuses to delay the inevitable, kills off Mah Ling in Chapter Ten and contrives a way for Jack to be accused of the crime. Returning to Mandon and proving his innocence to the satisfaction of religious leader Lo San (Nigel De Bruilier), the American pilot finally secures the route's location and alerts General Kai Ling that he's bringing it in. Fraulein Von Teufel makes one last attempt to get the secret, in the process revealing her identity to Jack and the others. But she dies when the treacherous Kageyama has the Black Samurai's waterfront headquarters bombed in a bid to do away with his Nazi superior and take credit for her accomplishments. He, in turn, is shot by a fellow conspirator but guns down the assassin before expiring—thus tying up all the loose ends. With the Black Samurai smashed and the Mandon secret in Chinese hands, Jack accepts a commission with the U. S. Air Corps.

In synopsis, *Adventures of Smilin' Jack* probably doesn't sound all that impressive. But it's a thoroughly enjoyable serial, brightened by many offbeat touches and only slightly marred by minor production shortcomings and errors of continuity. Clearly, producer Beebe (himself a writer of silent and early sound Westerns and serials) worked closely with Cox to develop a story that has logical underpinnings yet abounds in melodramatic situations.

It was Bertram Millhouser, prolific writer of early silent-era chapter plays, who said that the key to a successful serial was a strong villain. *Smilin' Jack* certainly has one in Fraulein Von Teufel. In her Trudy Miller guise she enjoys the complete confidence of Jack and his friends, only briefly coming under suspicion after dispatching several people with a mechanical pencil tricked out to shoot poisoned darts with a click of a button. Hobart plays the role cleverly; as Trudy she's lighthearted and delivers her dialogue accordingly, but as the Fraulein she drops her voice an octave and speaks in cold, flat tones. That subtle shift in line reading shows the difference between a well-schooled stage actress and the typical "B"-picture ingénue who made her bones in six-day quickies.

Tom Brown is equally effective as Jack, who comes across as determined, resourceful, and indefatigable. He and his friends are captured repeatedly, but he always manages to contrive an escape. The script is laced with understated tributes to Jack's sterling character, the most specific coming from Mah Ling. While locked below deck on the aforementioned sub tender, from which there is apparently no escape, Jack figures out how they can get away, rolls up his sleeves, and puts his plan into motion. Mah Ling, long since resigned to his fate, turns to Wu Tan and says, "Do you not find this American's enthusiasm strangely contagious? Let us see if we can be of help." Without being obvious, Cox draws a comparison between the Eastern philosophy of submitting to one's destiny and the Western philosophy of changing it with dynamic action.

Adventures of Smilin' Jack is deficient in physical action, and directors Taylor and Collins—old serial hands—aren't bashful about taking shortcuts where possible. (For example, no less than three car chases are filmed from the same several angles, using the same vehicles.) But the scarcity of fistfights and stunt work is offset by unusual and clever chapter endings. The first episode closes with Jack having bailed out of a plane and struggling to open a defective parachute. We see him from above, plunging toward the ground and shrinking in size as he recedes from the camera, a look of panic on his face as he tugs desperately at the ripcord. (Chapter Two, of course, shows him releasing the silk just in time.)

Chapter Four ends with Jack trapped in the Black Samurai's waterfront headquarters. While chasing a disguised Fraulein Von Teufel, he drops through a hole and lands in a latticed net suspended above a pit with a wooden block from which long, razor-sharp knives protrude. The Fraulein opens a valve that releases a flood of river water into the pit, its pressure forcing the knife-studded block upward until it threatens to skewer the American tangled in the net.

Another water-based episode ending finds Jack locked in a coffin-like wooden box and plunged into the river. We see through the box (one side having been replaced by glass to give us a close-up, inside look) as water pours in, filling it rapidly as a terrified Jack pounds on the lid in claustrophobic terror. A simple effect, but extremely well executed.

The finale of Chapter Six is almost entirely composed of stock shots from Alfred Hitchcock's 1940 thriller, *Foreign Correspondent*. Jack and his friends are aboard a passenger plane that's shot down by a Japanese destroyer. We see the craft plunging toward the ocean and the unforgettable shot of water crashing through the windshield and flooding the cockpit. How could lowly serial producer Ford Beebe afford to purchase several minutes of stock from a major motion picture like *Foreign Correspondent*? He couldn't . . . and he didn't. The

Hitchcock film had been produced by Walter Wanger, who was making movies for Universal release when *Smilin' Jack* was filmed. He granted Beebe permission to use the footage as a courtesy, from one Universal producer to another.

Ford Beebe's 27-year association with the chapter play ended with *Adventures of Smilin' Jack*. Universal released a dozen more serials before abandoned the form in 1946, but none of them—with the possible exception of 1945's *Secret Agent X-9*—came remotely close to reaching the level of quality achieved by *Smilin' Jack*. And none boasted as strong a cast. Morgan Cox produced or co-produced seven of the 12, which relied even more heavily on stock footage and lengthy, repetitious dialogue exchanges. Of course, by this time Republic's serials were equally formulaic affairs: mind-numbing strings of car chases, choreographed fistfights in warehouses, and exploding miniatures. Columbia's mid-Forties chapter plays, produced by Sam Katzman as cheaply as possible, could best be defined by the word "lethargic." The movie serial's best days were long gone. *Smilin' Jack* was a noble effort, but it wasn't enough to save a dying format.

Dissed and Dismissed: Ten Underrated Serials

by Daniel J. Neyer

With a few exceptions, serials on ten-best lists compiled by fans and aficionados tend to be picked from a closed circle of about 30 chapter plays. They include Republics directed by William Witney and John English *(Zorro's Fighting Legion, Adventures of Captain Marvel,* etc.), Universal Pictures' three *Flash Gordon* serials, pre-1945 Republic serials directed by Spencer Gordon Bennet (The *Masked Marvel, Secret Service in Darkest Africa,* etc.), and, occasionally, late 1930s and early 1940s Columbia serials such as The *Spider's Web* and *Deadwood Dick.* I have nothing against any of these serials or others from the closed circle. However, the habitual listing of the same titles over and over leads some people to believe these are the only serials worth watching-which leaves some 200-odd others relegated to the also-ran department. And yet, there are many serials well worth seeing among these discounted titles. Here, in chronological order, are ten highly entertaining chapter plays that, for one reason or another, have been rejected by the "ten-besters." Some have been stigmatized by false rumors or critical snap judgments; all of them deserve a closer evaluation than they've generally received.

(1) *Pirate Treasure,* a 1934 Universal cliffhanger starring ace stuntman Richard Talmadge, has never been released on home video, and its hard-to-find nature has kept it from being seen and commented upon. But this isn't the only reason *Treasure* has been dismissed by ten-besters. Some feel there's no reason to seek out this title, based in part on the claim of noted serial historian Alan G. Barbour in his book *Cliffhanger* that *Pirate Treasure* was completely lacking in action. Other critics have parroted this statement, and as a result it's not easy to find a serial fan who's actually seen the film. This is truly a shame, since *Treasure* is an archetypal adventure tale, full of lively action and uninhibited derring-do. The plot incorporates one of the basic staples of adventure fiction-a hunt for buried pirate treasure on a tropical island. There's a treasure map, a mutinous crew of sailors, a gang of crooks out to steal the map, a tropical island, dangerous natives, and lots of miscellaneous skullduggery.

Director Ray Taylor, an accomplished serial hand, handles this hackneyed plot with such freshness that you can almost believe *Treasure* is the first fictional treatment of such an adventure. A lot of this sparkle derives from the enthusiastic, larger-than-life performance of leading man Richard Talmadge, He's an ideal serial hero: chipper, bursting with energy, and ready to tear off after bad guys at a moment's notice. He's certainly not the world's greatest actor, and he does possess a rather thick Swiss-German accent, but such points seem minor in view of the infectious enthusiasm of his performance. And then there's all the spectacular stunt work he delivers throughout the serial (contrary to Barbour's appraisal). It's hard to pick a highlight among the various acrobatic action scenes in *Treasure,* but a rooftop chase at the end of Chapter Two, the later shipboard fight during a mutiny sequence, and the car/motorcycle/train chase and fight sequence that spans Chapters Four and Five are among some of the best. Talmadge performs all these stunts himself, which supplies an added thrill for viewers.

Pirate Treasure's varied action set pieces are complemented by a varied backdrop, as the serial's setting moves from metropolitan America to sailing ship to tropical island.

Talmadge's infectious enthusiasm carries over to the rest of the cast-Lucille Lund as the lovely, blonde and blue-eyed heroine, Pat O'Malley as her stalwart and dignified father, William Desmond as a salty old sea captain, Walter Miller as a slick and greedy villain, and Ethan Laidlaw as a nasty, cranky henchman. From the first chapter's opening credits—which roll to a rollicking arrangement of "Yo Ho Ho and a Bottle of Rum"—to the final fadeout, *Pirate Treasure* is sheer serial delight.

(2) *Wild West Days* was released in 1937, and, like most of Universal's 1930s Western serials, is usually written off as a creaky, clunky failure, loaded with melodramatically bad acting and ill-matched stock footage. Most chapter play aficionados would probably tell you not to waste your time on it until you'd seen all the "good" serials. But you'd be robbing yourself of a lot of fun. *Wild West Days* is rollicking, fast paced, and full of exuberant acting and lively action. Stock footage from silent films *is* utilized during Indian-attack sequences, as is the case in nearly all Universal Western serials, but it certainly doesn't detract from the exciting nature of the original footage.

The plot, while simple, provides ample space for full-blooded and slightly humorous adventure. Carefree cowpoke Kentucky Wade and his equally carefree pals Trigger, Mexican Mike, and Dude come to the aid of their pal Larry Munro and his sister Lucy, who are being threatened by a vicious band of rustlers known as the Secret Seven. The rustlers' secret leader, the supposedly kindly newspaper editor Matt Keeler, is out to grab Larry's ranch and his newly discovered platinum deposit, and our heroes have their hands full protecting the Munros from the Seven and Keeler's outlaws and Indian accomplices.

Directors Ford Beebe and Clifford Smith stage *Wild West Days'* action scenes against varied and picturesque terrain, giving the serial a wild and rugged feel ideal for a Western. The audience is treated to horseback chases up and down rolling hills, lengthy shootouts on mountain ledges and atop suspension bridges, and ambushes in rocky canyons.

The leading characters of *Wild West Days* are as varied and picturesque as the locations. Johnny Mack Brown, Frank Yaconelli, George Shelley, and—of all people—Bob Kortman are a wonderful quartet of heroes, fun loving, easy-going, yet always ready to leap into action. The byplay between Shelley and perennial heavy Kortman (who resents Shelley's attempts at singing and always tries to sabotage them) is most amusing, as is Yaconelli's continual excitability. The sidekicks in this serial are funny and colorful without being stupid or inept. Russell Simpson is excellent as Keeler, hearty one minute and ruthless the next, and Charles Stevens is unusually tough and swaggering as his half-breed henchman Buckskin Frank.

Any serial fan who cares to give *Wild West Days* half a chance will, I predict, be quickly swept up in the adventures of Kentucky Wade and friends, and find himself wanting more when the serial winds to a close.

(3) I've never understood why Republic's 1938 thriller *Hawk of the Wilderness* is routinely overlooked by serial fans, despite the fact that it's directed by the famed team of William Witney and John English. It definitely doesn't deserve this fate; in my estimation, it's among the best of the Witney/English classics, and perhaps one of the best serials that Republic ever released.

The serial deals with an expedition undertaken by one Dr. Munro to find the Lincoln Rand expedition, which disappeared in the Arctic Circle years ago. Munro, his daughter Beth, and a group of friends discover a mysterious island inhabited by primitive and hostile Indians, and are soon trapped between the tribe (led by witch doctor Yellow Weasel) and a treasure-hungry, mutinous crew (led by the smuggler Salerno). Fortunately for Munro's party, Lincoln Rand's orphaned son has grown to manhood on the island as a resourceful, Tarzan-like lord of the forest known as "Kioga," or "Hawk of the Wilderness." He first comes to their rescue at the end of Chapter One. The following thrill-packed episodes chronicle Kioga's attempts to keep his newfound friends alive as Munro seeks a way of getting them all safely off the island.

Hawk of the Wilderness is quite different from the run-of-the-mill Republic serial. The plight of the good guys attempting to survive on the perilous island is much more involving than battles over the "MacGuffin" (in this case, a cache of gold) that furnishes the action in most cliffhangers. The island itself provides an ideal setting for robust outdoor adventures: practically the entire story unfolds in lovely pine forests, on the shores of mountain lakes, or on breath-taking mountain slopes. The stockade-like Indian village is most impressive, and the mysterious "Valley of Skulls," with its taboo "Caves of Death," is memorably eerie. The serial's stirring action scenes include Kioga's frequent displays of treetop acrobatics (undertaken to elude pursuing Indians), his fight with a tiger in a deep pit, and his climactic confrontation with Yellow Weasel.

Wonderful location cinematography (in the picturesque Mammoth Lakes region) and top-flight action sequences are backed up by more dimensional characterizations than usually found in serials. Herman Brix brings the necessary physical prowess to his role and imbues Kioga with dignity and quiet strength. William Royle is excellent as the seedy but audacious Salerno; George Eldredge does a fine, nuanced job as an expedition member who deteriorates from good guy into rotter; Noble Johnson underplays effectively as Kioga's wise mentor Mokuyi; and Jill Martin makes an appealing heroine.

In short, *Hawk of the Wilderness* has everything a serial fan could want, and a good deal more than a serial fan might reasonably expect.

(4) Universal's The *Green Hornet* (1940) has been the victim of some off-the-wall criticism. It's remarkable that such a well-done and faithful adaptation of a once-popular radio show has been so frequently dismissed as a failure. Alan Barbour criticized the serial because its "routine script had the Hornet battling conventional racketeers"—overlooking the fact that the Green Hornet had been depicted on radio as a crusading vigilante who battled such realistic villains as gangsters, con artists, and corrupt politicians. Subsequent critics have taken the same view, lambasting the serial for its lack of fantastic elements and choreographed Republic-style fistfights; they've missed the point in the same way Barbour did. It's more than slightly unfair to fault a serial simply for being faithful to its source material.

Another popular criticism of *Green Hornet* concerns the actor who plays the title role. Conventional wisdom holds that Gordon Jones was miscast as the Hornet. In the main, these fans have come to this serial after watching an overweight, middle-aged Jones playing comedic roles in Roy Rogers films and TV's The *Abbott and Costello Show*. They don't realize that Jones, a familiar face in films of the mid and late Thirties, had a well-established screen persona as an All-American athlete and/or tough guy when he was cast as the Hornet. He's eminently heroic and convincing as tough, civic-minded newspaper editor Britt Reid, and the dubbing of his Hornet dialogue by Al Hodge—who played the character on radio—was due to Universal's mandate to tie the serial more closely to its etherwaves inspiration, not to Jones' reputed inability to handle dialogue (as at least one critic has claimed).

The Green Hornet finds its hero and his trusty aide Kato (Keye Luke) taking on racketeers who participate in such relatively mundane criminal activities as bus-line sabotage, insurance fraud, election-rigging, and extortion. Each racket is headed by its own boss, but each boss answers to a Syndicate led by a mysterious Chief. Every episode has Britt Reid discovering one of these rackets, and then setting out as the Hornet to smash it, getting ever closer to the Chief. It's very enjoyable to watch the Hornet bring down each racket boss in a different way, and the introduction of a new set of bad guys in each chapter enables the Hornet to hold center stage throughout the cliffhanger-and helps the audience to identify with him, as we follow his crusade step-by-step.

The pace of the serial is swift, and the action scenes-car chases, explosions, and fistfights-are satisfactory if non-spectacular. Acrobatic fight sequences and daredevil stunting of the sort found in Republic serials would only have interfered with *Green Hornet*'s relatively realistic atmosphere.

(5) Universal went all out to promote their 1941 Western chapter play, *Riders of Death Valley,* touting it as a "Million Dollar Super Serial." The blatant exaggerations of this overwrought publicity campaign subsequently proved counterproductive, prejudicing latter-day fans against the serial and blinding them to its many solid merits.

Oliver Drake, who penned the serial's original screenplay, set this ball rolling by revealing in later years that it had been written as just another Western, that the presence of so many well-known actors in the cast (Dick Foran, Buck Jones, Charles Bickford, Lon Chaney Jr., Leo Carrillo, Guinn "Big Boy" Williams, et al) was a result of them just happening to be available all at once. Moreover, said Drake, stories trumpeting the serial's "million dollar" budget were strict fabrications. To make matters worse, Alan G. Barbour, obviously irked by the bombastic publicity, condemned *Riders* as a "grossly overrated and over-publicized serial whose only real merit was its large star-laden cast." The statements of Drake and Barbour only reinforced *Riders'* pretty dismal reputation; even today, many serial fans are quick to dismiss it as an abysmal failure or, at best, a seriously flawed effort.

Riders might not be a Million-Dollar Serial, but it definitely *is* fast-moving, action-packed, and well acted. The plot, dealing with the heroes' attempts to stop the villains from taking over the heroine's mine, is standard Western fare, but it never really seems formulaic. Nor do any of the serial's 15 chapters seem padded. The serial's first half is devoted to the heroes' attempts to locate the mine; the second half depicts their efforts to finance and develop it. Throw in assorted attacks by the villains and you have more than enough material to avoid excessive repetition, the bane of many Western chapter plays.

The serial's stunning locations (especially Red Rock Canyon) are neatly incorporated into the action sequences, with our heroes and villains clambering up and down awesome cliffs or chasing each other across wide plains and through narrow canyons. The action sequences themselves are well-staged and exciting, and many of the cliffhanger endings are excellent, especially one in which hero and heroine are trapped in a shack as a blazing wagon rolls down a hill towards them, and another in which two of our heroes plunge down a mine shaft on a runaway elevator.

The many stars of *Riders* handle their parts with gusto and enthusiasm. Foran and Buck Jones bounce wise-guy remarks off each other with obviously good-humored enjoyment, Williams and Carrillo are quite amusing as bickering sidekicks Borax and Pancho, and Bickford's Wolf Reade is perhaps the toughest and meanest villain in serial history. *Riders of Death Valley,* for sheer entertainment value, should rank high among Western serials. Even though its budget was nowhere near a million dollars, it certainly contains a million dollars' worth of entertainment.

(6) Like its fellow Hawk (of the Wilderness), The *Desert Hawk* enjoys no evil repute among serial fans-it's simply been ignored and forgotten. Part of the reason for this, I think, stems from the fact that it was released by Columbia in 1944, not long after The *Phantom* and The *Batman.* These Columbia releases featured well-known superheroes, and they overshadowed the less saleable *Desert Hawk.* This title is also overlooked because it's so hard to find, having never been legitimately released on home video.

The Desert Hawk deals with Kasim, young Caliph of the mythical Arabian kingdom of Ahad, who is deposed by his evil twin brother Hassan. Unable to prove his identity even to his own servants, Kasim assumes the guise of a legendary bandit called "the Desert Hawk" in order to protect his people and his bride-to-be from the usurper. This simple plot is nicely spread out over 15 chapters. While *Hawk* could easily have been a sloppy mess, given the difficulties inherent in transferring a cliffhanger to Arabian Nights territory, it nevertheless emerges as a successful experiment. The serial's writers (Leighton Brill, Sherman Lowe, Jack Stanley, Leslie Swabacker) and director (B. Reeves Eason), given an adequate production mounting, succeed admirably in capturing the atmosphere of an "Arabian

Nights" film, with the help of exotic locales including the Caliph's palace and its garden, the underground caves of the mysterious Grey Wizard, the rocky hideout of the bandits called "the Brothers of the Sword," the sandy desert, and the crowded streets and marketplaces of the city.

The serial also features fierce action, including many well-staged sword duels. The Chapter One swordfight, with Roland taking on a gang of henchmen atop a balcony and then sliding down a long tapestry, is a standout. A subsequent battle between Roland and henchmen in the marketplace in Chapter Ten is also well staged, as is the final showdown in the Caliph's throne room (this last fight being shot partly from above, an unusually stylistic touch for a serial).

Another point in *Hawk's* favor is its terrific final chapter, which climaxes just the way a classic swashbuckler should climax. The Hawk leaps from a balcony at the last minute to save the heroine from marrying Hassan, and battles against the usurper's swordsmen as loyal peasants storm the palace gates to aid their rightful ruler.

The whole cast is good, with Gilbert Roland's stellar dual performance giving the serial the added spark that lifts it to classic level. He's miles ahead of the average serial hero in acting talent, and invests Kasim with true charisma while making Hassan utterly despicable. Mona Maris is ideally regal as the heroine, Princess Azala, and Ben Welden—usually a bumbling, comical villain—makes an excellent sidekick for Roland: loquacious, crafty, somewhat jittery, but loyal and brave when the chips are down. The *Desert Hawk* is a grade-A Columbia outing, and deserves to be considered for membership on any list of that studio's "ten best" serials.

(7) *Son of Zorro*, released by Republic in 1947, had the poor luck to follow two classic chapter plays based on the Johnston McCulley character *(Zorro Rides Again* and *Zorro's Fighting Legion),* and a more routine but still fondly remembered pseudo-Zorro serial *(Zorro's Black Whip).* As a result, *Son* is usually panned as a cheap, stock-footage-filled knock-off of its three predecessors, containing no worthwhile or original plot elements or action sequences. But these frequent charges and condemnations simply are not accurate. *Son of Zorro* contains little, if any, stock from previous Zorro serials, as a quick comparison of costumes will show: John Carroll and Reed Hadley wore stiff full-face masks with mesh over the mouth, while Linda Stirling wore a half-face cloth mask and *Son of Zorro* star George Turner wears a full-face cloth mask with eyeholes.

Far from being composed of stock, the chapter endings and action scenes in *Son of Zorro* exhibit more creativity than was generally displayed in Republic serials of the post-WWII period. These creative cliffhangers include the hero trapped in an alleyway by a burning wagon, the heroine about to be crushed by a huge millstone, the hero apparently stomped by a wild horse, and the heroine being lowered into a deep well by the bad guys. The fight scenes, staged by directors Spencer Bennet and Fred Brannon and stuntmen Tom Steele and Dale Van Sickel, are quite energetic and benefit from slightly larger, more extensive sets that give the combatants more room to tussle.

The serial's screenplay takes a fine approach to the Zorro story, making the hero a Civil War officer who returns to his hometown to practice law, only to find the county administration controlled by outlaws. This leaves him no choice but to work outside the law in the guise of Zorro, a relative of his. This storyline gives the hero a more plausible motive for concealing his identity than did the plots of *Zorro Rides Again* and *Zorro's Black Whip* did, and the hero's initial reluctance to don the mask lends Zorro's debut at the end of Chapter One a dramatic and satisfying feel.

Another satisfying aspect of *Son* is its unusually large and varied supporting cast. Most Republic serials from this period only feature a hero, a heroine, a sidekick, and three villains, but in this one we have Ernie Adams' cowardly judge, Roy Barcroft's tough and cunning outlaw, Ed Cassidy's nasty sheriff, Edmund Cobb's grouchy rancher, Tom London's jolly storekeeper, and Stanley Price's trusty Mexican ranch hand to add interest and color throughout the serial. The gorgeous and athletic Peggy Stewart makes a perfect, spunky heroine. And though he's not as familiar as earlier Zorros Carroll or Hadley, George Turner (getting his one and only shot at stardom after years of bit parts) makes a fairly strong hero. His large size and tough countenance are tempered by a cheerful grin and a pleasant voice, and he handles dialogue with conviction. *Son of Zorro* might not be as good as *Zorro's Fighting Legion* or *Zorro Rides Again,* but there's no reason why it shouldn't be accepted as a satisfying, engrossing, and well-made Republic serial.

(8) Republic's *G-Men Never Forget* (1948) is generally dismissed as a dull cops-and-robbers serial, a typically unimaginative post-war rehash of story elements and footage from earlier and better serials. It's true that the central plot gimmick-a villain who kidnaps a good guy and impersonates him throughout the serial-had been used before in *Daredevils of the Red Circle* and *Secret Service in Darkest Africa.* It's also true that many cliffhanger endings in this serial come from earlier Republics, including *The Purple Monster Strikes* and *King of the Mounties.* And it's true that the serial contains no colorful mystery villains, fantastic gadgets, or costumed heroes. But *G-Men Never Forget* needs none of these trimmings, emerging as possibly the best Republic crime serial of them all, thanks to the uniquely hard-boiled and realistic nature of its screenplay and direction.

To enumerate a few of these hard-boiled elements: The villains of the piece are true racketeers, who engage in extortion, industrial sabotage, and armored car robbery; our hero is almost framed on bribery charges at one point; and our hero and heroine pose most convincingly as a tough hoodlum and a gun moll while going undercover. The chief henchman in *G-Men* is a trigger-happy, wise-cracking young punk (well played by Drew Allen), as opposed to the more typical seasoned thug. Chapters Five and Ten feature unbearably tense murders committed by the Murkland gang, and in both cases the victims are characters who have appeared throughout the serial-which makes their deaths all the more shocking. These two murders are shot in a suspenseful and shadowy style, as is a sequence in which Allen silently waits in a darkened hotel room to assassinate Clayton Moore, playing the serial's hero. The only light in the scene is the intermittent flashing of a neon sign outside the room window. Heightening the tension, no background music is featured during this sequence.

These touches make *G-Men Never Forget* seem more like a vintage cops vs. gangsters picture than a serial. But the chapter play nevertheless maintains the basic Republic formula, including the regulation fistfights and gun battles. The serial's fight sequences (handled in part by co-director Yakima Canutt) are exciting, and feature the welcome presence of acrobatic Duke Green in one of his last serial stunting assignments. The final shootout between Moore and Allen in the commissioner's cramped office is very tense, and an earlier shootout at the used car lot is especially memorable for Moore's use of a tipped-up dump truck as moving cover.

The serial's gritty atmosphere is admirably enhanced by its fine lead actors. Clayton Moore and Ramsay Ames portray their characters as competent, resourceful, and dedicated. Veteran screen heavy and Republic regular Roy Barcroft is brilliant in his double turn as tough, brutal gangster Vic Murkland and courageous, honest police commissioner Angus Cameron. Don't be deceived by the generic-sounding plot of *G-Men Never Forget;* its familiar storyline is seasoned with some unique touches.

(9) *Federal Agents vs. Underworld Inc.* is a rather dull title leading many serial fans to assume that the film itself is a rather dull serial—especially since it was released by Republic in 1949, during a period that saw imagination waning and budgets declining. Seldom cited as a bad serial, it's generally ignored in discussions of good serials. The first chapter sets up tried-and-true serial formulas, but *Federal Agents'* plot is unexpectedly twisty and devious, putting this chapter play above other technically competent but unsurprising serials from Republic's postwar years.

In an unnamed American city, members of an archeological

expedition are endangered by a Middle Eastern fanatic named Nila and her chief accomplice, an American gangster named Gordon. This nasty pair is after the Golden Hands of Kurigal, artifacts recently discovered by said archeologists in the Middle Eastern country of Abistahn. These hands are keys to the location of the treasure of Kurigal, a legendary king. Nila hopes to use Kurigal's wealth not only to make herself ruler of Abistahn, but also to organize the American underworld into one vast combine. The expedition's head, Professor Clayton, has already disappeared along with one of the Golden Hands, and Nila and Gordon begin menacing Clayton's associate Evans in order to gain possession of the other. Federal agent Dave Worth sets out to protect Evans, unravel the mystery of Clayton's disappearance, and thwart Nila's mad bid for power.

This plot may sound cut-and-dried, but things aren't always what they seem, and the writers of *Federal Agents* spring some surprising plot twists on us as the serial progresses, lending pizzazz to what might have been a routine storyline. These twists-which include a prominent character being revealed as a villain, the finding of a Golden Hand halfway through the story, a change of locale from urban America to exotic Abistahn, and the introduction of a new major villain in the chapter play's last third-hold our interest throughout and keep *Federal Agents* from becoming formulaic.

There are many good fistfights and gun battles, the former contributed by Tom Steele, Dale Van Sickel, and a welcome Dave Sharpe, who doubles sidekick James Dale and incorporates a few of his acrobatics into the fight scenes. Hero Kirk Alyn, while typically serious and devoted to duty, is a far more lively and effervescent hero than most Republic leading men from this era. Carol Forman and Roy Barcroft playoff each other beautifully as the villains; her aristocratic arrogance and his down-to-earth cynicism contrast perfectly. Add lovely Rosemary La Planche as the heroine and James Craven as the urbane Professor Clayton, and you have a compact and solid adventure that compensates for its low budget with a creative storyline.

(10) There's no earthly reason why *Roar of the Iron Horse* should be any good, seeing as it was released in 1950, during the dark days of Sam Katzman's tenure as Columbia's serial producer. Most Katzman serials are low-budgeted, slow-paced, and talky affairs, filled with clumsy action scenes, incoherent plots, and infighting villains who occasionally usurp the nominal hero's screen time. The generally low quality of such Katzman-produced chapter plays as *Batman and Robin, Jack Armstrong, Brick Bradford* has led most fans to give Katzman serials like *Roar of the Iron Horse,* which aren't even based on popular comic book or radio heroes, little or no attention. But it's not always fair to judge a serial by the company it keeps, at least not in the case of *Roar of the Iron Horse.*

Roar is a highly satisfactory Western adventure that falls into none of the pitfalls that typically beset Katzman serials. The worst of these pitfalls—a lack of fast, hard action—is avoided through the presence of Jock Mahoney in the leading role, and through the creative use of railroad action. Mahoney does all his own stunt work and makes the fight scenes look ten times more dynamic than they usually do at Columbia.

Action sequences centered around the train are also exciting and inventive. A shootout between the henchmen and the rail crew (who take cover aboard the stationary train) in Chapter Three is memorable, as is an Indian attack on the railroad crew (who fight back from a moving flatcar) in Chapter One. Chapter Ten features a decidedly unusual cliffhanger that shows heroine Virginia Herrick, riding a handcar, on a collision course with a locomotive. In this case *Roar's* co-director, Spencer Bennet, was recreating a chapter ending he originally staged in 1928 for *The Yellow Cameo,* a 1928 Pathé serial starring Allene Ray and Edward Hearn.

The serial's plot, while simple, never blunders into incoherence: the hero battles two different factions of villains attempting to stop work on the railroad for (varying) nefarious purposes. Nor do these two teams of villains use up screen time by shooting each other while the hero watches from the sidelines-the two factions never even meet until Chapter

Fourteen. The focus stays on the hero and *his* struggle against the villains, which is as it should be.

Veteran serial director Bennet wasn't always able to overcome Katzman's budgets, but in *Roar of the Iron Horse,* he and Thomas Carr do a great job, backed by Mahoney, Herrick, crusty sidekick William Fawcett, and a fine assortment of rogues that includes Jack Ingram, Dick Curtis, and George Eldredge as the genteel but nasty Baron. I think any train buff, Western buff, or serial buff would find *Roar of the Iron Horse* a pleasant surprise, Katzman serial though it might be.

Appendix

My Dinner With Nita: Remembering Iris Meredith

by Ed Hulse

In the summer of 1976, I had an experience most serial fans could only dream of. I actually met, interviewed, and broke bread with the Spider's paramour, Nita Van Sloan!

Not the real Nita, of course. That would have been impossible. Because there *wasn't* any real Nita. No, I attended a dinner with the *reel* Nita, the beautiful actress who played opposite Warren Hull in *The Spider's Web* (1938), first of two fast-action Spider serials made and released by Columbia Pictures.

Her name was Iris Meredith, and she had come to Nashville, Tennessee as a guest of the Fifth Annual Western Film Fair, a movie-buff confab sponsored by *Western Film Collector* magazine. Over the course of this four-day convention, some 160 feature-length films and a couple dozen serials—among them The *Spider's Web*—unspooled in six makeshift screening rooms outfitted with 16mm projectors manned by bleary-eyed collectors. Movie showings began at 10 a.m. every day and continued until the wee hours of the next morning. The hucksters room included well over a hundred tables, some of them covered by boxes bulging with movie memorabilia, others sagging beneath the weight of film cans containing 16mm prints. Film Fair atten-

APPENDIX: MY DINNER WITH NITA

dees could either screen themselves blind or spend themselves poor. Some did both.

Much-needed diversions were provided by panel discussions (in which the many guest stars reminisced about filmmaking in the Good Old Days) and the yearly Saturday-night awards banquet, when actors long forgotten by the public at large accepted handsome plaques and standing ovations from True Believers who still cherished the Saturday-matinee movies of their youth.

I had already attended several such events and would likely have returned to Nashville even if Iris Meredith *hadn't* been among the dozen or so performers invited to this year's convention. But her presence was the icing on the cake for me. Iris Meredith—the silver screen's Nita Van Sloan! (Those of us who had seen both Spider serials rarely spoke of The Other, that garish, brassy floozy so obviously miscast as Nita in the 1941 sequel, The *Spider Returns.* As far as we were concerned, there had been only one Nita, and that was Iris.)

Born on June 3, 1915 in Sioux City, Iowa, Iris Shunn didn't have an easy childhood. By the time she was ten, her family had moved twice, first to Minnesota and then to southern California. By the time she was 13, both parents had died, leaving her to support three younger siblings with a Depression on the way. She attended school in the morning and toiled as a theater cashier in the afternoon and evening. Legend has it that Iris was discovered by a talent scout while working at the Loew's theater in downtown Los Angeles. Still just a teenager—albeit a beautiful one—she briefly joined the fabled Goldwyn Girls and first appeared on screen with them in a 1933 Eddie Cantor vehicle, *Roman Scandals.*

Iris worked as a chorus girl in several movie musicals before landing her first substantial part: an ingénue role in The *Cowboy Star* (1936), a better-than-average "B" Western in which she played opposite Charles Starrett for the first time. (This film was the first in which she received on-screen billing, and for it she assumed the Meredith surname.) Starrett, scion of a wealthy northeastern family, had taken up acting while attending Dartmouth College. In the early Thirties he appeared in numerous major-studio productions, among them M-G-M's The *Mask of Fu Manchu,* which starred Boris Karloff and Myrna Loy. But Starrett never really caught on with adult moviegoers and in 1935 began starring in low-budget horse operas released by Columbia. He spent 17 consecutive years making Westerns for that studio, appearing exclusively as The Durango Kid from 1944 to 1952.

When Iris landed a Columbia contract, she was initially assigned to the unit cranking out Charlie's pictures, and she co-starred with him in some 19 Westerns released between 1937 and 1940. The Starrett vehicles of this period maintained a fairly high standard, but their strict adherence to formula on formula made one virtually indistinguishable from another. The Sons of the Pioneers, a Western-music group to which Roy Rogers once belonged, worked with Charlie and Iris in every picture. The supporting casts nearly always included Dick Curtis as the principal heavy and silent-screen veteran Edward Le Saint as either Starrett's or Meredith's father. Even the bit players were the same from picture to picture, and they almost always wore the same clothes. For that matter, so did Iris: she generally showed up in an ensemble consisting of plaid shirt with vest and split skirt.

Iris pressed for roles in better movies but rarely escaped the Western and serial unit headed by producer Jack Fier. And when she did, it was only temporarily and usually in a thankless part. In late 1940, after appearing in 22 Westerns and three serials, she left Columbia. For the next couple years Iris freelanced, but she found it difficult to land roles outside of Hollywood's Poverty Row. By 1943 she had married director Abby Berlin, himself a Columbia contractee, and shortly thereafter she had a daughter and settled into domestic life.

Unlike some of her contemporaries, Iris never attempted a comeback when television series production created new opportunities for technicians and performers used to working at top speed on short budgets. She never dreamed that people still remembered her fondly, or that she had won new fans thanks to TV reruns of her old movies and the proliferation of 16mm dupe prints of the old Westerns. By the mid Seventies, however, the word was out. The "B"-Western stars, starlets, and supporting players were very much in demand at nostalgia-oriented film festivals, and Iris eventually accepted an invitation to appear at one such event.

Of course, those of us who attended that 1976 Western Film Fair had no way of knowing what hell Iris Meredith had been through. Some ten years earlier she had been diagnosed with oral cancer. She endured 14 operations, surrendering part of her jaw and tongue in her fight against the disease. None of us expects our film favorites to withstand indefinitely the ravages of time, but we weren't fully prepared for the severely disfigured, prematurely aged woman who courageously greeted her fans.

However shocked Film Fair attendees may have been, they never let on. Iris bravely met and talked with her fans, laboring mightily to make herself understood. Losing part of her tongue made it impossible to clearly articulate certain words, and her slurred speech was reminiscent of someone who'd had way too much to drink.

But ultimately this didn't matter to her fans, whose outpouring of love plainly lifted her spirits. As the convention progressed Iris seemed demonstrably happier; by the second or third day one could see a twinkle in her rheumy eyes. Initially reluctant to speak, she pushed herself to engage fully with fans who approached her with questions, often bearing stills and lobby cards for her to sign.

She was accompanied by her grown daughter, who occasionally sat with her mom when Iris elected to watch one of her old movies. During a screening of *The Spider's Web*—all 15 chapters in one marathon session, interrupted only by the projectionist's reel changes—the daughter excused herself, leaving Iris all alone. The screening rooms were sparsely attended at that moment; my recollection is that another guest-star panel was just getting underway. Only a dozen or so people remained to see the Spider battle his arch-foe, the Octopus, to a standstill.

A few rows behind and to the right of Iris, I stared at her as the next episode began. She sat very still and very straight, apparently transfixed by the flickering image of a younger, beautiful version of herself. I couldn't help but wonder what might be going through her mind. Having already seen the serial several times, I left the room after one more chapter to attend another screening. As I eased through the door, I shot a glance back at Iris. She was still riveted by the adventures of Dick, Nita, and the others.

On the third day of the convention, I persuaded Iris to sit for an interview. She briefly stiffened when I brought out my portable cassette recorder, but after a few seconds—just as I was about to stuff it back into my briefcase—she relaxed again. "What would you like to know?" she asked.

Naturally, I was most eager to hear whatever she had to say about The *Spider's* Web. "You know," she said, "a year ago I couldn't have told you anything about it. But now that I've seen it again, little things come back to me.

"Those serials were very hard to do. With the Westerns, you worked for a week or two and then you had time off. But those damn serials went for four, or five, or six weeks at a time. And we worked very long days, sometimes 12 or 14 hours. So every night you came home exhausted. It was all we could do to remember our lines the next day. The directors had it bad because they had to keep track of everything, all those little things that happened in the chapters."

I asked her what she remembered about her castmates.

"Well, of course, I knew Richard Fiske already. We worked together on some of the pictures I did with Charlie [Starrett]. Warren Hull was a dear. Between takes he was a great kidder. And he loved to sing. He had a lovely voice. But then we would get in front of the camera and he would get so serious and squint, you know, and starting shooting at people.

"I remember we all thought it was funny that Kenny Duncan was playing this Hindu [Ram Singh]. He was Canadian! And they gave him some of the craziest lines to say." (I imagined Iris referred to Ram Singh's snarling threats, like my favorite: "Dog with a pig's face! If I had my knife, I'd carve my name in your heart!")

"The other thing I enjoyed was that I got to wear nice clothes. I only had a few changes of wardrobe, but it was so much fun to wear nice dresses after all those Westerns in that damn split skirt. And of course, I didn't have to deal with horses."

Iris insisted, as have so many serial actors before and after her, that she barely remembered making the chapter plays. "Really, we were rushing around so much we didn't know half the time whether we were coming or going."

She did, however, have specific memories of *Overland with Kit Carson,* the 1939 serial she did with newly minted cowboy star "Wild Bill" Elliott. "We went to Utah to shoot most of it," she told me. Then she tried to pronounce the name of the town where the company stayed while on location, but I couldn't understand what she was trying to say. Finally she scribbled the name on my note pad: "Canab." Several Westerns were made in and around that community, which the town fathers hoped would attract Hollywood producers in greater numbers. A Western street was built in the area to make Canab a more appealing location for filmmakers; *Overland with Kit Carson* was the first production to utilize it.

Iris was fond of her *Kit Carson* co-star, with whom she also made three feature films. "Bill Elliott took his work very seriously," she said. "The first picture I made with him, he wasn't much of a rider yet. But he always practiced between takes. He got to be very good at it. And you know how he wore his guns, backward in the holsters? Well, he spent *hours* practicing a quick draw with those guns. I really admired him for working so hard to be convincing."

She also had kind words for Ed Le Saint, another member of the Starrett stock company. "He was such a dear man. Very kind to me. But, you know, he was so *old!* I could never understand why they cast such an old man to play my father. Really, he was old enough to be my grandfather."

By this time Iris seemed to be enjoying herself. She was no

longer self conscious about the tape recorder, or about the effort it took to pronounce certain words. But I inadvertently brought our chat to a awkward halt with my next question:

"In 1940 you did your last serial, *The Green Archer,* for one of your *Spider's Web* directors, James W. Horne. What do you remember about that film?"

Her face clouded and the spark went out of her eyes. She seemed more than a little sad as she quietly replied: "I don't want to talk about that film. Please don't ask me about it."

I was stunned. What on earth could have happened during the making of that serial to elicit such a reaction? Fortunately, *Green Archer* was the last film about which I'd wanted to ask, and with nothing else to say I cleared my throat nervously and mumbled, "Well, I think we've pretty much covered everything."

That night at the banquet, following the typical rubber-chicken dinner, Iris Meredith was one of a dozen people presented with the inscribed plaque traditionally given to Western Film Fair guest stars. As she made her way to the podium, every person in the ballroom rose to give her a lengthy standing ovation. It was our way of honoring her for the courage and grace she had exhibited during the show. The room fairly crackled with electricity. Even from where I was, some ten feet from the dais, I could see her eyes welling up with tears. When the applause died down, she said just two words: "Thank you." Then, as it swelled again, she took her seat and stared intently at her award.

Subsequently Iris Meredith attended another film-fan convention, but she never became a regular on the "nostalgia circuit," as did some of her contemporaries. She continued her struggle with cancer, but the disease eventually overtook her. Not yet 65 years old, Iris died on January 22, 1980.

In 40 years of convention-going, I have met dozens of the actors, writers, directors, and stuntmen who worked on my favorite serials, Westerns, and "B" movies. I've enjoyed my encounters with all but two or three of them. But none ever affected me quite the way Iris Meredith did. It's difficult to explain, but even now, decades later, I get a little thrill whenever I run a chapter of The *Spider's* Web and see the optical player credits—you know, those pictures of the principal actors with their names across the bottom of the frame. Iris always stands there, clad in Nita Van Sloan's flying togs, smiling sweetly and placidly even though she will shortly find herself menaced once again by the minions of the Octopus.

In those moments, I like to think she's smiling at me.

Made in the USA
Las Vegas, NV
17 January 2024

84496459R00184